RULES
FOR RADICAL
CONSERVATIVES

★ ★ ★ ★ RULES FOR RADICAL CONSERVATIVES

Beating the Left at Its Own Game to Take Back America

DAVID KAHANE

BALLANTINE BOOKS · NEW YORK

Copyright © 2010 by David Kahane

Published in the United States by Ballantine Books, an imprint of The Random House Publishing Group, a division of Random House, Inc., New York.

BALLANTINE and colophon are registered trademarks of Random House, Inc.

Library of Congress Cataloging-in-Publication Data
Kahane, David.
  Rules for radical conservatives : beating the left at its own game to take back America / David Kahane.
     p.   cm.
  Includes bibliographical references.
  ISBN 978-0-345-52186-6
  eBook ISBN 978-0-345-52187-3
  1. Conservatism—United States.   2. Liberalism—United States.   3. Conservatism—United States—Humor.   4. Liberalism—United States—Humor.   5. Political satire, American.   I. Title.
  JC573.2.U6K34 2010
  320.520973—dc22   2010032944

Printed in the United States of America on acid-free paper

www.ballantinebooks.com

9 8 7 6 5 4 3 2 1

First Edition

For Kathryn Jean Lopez

What's the constitution among friends?

—George Washington Plunkitt, Tammany Hall

Contents

Sympathy for the Devil

An Introduction by "Che" Kahane

Please allow me to introduce myself.

I am the father of David Kahane, whose work you know from the Internet and from the pages of *National Review Online,* and whose *Rules for Radical Conservatives* you are now holding in your hand. Whether you have purchased this volume or stolen it, as my old friend and compadre in the Revolution, Abbie Hoffman, famously urged in the title of one of his own works, I already know one very important thing about you: in the great grim battle between Left and Right, between good and evil, between Satan and Saint Michael, between Wormwood and the Patient, you have already lost. Welcome to the Permanent Campaign, permanently to be waged against you until the end of time or our total victory, whichever comes first.

Look at yourself in the mirror. What do you see?

Don't tell me—I already know. You see a coward, a weakling, a quivering mass of protoplasm, a spineless jellyfish, a neutered creature stripped of dignity and cowering in fear. With what seems like "lightning suddenness," as the old sports cliché goes, your world has been turned upside down, the old verities tossed onto the ash heap of history, and you are now face-to-face with . . .

Us. In all our glory. Finally freed from the masks and the chains, able to reveal ourselves as we really are, cloaked for one brief moment not in the shade but by the sun, like something out of Blake. "You owe me awe!" as Mr. Dolarhyde says in *Red Dragon,* and see how neatly I tie up my pop cultural, literary, and artistic allusions. Who on your side can do that?

This is our time. This is our moment. Stop us if you can.

But you won't. Even as we draw the knife blade of nihilism across your throat, you will never muster the will to resist. You are the boiling frog, incrementally heated, accepting of every diminution and indignity, each hotter than the last, until at last you slip blissfully into that dark world to which we pay homage, but in which we ourselves at root fear to tread. Because this one thing we know:

You will never fight back against people like us.

We have done this to you, and we have done it by design. We have changed up to down, right to wrong, black to white, night to day. Via our silken garotte of "political correctness," we have undermined and hamstrung your very ability to think with clarity, to judge with confidence—and to see us for what we really are.

We not only want resistance to be futile, we want it to be *unthinkable*.

After all, it's exhausting, this constant fear and worry. Eternal vigilance is a price you're no longer willing to pay for your liberty. Let me whisper in your ear: Lay down your burden. It's easier this way. Come, lay down your heavy load. Go along. Get along. Join us.

You'll pardon, I trust, such candor from an ostensible stranger. But, in fact, you have met me before, many times over the course of the centuries. I was present when the Sodomites came for Lot's guests and rejected his living daughters, and again when his wife turned toward the burning city, listening to the tempting voices in her ears before the Enemy transformed her into a pillar of salt for the simple crime of feminine curiosity. I was there at Belshazzar's Feast, when the moving hand writ large upon the wall: *mene, mene tekell upharsin.* As the poet sings, I was there when Pilate washed his hands of the Christ, when the Czar and his family were murdered, when Oswald's bullet went through the back of Jack Kennedy's head. And speaking of poets, the great Alighieri knew me well, and my allies, consigning us to the various lower circles of his imaginary hell, an amusing anticipatory revenge that we have now rendered moot.

Your poets have long warned you about the likes of me: O That Anthropomorphical Rag that has such demons in't! You agree with Baudelaire that the Devil's best deception is convincing you that he doesn't exist—a trick that I, dear reader, would never dream of attempting. For I am one with my hero, Satan, the true hero of *Paradise Lost*: "Which way I fly is Hell; myself am Hell. And, in the lowest deep, a lower deep still threat'ning to devour me opens wide, to which the Hell I suffer seems a Heaven." That Milton sure could write dialogue.

But I digress. What we offer here is a guided tour through the new circle of hell that we have laid out for you. Something that even Dante could not have envisioned: a hell of your own making, and in which you freely choose to dwell.

To that end, I now send you my only begotten son, David, in whom I am so well pleased. It is he who will explain to you what we have done to you, so carefully, so methodically, over the decades of my lifetime, he who will explain to you our tricks and wheedles, our seductive lies, our entirely reasonable exhortation to self-destruction. It is he who will give you the tools and the weapons with which to fight back, secure in the knowledge that you will never use them.

I have to admit, despite my fatherly pride, that occasionally he gets carried away and actually tries to see things as you see them; he has in him a great weakness, which is occasional compassion for the Enemy. He blames it on something or somebody he refers to as the Amanuensis; I suspect it is one of the Principal Enemy's little tricks. If, at times, he seems actually to mean the advice he so freely dispenses, put it down to youthful exuberance; in time, he will be mine completely. As, of course, will you.

And why am I encouraging young David to this? Because even a bully every now and then enjoys an honest fight, if only by which to measure his own magnificent stature and moral rectitude.

So consider this a formal introduction to my boy's book—Bulgakov would know what I mean—and with it an over-the-shoulder paraphrase of the great Alinsky:

To the Enemy—from all our legends, mythology, and history (and who is to know where mythology leaves off and history begins—or which is which), the very first conservative known to man, whose ludicrous "mercy" and "goodness" created the establishment against which I and my kind are privileged for all eternity to rebel, and who did it so ineffectively that he allowed us our own kingdom, from which to wage war on his—God.

Enjoy. If you can.

First Things

or Whose Book Is This, Anyway?

Well—thanks a lot, Dad. To say your Introduction puts a burden on me, as usual, would be only a slight exaggeration. To say it gives the game away would be a mild understatement. To say it promises to telegraph to the Principal Enemy *every* element of our grand strategy . . . well, even you can't be that dumb. Or vengeful. Or maybe you can. So there must be a method to your apparent madness, a cunning plan behind your apparent magnanimity, and I merely your humble servant.

Please allow *me* to introduce myself. I am David Kahane, the only progressive yet to successfully infiltrate and co-opt the Vast Right Wing Conspiracy, principally via the pages of *National Review,* both dead-tree and online, and now in this book. Dedicated as I am to destroying you and your precious "American way of life," your implacable enemy who will fight, fight, fight you until the Last Trump, I nevertheless just can't take your ridiculous bumbling around anymore. For Gaia's sake, you idiots, wise up! Here, at the end, when we have you down for the count, go ahead—take a swing.

I must have a soft spot either in my heart or in my head, because I am about to let you in on a little secret—okay, a great big secret—which is this:

You can fight us.

You can beat us.

You can even destroy us forever.

If only—

You have the will.

Which you don't—not yet, at least. But I am now about to show you the way.

First, I'm going to take you on a little tour of our world. I want you to fully understand what we have done to you and, in retrospect, how relatively easy it all was. Sure, there were some broken heads along the way, but in the main we have effected our revolution—a near-fundamental transformation of American society that didn't have to happen, but which we have convinced you through our friends in academe and the media—and by our own incessant posturing and preening and preaching—was not only morally necessary but inevitable.

I want you to get mad. Good old-fashioned all-American furious, as you realize that we've been playing you for suckers for decades now, relying on your goodwill and sense of fair play and willingness to entertain any theory, no matter how ridiculous. Slow to anger, that's you guys, whereas our side usually resembles nothing more than visiting day in the insane asylum, what with all the shouting, shrieking, screaming, begging, whining, imploring, and general carrying-on. Whereas you tend to sit there, smiling and nodding, welcoming us into your homes via the evening news, and into your children's noggins via the state-controlled educational system, and into your purses and bank accounts via the ever-expanding reach of the federal government and its insatiable appetite for your money and your property. Not realizing that slowly we are squeezing the life out of you and what used to be your country, slow-boiling the frog, delay-poisoning you with our arsenic biscuits, the way Miss Madeleine Smith eventually rid herself of her inconvenient lover, Emile L'Angelier, in long-ago Scotland.

I want you to understand that very little of what you are about to read has happened by accident, that most of it was done with malice aforethought—not in any vast-left-wing-conspiracy sort of way, controlled from Moscow Center by a giggling psychopath stroking a white cat, but still deliberately—and with the clear intention of bringing down your society and replacing it with something else. Something that will still be called "the United States of America" (maybe; we haven't decided yet) but will bear as little resemblance to the land of Lincoln as nineteenth-century Britain does to its twenty-first-century incarnation.

I want you to understand that with each passing day, as we wrap our tentacles more tightly around you, binding you with a million small pieces of petty legislation, harassing legal tactics, intrusive law enforcement, and the criminalization of just about everything, we are doing this for a reason: to weaken you enough so that in the unlikely event you actually do decide to fight back at last, you won't be able to.

I want you to understand that when we say it's for your own good, we mean that it's for our own good.

When we use a term like "social justice," what we really mean is that payback's a bitch.

When we speak of "affordable housing," what we really mean is that we want to destroy your communities by attacking your property values.

When we start complaining that something is "unsustainable," we have not the slightest shred of evidence to support that assertion, and what we really mean is that it is, in fact, entirely sustainable, but that we are doing our best to wreck it.

When we start babbling on about "advocacy" and "activism"—only we men of the Left could invent out of whole cloth the twin nonprofessions of "activist" and "advocate" and have them taken seriously in the pages of *The New York Times*—what we really are talking about are what used to be known as "agitators."

Whenever we accuse you of something nefarious—and our usual litany includes such well-worn staples as racism, sexism, ageism, heightism, weightism, carnivoreism, antidisestablishmentarianism, homophobia, tridecaphobia, hydrophobia, and glossolalia—or of adopting a particularly mean, dirty, and low-down tactic, it simply means that those are the very things we are thinking of at that exact instant, and would actually indulge in ourselves if we thought you weren't looking.

When we say "hate speech" we pretty much mean every word that comes out of your mouths.

When we speak of such things as "fierce moral urgency," our "morality" is based on absolutely nothing more than whatever suits our purposes, and bears only an accidental resemblance to anything found in such traditional sources of morality as churches and synagogues, or basic common decency.

We really do believe, as far as you're concerned, that the perfect must be the enemy of the good, and that the impossibly perfect must always and everywhere be the enemy of the good enough right now. Therefore, nothing you can ever do will please us, and we will always hold it against you.

I **WANT YOU TO UNDERSTAND** the truth of Frost's observation that a liberal is a man too broad-minded to take his own side in an argument.

I want you to understand the truth of Chesterton's observation that tolerance is the only virtue left to the man who no longer believes in anything.

I want you to understand that, though we may profess to celebrate life, in fact we are little more than a suicide cult, intent on doing in our rage and self-loathing as much damage as possible before finally shuffling off into the darkness that we are sure awaits us.

I want you to understand that we will not be happy until you agree with us—one way or another.

I want you to understand that you have met the enemy, and he is us.

And then I want you to do something that under ordinary circumstances you should never, ever do.

I want you to trust me.

C'mon—what do you have to lose? You've been willing enough to buy into just about every other crackpot proposition we've been peddling over the decades, so why not this one?

Why am I doing this? In part because it's been so pathetically easy to defeat you up to this point, you've taken all the fun out of it. As Dad said, we thought we'd level the playing field a bit, and give you wingnuts a chance, the better to make our ultimate victory the sweeter. After the beating you have taken, you need all the help you can get, and that's what I'm here for, even though, when all the chips are counted, we will still be doing a victory dance in your end zone, pointing our fingers at you and taunting you like the trash-talking schoolyard bullies we so desperately wanted to be as kids, but put off until we could gather lots more of our own kind around us.

You have to admit that our brilliantly insidious game plan has been a thing of beauty to watch as it's unfolded—in conception, at least, if not at the messy street level, where as Uncle Joe Stalin once observed, you can't make an omelet without breaking a few heads, or something like that. Who else could have systematically dismantled the *soi-disant* "greatest" country the world has ever seen, all from the inside and without firing a shot—okay, maybe a few here and there, along with a couple of bombs courtesy of Bill Ayers and his pals—*and all the while claiming the moral high ground?* It's annoying but true: somehow your crowd—at least the diabolical Dick Cheney contingent—seems better equipped to appreciate our genius than the useful but, shall we say, "cognitively challenged" moonbats who make up so much of our own constituency.

So stick with me as I roll out a few tried-and-true principles that have served us very handsomely over the years, principles that, along with everything else in these pages, you might consider taking to heart. That is, if you want to take your country back. Otherwise, you'll be just another bunch of losers, standing on the sidelines as the triumphal parade marches by. And I'll be on the lead float.

Because, in the end, you can't win—you know that, don't you? You are on the side of everything that's reactionary, that's obstructionist, that's—not to put too fine a point on it—doomed. Therefore, I'm offering you this last, sporting chance before our armies of the night close in around you.

Go for it, Amerikkka—I dare you!

RULES
FOR RADICAL
CONSERVATIVES

As you probably know, out here in Hollywood we often work with partners when we're writing scripts or developing TV pilots. It's a lonely, cold, and cruel life we liberals lead in sunny SoCal and, like everybody else's wealth but our own, we like to spread the misery around. Which is why most scribes have a writing partner who more or less complements them in just about every aspect of screenwriting. One guy's good at dialogue, while the other handles story structure. One gal writes terrific action sequences while the other fella handles the mushy stuff. We are absolutely diverse in every possible way, if you don't count race, creed, color, or national origin, or, naturally, political affiliation. A glorious mosaic of monochrome, that's us!

Being my own man, I have ventured to break from the prevailing orthodoxy of independent sameness, and have decided to write a miniseries with an old friend, whom I'll call Max Jeffries, on account of everybody out here is named either Max or Jeff. Our working title is *A Tale of Two Citizens: This Time, It's Personal,* and if you think of it as a cross between that Dickens novel and *The Odd Couple* with lots of babes and cool weapons, you'll not be far off.

Well, here's the funny thing: as we're writing, we're realizing that the two of us, Max and Dave, are sort of like Charles Darnay and Sydney Carton, or Felix Ungar and Oscar Madison, ourselves. I mean, it's amazing—we're polar opposites, even though we both grew up in the same neighborhood in New York, both live out here near each other, even date some of the same chicks. Except for one thing, which is something I promised Max I'd never tell anybody in a million years, especially not out here, on account of it would end his career immediately if anybody ever found out, but I know I can trust you:

Max is a closet conservative. Which is why I write with him. There, I said it—now you can finish *both* our careers, so please use your power wisely. I like the intellectual give-and-take of an alternative viewpoint, and while I don't subscribe to a single thing he says (retrograde, revanchist opinions like his are best kept to oneself), they do come in handy when we're fleshing out our villains. In fact, people often come up to me on Hollywood Boulevard near Highland, while I'm scouting a suitable bit of sidewalk for my inevitable star on the Walk of Fame, and ask me just how I get those slobbering, rapacious capitalist creeps from Halliburton and Bechtel so right, but I just smile my Mona Lisa smile and walk away.

Anyway, to give you a flavor of the life I lead out here, and to help you make sense of all that follows, I'm going to give you a sampling of our thought processes and working habits, so that you can see how the sausage that lights up your jumbo plasma TVs is made:

MAX: So, who's the hero here?

DAVE: It's obvious, isn't it?

MAX: To me, yes. The Darnay–Felix Ungar character. Or, as we like to call him, the good guy. Honest, upright, neat, clean. A little fussy and lovable maybe, but the real spine of our story.

DAVE: Are you kidding? Everybody hates those guys! Darnay's a hard-luck sap, Felix is a prig—nothing lovable about either of them. Whereas old Syd is a dissolute opportunist with a yen for Chuck's hot girlfriend, Marie, while Oscar is a world-class slob: Everymen!

MAX: That is so typical of you lefties. Always rooting for the bad guy, the rogue, the outlaw biker type. You're like the Catholic schoolgirl who runs off with the first Hell's Angel she meets. You think everybody in the country shares your taste for your dark Bizarro-world, your fantasy of heaven if heaven were hell.

DAVE: This is why your movies stink. Colorless stories about colorless people, *In the Bedroom* without the bedroom scenes—

MAX: —we prefer the phrase "uplifting stories about role models."

DAVE: Earth to Max: role models died out with *The Pride of the Yankees,* and I always root for Babe Ruth in that picture. Where've you been since *Bonnie and Clyde*?

MAX: Let's get to work, shall we?

So we went to work and came up with the premise for the show: each week, from their "home base"—that's TV-speak for the main set of the show, the place where nearly every episode begins and ends—our two main characters get an impossible, save-the-world assignment, like rescuing Osama bin Laden from a secure holding facility in Afghanistan or else capturing him and sneaking him in there, depending on which way the political winds are blowing when we finally go over to HBO to pitch. In the grand tradition of *I Spy*, we combine quips and one-liners with exciting action sequences, then wind up back where we started: a nondescript brownstone in Greenwich Village, which the two bachelors share.

Here's the hook: the two guys look *exactly alike.* (That's the part we stole from Dickens, who's dead so no harm no foul.) Their own mothers couldn't tell them apart. Which means we can have great fun with identity switching, making love to the same girl, even a little Superman/Clark Kent dichotomy type of thing whenever we want to go full Freudian. The possibilities are endless. Plus, there's this:

They hate each other's guts.

DAVE: We need some backstory.

MAX: Let's keep them mysterious.

DAVE: Viewers are too impatient for mystery. How's this: they were both born at the same hospital at the same time and possibly switched at birth? Brothers from another mother! I tell you, the possibilities are endless. So, before you say it's—

MAX: —the stupidest thing I ever heard—

DAVE: —think of the mistaken identity fun we can have. The bed hopping—

MAX: —but the show's not about bed hopping. It's about saving the world. Doing the right thing. Besides, the switched-at-birth thing went out with *Il Trovatore*, or maybe *Big Business*.

DAVE: Who cares? We've got to give the audience a few yucks along the way; since this is HBO, a little skin too. Come on, Max—this is Amerikkka in the twenty-first century we're talking about here. Anything goes!

MAX: Well, that's just our problem, isn't it?

DAVE: Now, don't go getting all weepy on me. Just because I used to trip you when we played fantasy dodge ball over on the St. Luke's playground—you remember, without the ball so no one would get hurt—you don't have to get sore.

MAX: Sore? You were always jealous because I was an athlete and you were . . . well, a little runt. You were always afraid I was going to kick your ass. Maybe I should have, taught you some sense . . .

DAVE: So that's why you write all those macho hero parts? Revenge fantasy for your boring childhood?

MAX: Okay, so they're in the brownstone. Chuck's basement apartment is neat as a pin while Syd's penthouse is a mess . . .

DAVE: And then the secure PDA designed to look like a Cuisinart rings and it's the President of the United States—

MAX: Why does it always have to be the President of the United States?

DAVE: Because he's the only federal official people know anymore. Who would you call, the Secretary of Health and Human Services? Anyway, the Prez calls, and it seems that—

MAX: —the country's in a pickle. Half the people are practically in open revolt, while the other half are mind-numbed robots, who answer to the man they call the Dear Leader—

DAVE (getting excited now): —right, Rush Limbaugh, who's ordered his dittoheads into action against—

MAX (ditto): —the PRESIDENT OF THE UNITED STATES. I can see it now: it's a remake of *Seven Days in May*, but this time with a happy ending.

DAVE: The last one had a happy ending. Besides, remember our subtitle, *This Time, It's Personal*.

MAX: That's always your subtitle. It's become a cliché.

DAVE: I prefer to think of it as a trademark. Anyway, spitballing now, what if subtextually our show's really about a country that appears to be one unified place but—like our main characters—is actually a hotbed of resentment and barely disguised hostility?

MAX: Ontogeny recapitulates phylogeny, eh?
DAVE: Huh?
MAX: Didn't you learn anything at Columbia?
DAVE: No. Did you?

Silence for a moment, then—

MAX: What did you mean, "switched at birth"?

To be continued . . .

★ PART ONE
THE PROBLEM

or The Beginning of Wisdom Is Understanding How You Got Here

There is never a democracy that did not commit suicide.

—John Adams

YOU HAVE MET THE ENEMY, AND HE IS US

W E DIDN'T REALLY KNOW each other as kids, and why would we? We come from two different worlds, you and I, and I very much doubt if you would have traveled in the elite circles of Greenwich Village the way I did growing up in New York City. I moved easily from the Little Red School House to the cannoli shops over on Bleecker Street, the small, intimate reading circle that my father, whom you've just met, hosted in the basement of the old Café Society building at One Sheridan Square, where I was instructed in the finer points of Marxism-Leninism and Billie Holiday more or less at the same time. I could sing the "Internationale" by the time I was four, and still know all the words, in Russian, to the old Soviet national anthem. There was hardly a progressive school I didn't attend, an essay by Adorno or Horkheimer or Fromm I didn't read, a Pete Seeger song I didn't love. I was politically correct before it was politically correct to be politically correct.

You, on the other hand, were probably trudging from shop class or home economics to some dumb English class where a droning professor who made Ben Stein in *Ferris Bueller's Day Off* seem like Robin Williams on speed forced you to read reactionary literature like *Lord Jim* and other criminally exploitative trash while you gazed out the window and waited for football or cheerleading practice to begin. Being a New Yorker and all, I didn't even have a driver's license until I moved to Los Angeles, while you probably got yours at fourteen so you could drive your daddy's tractor, right about the same time as you got your first pis-

tol permit. You were the big, strong guy who respected his parents, dutifully got good grades, went out for all the sports teams (whether you
made them or not didn't seem to crush you, the way it crushed lesser
mortals—like me, for example), knew how to shoot a rifle, and even
darkened the door of a house of worship once in a while. Or you were
the hot chick, nice Miss Goody Golightly, the one who wore her skirts
to the knees, who knew how to cook but could also go to the hoop with
any of the guys, the girl guys like me knew we could never have until either we a) learned to shoot or b) made a lot of money.

Because, despite my ambiguous but inarguable intellectual prowess,
I was also the unpleasant misfit who never got picked for any sport, the
affirmative action right fielder way back before they had affirmative action, the wiseacre in the back of the classroom who could make everybody laugh, *just* manage not to piss off the teachers too much, and only
get beaten up every once in a while. The class presidential candidate
who ran on a platform of getting IBM out of South Africa and getting
the U.S. out of the U.S. (Wildly popular, even back then.) I was the
snitch, the weasel who threatened to tell your mama whenever anything
didn't go my way. Eddie Haskell was my hero, the creep who would
start fights and then run to Mrs. Cleaver and blame the other guy. It was
from him that I learned that it didn't matter what you did, it only mattered what you *said,* and what you could get away with. Contrary to
your idiotic "realist" mantra, words *don't* have fixed meanings and actions usually *don't* have consequences. In fact, almost *nothing* has consequences, at least not in this life, and I was raised to believe in the here and
now, and not the hereafter. You fools, with your faith in good works
and, well, faith itself, reliably undercut yourselves and hold yourselves
back; it is your fatal weakness, and boy oh boy do we know how to exploit it. Advantage: atheists! Just as long as we win—or fix—the next
election.

In short, I was a born liberal.

Remember that old Three Stooges routine? You know, the one
where they're counting out the swag and Moe says to Larry, "One for
you, one for me. One for you, two for me. One for you, three for me . . ."
It takes Larry an agonizingly long while to catch on to the scam, which
only sounds reasonable if you buy Moe's arithmetic in the first place.

But why wouldn't you? You've been buying our arithmetic since the dawn of the Progressive Era, back in the days of Marx, Engels, and Lenin, and have been falling for it ever since. The point is simple: what's mine is mine and what's yours is either ours or negotiable. Once you understand that, we're going to get along just fine.

Got it? Yeah, we might not have met, but we nevertheless recognize each other from the old neighborhood, if you know what I mean. Now my pals and I are the ones who run your neighborhood associations and co-op boards and "concerned citizens committees"—we never get tired of this stuff!—the people who meddle in every aspect of your lives, not only because we want to, having nothing better to do ourselves, but because *we can*. We *are* Eddie Haskell, on steroids, a malevolent, empowered Eddie Haskell, come to living, breathing life, and sent back to earth by a lower power to annoy you. It's no wonder that we still secretly mourn the death of our beloved Soviet Union, because we pine for a world we never quite knew, but are busy bringing into existence right here in Amerikkka: a cleaner, greener, better place, in which people like me occupy every interstice, Comrade Strelnikov, telling you at every turn what you may or may not do, what you should eat and shouldn't smoke, where you must put your trash, your "recyclables," even your grass clippings—and all for your own good.

At nearly every juncture of your lives, people like me are there with our hands out for a little of the old palm-crossing ho-ho-ho. You used to call them bribes, shakedowns, *pourboires*. Today, we call them "fees," or "permits." Want to build a new bathroom? Pay me. A fence? Pay me. Change the front of your home in a historic preservation zone? Accommodate me and then pay me. Gaia forbid you want to do anything major on what we laughingly used to call "private property." Then you're really going to pay. And all for the privilege of "participating" in a system that is fast becoming as much an illusion as your religion.

There is no God but Caesar, and we am he and he is me and we are all together and . . . whoops! Get used to it, walruses.

Or do something about it. Which is the whole point of this book. Although we've been able to attract a great many well-intentioned or well-indoctrinated or, well, let's call it confused people to our side, that's

mostly because we've so stridently claimed, with no factual basis whatsoever, the moral high ground for so many years that it is now socially
unacceptable to oppose us. *We're* the cool kids these days.

Admit it, you've always hated people like me, even though "hate" is
a hateful word and ought to be punishable under hate crimes laws, if it
isn't already. And yet you follow your leaders—presidents you never
heard of a few years ago, and weak little men with voices like straw
reeds, and gangster gun molls from cities back east—because you believe
the sound of sweet nothings on their lips. Or, more likely, because it's
the "right thing to do." Well, as Texas Guinan used to say to the patrons
of her speakeasies, just before she and Owney Madden fleeced them—
"Hello, suckers!"

And yet . . . you will follow. Because you are postmodern men and
women, which means that you've come to accept, if not fully believe,
our contention that words mean more than deeds, that good intentions
mean more than results. That feelings are far more important than facts.
And, speaking of which—

The *fact* is, we are all around you. We are those people you complain
about when you get home from work at night, if you even still have
work. Or a home. We are the bureaucrats, the regulators, the lawyers,
the administrators. We are the tribunes of the Great Liberal Empire,
which exists for one reason and one reason alone: to tell you what to do.
We are the people who control nearly every aspect of your lives, the unelected pygmy functionaries whose jobs have been created by legions of
lawyers in order to tie you—the heroic Gulliver—to an infinite series of
pegs and stakes until you are finally completely immobilized, at which
point we will at last be able to pick your pockets clean. Call it the Revenge of the Nerds.

Indeed, we are obsessed with shoving our lifestyle choices down
your throat, if you don't mind the metaphor. We need to see you grovel
before us and publicly disavow all your previous standards, because
when you don't—shhhhh! Don't tell anybody I told you this—it robs us
of the moral absolution we so desperately seek, if you'll pardon my use
of the word "moral."

Because, the sad truth is that as much as we love the People, we don't
trust you to be left to your own devices. Having done our level best to

rig and then wreck the marketplace, we can point at it in alarm, and convince you to abandon it to tender mercies. Because we are, in effect, a kind of suicide cult, unable to deal with our own feelings of narcissism and guilt and free-floating anxiety, we've decided to take our anger out on you. Because you represent everything we hate:

Freedom.

Personal choice.

The right to privacy.

The triumph of the individual over the collective.

Because we cannot compete with you on this field of sporting endeavor, we have worked assiduously to change the rules of the game. Even when we succeed, as I and my pals out here in Hollywoodland have done so spectacularly, we work to undermine the system in nearly everything we do—except, of course, our own personal lives—and continue our work to convince you that everything you used to believe in is false. We intend to show our love for the Little Guy by making him our permanent ward, by crushing his foolish belief in Santa Claus, the Tooth Fairy, and the antiquated notion of America as a "free country." Only in slavery is there true freedom, and we intend to give it to you, in spades.

And if you so much as think about doing anything about it, about fighting back, about "taking back your country"—we co-opted that slogan from you years ago—or even looking a little bit askance at us, well . . . that's what we have lawyers for.

Now you know why Eddie Haskell is my hero. Like him, we are free to push, poke, prod, plot, whine, wheedle, whinge, incite, moan, and connive and you have to sit there and take it. Have you forgotten two centuries-plus of your own history and the tenets of your own culture: that there are some things a man doesn't have to take, and that real men, when they have to, put up their dukes or pick up their guns and go to war? They don't let threats of lawsuits deter them, they treat domestic enemies with disdain, and when it's time to do what a man's gotta do, they do it.

Not anymore. We have undermined manliness, feminized your culture, elevated fretful safety and excessive caution into virtues instead of weaknesses. A man doesn't have to do a damn thing anymore, and some of you, against your better judgment, have bought into it. You're one of us now.

And you know what? We despise you for it. So put down the remote, get up off your keister, grow a pair, and pay attention. This is your last chance.

The Cold Civil War

Despite all the evidence of the past several decades, you still have not grasped one simple fact: that, just about a century after the last one ended, we engaged in a great civil war, one that will determine the kind of country we and our descendants shall henceforth live in for at least the next hundred years—and, hopefully, a thousand. Since there hasn't been much shooting, so far, some call the struggle we are now involved in the "culture wars," but I have another, better name for it: the Cold Civil War.

In many ways, this new civil war is really an intragenerational struggle, the War of the Baby Boomers. America's largest generation, the famous "pig in the python," has affected everything it's touched, from the schools of the 1950s (not enough of them) through the colleges of the 1960s (changed, changed utterly), through the political movements of the 1970s and 1980s (revolution and counterrevolution), and into the present, where the war is still being waged. For the dirty little secret is that all those fresh-faced kids, crammed together in public school classrooms, have hated each other almost from the moment they first drew breath, and realized that they were to be locked in lifelong, mortal competition with the dozens, hundreds, thousands, millions of other kids their same age. From their first moment of self-consciousness, they were aware that they would have to fight for everything they got: for the love of their parents, for a desk in the classrooms, for a place in the elite colleges, for a job, for a title, for money, for everything.

It was back then, shoulder to shoulder in those crowded, stinky classrooms, benighted places where there was scarcely a grief counselor to be seen, where Attention Deficit Disorder and the whole host of other imaginary diseases we have since inflicted on you had not yet been invented (any kid claiming ADD would have been laughed at and, in Catholic school, probably slapped upside the head by the nuns), and where the idea of filing a lawsuit on just about any pretext would have been considered trashy, that our respective sides developed our deep antipathy for one another. My crew was resentful that we had to share space, not only in the classroom but on the planet, with inexplicably happy alien beings like you, who, at best, ignored us as you got on with your lives in pursuit of the chimerical "American Dream," or worse, treated us with contempt as we whined, moaned, bitched, and complained about the awful unfairness of life and the vast evil all around us and all that jazz. Just because you happened to be the so-called "majority" at the time didn't mean we couldn't start planning ways to take you down, to change things, to effect a fundamental transformation of your society. Which, in case you haven't noticed, is now ours.

You admired strength, resolve, and purposefulness; we were stuck with weakness and indecision. You saw the world as something to be conquered; we saw the world as a hostile force needing to be appeased. You dealt with life head-on, never complaining and never explaining; we ran home and told our mommies. You cheered when macho neanderthals like John Wayne or Steve McQueen kicked some "bad" guy's butt, and swelled with pride at that whole faked "moon landing" charade, while we ogled Jane Fonda as *Barbarella* atop that antiaircraft gun in Hanoi, and rolled around naked in the mud at Woodstock. Think of us as Cain to your Abel, hating you from practically the moment you were born, hating you for your excellence and your unabashed pursuit thereof while we were the ugly stepchildren. Well, Cinderfella—how do you like us now?

Today, we are cock of the walk, king of the world, all our vices made virtues, and all us sinners, saints. While you were out trying to make your way in the world, earning a living, being responsible, raising a family, paying your taxes, we infiltrated your every institution: the schools, the law, Hollywood, the culture, the government. We learned to train your own weapons upon you and, while you weren't looking, we shot you in the back with them, metaphorically speaking.

And sometimes literally. The Cold Civil War, in its early stages, was marked by repeated clashes between the visionaries among the baby boomer youth (my dad, the sainted "Che" Kahane, was of course one of them) and their parents, between students and the pigs, between the Free Speech Movement of Mario Savio and the other Berkeley protesters, and the university deans and presidents who at first resisted them but quickly and cravenly capitulated to hordes of unwashed goliards and at Cornell in 1969 to an actual armed takeover of the school's Willard Straight Hall on, fittingly, Parents Weekend, by gun-toting black students. Heck, we (and I'm talking Movement here, since I had yet to make my debut and missed out on the whole thing) even got our heads proudly bashed in on the streets of Chicago during the 1968 Democratic convention.

Those were heady early days, marked by the Left's generational blitzkrieg against an unprepared and astonished establishment. To hear my dad tell it, our side couldn't believe how easy it was. I mean, here we were, ready to almost lay down our lives for what we believed in—and what we believed in was basically nothing, disguised as "protest." We were the bastard idiot children of Rousseau as filtered through the nihilists of the nineteenth century (no wonder we all read the Russians in those days, for Dostoyevsky spoke to our suffering souls as did no other nineteenth-century novelist, certainly not the overrated bourgeois Dickens or the impenetrable Thomas Mann), seething with rage against the Burroughs Soft Machine, but otherwise pretty much clueless as to what, exactly, we were protesting—except, of course, the draft; "Hell, no, we won't go," was our ultra-patriotic battle cry. We sure knew what *that* was about. And yet we rolled through our parents' and grandparents' generation like the panzers through Poland.

In retrospect, it's almost tempting to feel sorry for them. They capitulated so quickly and so completely—especially the academics, who made the French in 1940 look like the heroic Warsaw Ghetto fighters under Anielewicz in 1943. That was the moment when we realized that the universities, far from being instruments of the oppressor, were actually ours for the taking and a natural nesting place for the long term, pretty much in perpetuity. Even after we so clearly provoked Mayor Daley's coppers during the convention, and later during the "Days of Rage"—"direct action" was our euphemism for violence and vandalism—the Walker Report blamed it all on the fuzz and said what happened in the streets was a "police riot." Can you believe that? By May 1970, what had begun on the steps of Sproul Hall at U.C.–Berkeley just six years earlier was essentially over, and we had won.

Alas, as is our wont, we didn't know where or when to stop. One thing you can say about us is that we just can't help ourselves, cannot control our appetites or inclinations in any way; try as we might, animosity, snark, and rage are in us, and they've got to come out. And so it was that the Cold Civil War moved to the trenches with the last battle of the shooting war, which came at Kent State in May 1970.

You remember that: it was in all the papers. Shortly after Nixon (who had replaced Johnson in our eyes as the chief villain) announced the outrageous and illegal Cambodian "incursion," students at the Ohio university protested and demonstrated. There were the usual brave calls to "bring the war back home." On the first day of the troubles, liquor and the late hour predictably ignited into a street riot that was finally quelled by the cops. But tempers and nerves were on edge, and so the National Guard was sent to "maintain order," and the governor called the kids "un-American." Unbelievable!

Well, you know what happened next. Faced with insults like that, the students upped the ante; to which the Guard responded with tear gas. (As "Che" tells it, you were nobody back then until you'd been tear-gassed, and then you could get laid anywhere, at any time. Never been tear-gassed myself.) Finally on Monday, May 4, a mass rally was held, the administration tried to cancel it, to no avail. The Guard tried to break it up. They fired tear gas, but the wind blew it away. The cry went up: "Pigs off campus!" The kids threw rocks and empty tear-gas canisters. And then the Guard fired back—not with rocks but with real, live bullets. In thirteen seconds, sixty-seven rounds were fired and when the shooting stopped, four kids lay dead.

And that, my friends, was the end of the student protest movement.

Sure, some of the *alter cockers* on our side will tell you that's not how it was, that the movement continued, that the fight went on and the dream never died. But that's a lot of hooey. The minute those young Guardsmen turned their M1s on the crowd, and the student protesters got an ugly lesson in the first rule of protest—never throw rocks at guys with guns—that was pretty much the end of the violent prelude to our current conflict. (Luckily for us, no one cares about newly declassified FBI files relating conversations among agitators planning to torch businesses and the campus ROTC headquarters and foment a riot, and credible reports of shots fired first at the Guards.)

But after Kent State, the movement went both underground, with the heroic Weathermen bombers (shame about that town house in Greenwich Village) and, much more effectively, aboveground: into the schools, the law firms, the journalism programs, the civil rights movement, the environmentalist movement (which, believe it or not, actually started in the 1970s, with the first Earth Day on April 22, 1970—inspired by a call from a Democratic senator and activist named Gaylord Nelson of Wisconsin), where, like the syphilis virus, it went dormant for decades until it finally burst forth, with what happy results we now enjoy. We are nothing if not incubators.

Now, just between us, I like my Prius fine. But I have no more intention of giving up my other car—an Escalade—than I do of jumping off a bridge: hardship and penury are for the little guy, not big-time screenwriters like me. But if you think back over the events of the past several decades or so, you will see how even the craziest notions that we introduce gradually get accepted, mostly by sheer dint of our repetition. So that what started as a "clean up the garbage day" back in 1970 has gloriously turned into the "carbon dioxide is a pollutant" transparent but potent nonsense of our own time. Really, you have to give us some credit: what other movement could convince you that the very air you exhale is dangerous to the planet, and will eventually charge you a tax for the privilege of not having to hold your breath until you turn blue and die?

There, I said it: die! The purpose of war is to kill your enemy, but after Kent State—when it was we who were getting killed—we had to stop fighting up front and out in the open, and instead begin a gradual process of getting you to kill yourselves. Now, that's what I call a Cold War! Probably for the first time in history, one side pins its hopes of winning on the other's gullibility and willingness to believe even the

most patently impossible things: Polar bears who can't swim! Melting
ice caps! Seas rising! And that's simply "global warming," the magnificent hoax with which we succeeded "global cooling" when that one
didn't work out thirty years ago.

But there's oh-so-much more:

Your kids are all crazy—give them drugs!

Your cars are going to kill us all—better to ride bicycles, even in sub-
zero weather! Right down the middle of the internal-combustion-
engine-propelled traffic we haven't managed to eliminate yet!

Religion is the opiate of the masses—so go see a shrink!

Cow farts are destroying the ionosphere, or whatever it is—eat veg-
gies!

Criminals should be allowed to vote!

Marriage is an outmoded, sexist, patriarchal institution—but let
gays marry!

And it's *all your fault*! So shut up and die, already.

It's like that scene in *Goldfinger,* when Bond, James Bond, is lying
there strapped to the table, with a laser beam (standing in for the usual
buzz saw) slowing sliding up his legs toward his crotch, and he asks the
villain, "You expect me to talk?" To which Goldfinger replies, "No,
Mr. Bond, I expect you to die. There is nothing you can talk to me
about that I don't already know."

Or, if it's a movie closer to our own time you're after, what about
this exchange from *Independence Day?* You remember, the scene where
the Area 51 alien has wrapped his tentacles around Brent Spiner's neck so
he can communicate via the hapless scientist with the pitiful earthlings:

THE PRESIDENT: What is it that you want us to do?
ALIEN: Die.

Well, those two scenes pretty much sum up our attitude vis-à-vis
you.

Now you may object: *"Hey holy cow Dave for crying out loud if you make
breathing illegal then what hope do we have huh?"*

And now you've reached the central conundrum, which is why
you're having such a hard time engaging us on the field of battle. And

for this I must reach for an unpleasant metaphor from the so-called War on Terror, now blessedly over, to explain our position.

Think of us as slow-motion suicide bombers. In the end, we understand that we will have to go too, certainly if we follow through on the logic of our positions, such as it is. But as proud atheists who see nothing beyond but darkness, we don't care. We don't care what happens in the long run, because, as John Maynard Keynes said, in the long run we're all dead. And he should know, because a) he's the guy whose cockamamie economic nostrums basically wrecked the soundness of the American dollar when Nixon took us off the gold standard in 1971 (I try to tell my progressive friends that Nixon was the greatest friend we ever had, but they're still mad about the "Pink Lady," Helen Gahagan Douglas), and b) he's dead. Meanwhile, we're damn well going to enjoy living in each and every "moment" while we're here—being atheists, we are nothing if not "in the moment"—and failing that, at least make sure that your lives are as miserable as ours are.

I don't want to bore you all with a lesson about, you know, ancient history that happened way before I was born, and about which I wouldn't care a fig were my family not so heavily invested in the outcome, but—given my marching orders from "Che" and his homies down there in Lanskyland to try and bring you up to speed, it's important that you get at least some of the deep background on the seminal events of our time. Much as we all would like to, we can't blame this fight on Clinton or Bush and the "polarization of our politics" that the chin-waggers like to wag about. You think we're polarized now, you should see the family photographs of "Che" and "Uncle Joe," blood streaming down their faces from the truncheon beatings they got as, for some reason now lost in the mists of history, they tried to prevent Hubert Humphrey from becoming President of the United States.

I mean, you could practically pick an arbitrary starting point just about anywhere in American history to kick off the fisticuffs between Left and Right, and I realize those terms have changed meanings a lot over the past three centuries, but the point I'm trying to make here is that the Cold Civil War started during the Nixon administration, and really is nothing new. The difference is that now it is no longer a battle between generations, but a civil war *within* a generation, yes, the good old baby boomers. If their parents were the Greatest Generation, what can we say of our glorious boomer forebears? The Worst Generation slips trippingly off the tongue. The Me Generation got hung on them long ago. The Narcissistic, Irresponsible, Arrogant, and Entitled Generation is a little long. So how about this: the Viper Generation.

For sure, weren't they like vipers in the breasts of all those schlimazels who came home from the war and promptly went about their duties to be fruitful and multiply the suburbs? And the thanks they got was the poisonous asps who lay in their cribs, played in their leafy yards, broke down the remaining social barriers that had previously kept their riffraff folks out of the Ivy League schools, and turned on their own kith and kin with a ferocity that hasn't been seen since Orestes whacked Clytemnestra and her boyfriend, although they obviously had it coming.

Dedicated as we are to striking, destroying, poisoning, and destabilizing, we naturally flocked to a party with a long criminal history such as the "progressive" Democrats had, as we shall see, and their admirably "flexible" and "nuanced" approach to such arcane notions as law and truth and morality and standards of right and wrong . . . well, you get the idea. As they ladled on the moral superiority even as they violated every law and moral tenet in the Enemy's book, well, who wouldn't fall in love? It was like a permanent "get out of jail free" card, a form of atheist indulgence buying, but instead of sinning no more, we went out and sinned our tushes off.

A party, a movement, that promised us one thing above all—that it would never be "judgmental"—was just the thing some of us were looking for after those eighteen dreadful years with Mom and Dad. In its warm, if slightly clammy, embrace, we could indulge our every childish whim and fantasy, from our earliest erotic impulses to our inner-four-year-old's appetite for destruction. All of those so-called rules went by the board as we realized that, with the defeat of our parents' generation, there was now nothing and no one to stand in the way of our complete hedonistic orgy of self-fulfillment, each vice now a virtue, each temptation an act of saving grace in the afterlife that we were sure would never come. Platoons, nay, brigades of shrinks and "social scientists" (novelists manqué without any talent, otherwise they would be real scientists) arose to counsel us not to suppress our deepest id, but to let it have free reign in the real world lest it damage us in the imaginary world in which they habitually dwelled.

Up was suddenly down. Black was suddenly white. In was suddenly out. How wonderful it all was. We never thought of the consequences, because consequences are for later and we are for the here and now. It's no accident that one of our standard rejoinders when you lot object to one or another of our social experiments that we've just implemented, usually by judicial fiat, is: "Well, the sky didn't fall, did it?" This is such an easy softball to swat out of the park one would have thought you would have long since figured it out, but no . . .

Only one thing stood, and continues to stand, in our way: you.

And by you I mean principally the other half of the baby boomer cohort, the ones who didn't, like Satan, rebel. Some of them, a few, were like the angel Abdiel, who flirted with joining the insurgents but quickly repented and returned to the Enemy camp. But most of them—kissing cousins to those murderous National Guardsmen at Kent State—were deaf to our siren song, and set about living their lives in much the same stultifying ways their fathers and grandmothers had. They got up in the morning and went to work, dealing with reality as if it was, you know, reality, instead of the elaborate artificial academic construct we had fashioned. Unlike us, the constant kvetches, they never complained. They worked for ten cents on our dollar, their backs worth less than the penny for our thoughts, and still the fools were under the impression they were living the American Dream. Try as we might, and we did, to convince them otherwise, they believed in this country, believed in American exceptionalism, believed that their children would have a better life, believed—even when, like Abdiel, they slipped and fell—in the power of redemption. And though we laughed at them, they persisted, which is one virtue we certainly know how to respect.

So the Cold Civil War continues, unto the generations, which would be mine. Because unless you finish us, we are most certainly going to finish you.

In the Future, Everyone Will Be a Criminal for at Least Fifteen Minutes (Except Us)

You probably don't think of yourself as the bad guy in this little morality play, but the first thing we have to get straight between us is that you are, and there's just no getting around it. Whether you couldn't help yourself from the get-go and always embraced "traditional" (and thus suspect) ideas about right and wrong . . . whether you're one of those so-called "September 11 conservatives," who let a little thing like the murder of nearly three thousand people irrevocably color their worldview—what you need to keep in mind is this: we don't care. You're a wingnut, and we hate you.

I realize this is hard for you to accept. All your life, you've worked hard and played as close to the rulebook as your conscience, your bank account, and your spouse allowed. You probably went to college (although not a very good college; a state school seems more your speed than one of the Ivies), you're more likely to work at a trade than a profession—although chances are you're probably not a member of a union, or at least not an enthusiastic one—and just about the only time you think seriously about politics comes around election time, when you do your civic duty and trudge to the polls, there to pull the lever, ink the dot, or punch the ballot for the candidate who hasn't promised you much of anything in particular except that he won't upset the applecart for the next two, four, or six years. The big issues that play themselves out on the national stage, the pitched battles between Right and Left, the boilerplate about "morning in America" and "fundamental change," don't mean much to you. You leave that sort of thing to the chattering classes, the people who write for *The New York Times* and then go on shows you don't watch on cable channels you hardly ever tune in to, to plug the books they write in their spare time . . . to tell the President why what he's doing is either right or wrong, and why the American people—guys like you!—are too dumb to understand any of this anyway.

In short, you don't ask for much except to be left alone. Surveys show that roughly 40 percent of Americans consider themselves to be "conservative," by which I believe they mean that they don't want things to change very much at the local level, that they'll be able to get up every morning pretty much as usual, get to work, assume that their working conditions and taxes pretty much will stay the same, commute home in a decent American or Japanese car, have a drink and some dinner, sleep, and then get up and do it all over again the next day.

Buddy, if that's what it means to be a conservative, then it's no wonder I'm a liberal!

In other words, you're a normal American. At least, that's the way you think of yourself, or used to, before it became unfashionable if not yet actually criminal and actionable. You respect the flag, root for your school's football team, don't think the paintings of Norman Rockwell are as kitschy as some of your better-educated friends say, have an appreciation of your ethnic heritage that ranges from nil to *Roots* to the Sons of Erin and the Knights of Columbus, and whether you attend church or synagogue regularly, you're probably not an atheist.

But lately you've started questioning some of your most fundamental beliefs. Lately, crazy—lunatic!—ideas that you never would have credited in a million years have begun to seem, if not normal, then at least plausible. You're feeling your world sliding away from you and, while you might resent it, you don't dare let on because to do so would seem somehow . . . bigoted. Yes, that's right! You're a bigot! For you to speak up, for you to even attempt to defend what we fervently and fondly hope will soon be your former way of life, for you to try and reassert the verities you were taught as a kid, the truths you once held dear (not just some of them but, as we shall see, *all* of them), the—hah!—so-called "moral principles" you once thought were unquestionable . . . for you to take any firm stand whatsoever—is not just acceptable.

It really is amazing. In just four or five short decades—they seem short to us because we always take the long view—your entire world has been turned upside down, and you have acquiesced, and sometimes celebrated, at each step of the way. Sure, we were there, leading the parade, cheering, lofting signs, waving placards, engaging in a mighty mutual orgy of self-congratulation as we applauded this or that "historic" moment. Naturally, we never told you that our definition of words like "historic" and "unprecedented" was simply "audacious," "brazen," or even "ridiculous," since we never in our wildest and most perfervid dreams ever believed you'd actually fall for half the "social change" we were selling you, but you did. And here we are.

From cock of the walk to borderline bigot and soon, Gaia willing, to hate-crime criminal, what a short, strange trip it's been! We hope you've enjoyed the ride so far.

I'm thinking that, right about now, you must be feeling a little bit like Josef K. in Franz Kafka's *The Trial*. Doesn't matter a bit that you've never read Kafka, or that you have no idea what *Der Prozess* is about (I'm deliberately referring to it in German so that when Rush Limbaugh attacks me and tries to pronounce the title, he'll hilariously mangle it, rube that he is). Here, as we say in Hollywood, is the pitch:

One fine day, Josef K. gets arrested for no apparent reason on unknown charges for an unspecified crime of which he has no knowledge. His attempts to uncover the source of his guilt come to nothing. His lawyer is useless. To his horror, he learns from some weird Italian dude, a painter, that no defendant has ever been acquitted. In the end, they kill him. End of story.

Not exactly the kind of triumph-of-the-human-spirit stuff we love in Hollywood, but if you think of this tale as a cross between *No Exit* and *The Texas Chainsaw Massacre* you'll begin to get some idea of what we've got in store for you—if only you'll stay quiescent and impotent long enough for us to finally win this battle that's basically been going on since Mike and Lucifer had their little disagreement in *Paradise Lost*.

Oh, you're surprised I know about that, eh?

That's because we're getting into your head. Making you feel uncomfortable in your own country. In your own home. In your own skin. Making you feel *guilty*.

In other words, making you feel just like us. Don't worry. What you're feeling is perfectly normal. It's all part of the plan.

"What plan?" you ask. After all, we seem like such nice people. We preach tolerance constantly (it's our protective cloak, our defensive shield, our Tarnhelm against your righteous anger), we never resort to violence when a ruinous lawsuit will do, and we're always ready with an explanation of why your behavior is wrong, immoral, selfish, aberrational, arrogant, or just plain nuts. We will "talking cure" you to death, set the rules for you, force you to stay inside your head while we romp around in the unoccupied sectors.

Stop and think. Don't you now, on some level, believe that up is down? That black is white? That freedom is tyranny? That good is evil?

Of course you do. Because that's what we want you to think. That's what we've been telling you for more than seventy-five years. There is no position or proposition too ludicrous for us to argue, and so beaten down are you that you're bound to at least consider what we have to say.

Face it, it's so much easier this way. All those "commandments" about right and wrong, all those bad childhood memories, all those fears and worries (the two favorite words of *The New York Times* for use in headlines)—let them go. They were all an illusion. All those moral scruples, that devotion to hard work, that crazy notion that what you were doing really mattered—give it up. Listen to our siren song. Carpe diem. Or, as my dad likes to say: if it feels good, do it!

As you probably know if you've been reading my columns at National Review Online for the past few years, I'm in real life a novelist and Hollywood screenwriter, living in my palatial mansion in Echo Park near Dodger Stadium and dating the hottest women in Tinseltown, who hop in my Prius along Sunset Boulevard like it was a '59 Corvette and I'm James Dean. Like my celebrated counterparts on the *Times*, Frank Rich and Maureen Dowd, I never reach for any deepthink when a cheap pop cultural reference will do. Long gone are the days of the dinosaur pundits, the Walter Lippmanns, the Stewart and Joseph Alsops, the Flora Lewises (not that I ever finished even one of her *bien-pensant*, soporific columns) et al.

And so the pop culture moment I reach for is that horrible scene in Steven Spielberg's brilliant *Saving Private Ryan,* the scene that for me, for some strange reason I can't quite identify, was the most emotionally powerful in the movie, the scene in which Private Mellish, the Jewish kid from Brooklyn, is killed by Steamboat Willie, the German whose life the platoon's liberal, Upham, has saved. Sure, we all remember the first amazing twenty minutes, the landing on Omaha Beach on D-Day, the vivid depiction of the carnage, the senseless slaughter, the irony of who lives and who dies. We all remember the opening shot of the men throwing up as their Higgins boats are about to discharge their human cargo into the teeth of the German machine gun fire, coming from the pillboxes atop those dreadful high hills. We remember the ending, when the Tom Hanks character is killed by the same Steamboat Willie he allowed to live, against his better judgment.

Still, it's the Mellish scene that, annoyingly, haunts me and should haunt you too, since it's the fate we have in store for you. Mellish, who's been carrying a Hitler Youth dagger, eventually winds up in a desperate hand-to-hand battle with Steamboat Willie, which ends with the German plunging the *Hitlerjugend* knife slowly into Mellish's heart, whispering softly to him to "give up, it's easier this way. Let's end this."

Well, think of us as Steamboat Willie. I guess you can figure out who you are in this scenario.

For the truth is, it really is easier our way. No more being sneered at and chastised for your superstitious beliefs and your impossible standards. No more thrashing about in the unequal struggle, no humiliating pleading for your life (as Mellish does, as would we all), no being conquered by a superior force and being forced to pay the ultimate penalty as your killer looks you in the eye and whispers sweet, nihilist nothings in your dying ears. You too can be one of the cool kids. Join us.

If not, well, you know the consequences. Look what we have done to you. We have made you a stranger in your own country. And if you continue to resist us, we will make you a criminal.

Yes, a criminal. Because that is the ultimate goal of our long march through the institutions, our long march from the philosophy of Rousseau, through the founding principles of Marxism-Leninism, through the arrival on your shores of the Frankfurt School, through the penetration of your institutions by waves of subversives and outright Soviet "illegals"—American-born agents-in-place, whose first allegiance was to International Socialism, prepped and fed and watered and cared for as they scooted through your civil society, and brought you to the pretty pass you find yourselves in today. We are so close. All we need is for you to stay asleep just a little bit longer.

My father, the sainted "Che" Kahane, has told me stories about a different America, one that existed not long ago. A country where in the summers kids were told to go outside and play and come home at dinnertime—and if you got into any trouble, Gaia help you. A country where not all priests were gay child molesters (for that's the way you think of them now, isn't it?), a country that was not afraid of inanimate objects like guns and Swiss Army knives, a country where public and private morality were riven by a Chinese wall and nobody wished it otherwise. A country where crime was an individual's responsibility, not society's, and where the guilty were punished, and only their relatives mourned them, instead of the press. What a horrible, reactionary, illiberal place it was.

Take *Gun Crazy*.

Few of you have seen it, although you film buffs might know it by reputation. Suffice it to say it is one of those American film noirs, made in 1950, when your country—I say "your country" because I do not yet think of it as "my country," although it will be soon enough—was fresh off its victory in World War II, and secure in its sense of itself. *Gun Crazy*, made on a shoestring, told the tale of a boy who liked guns, who falls in with a girl who also likes guns, and it all ends badly. But here's the thing: *it's not an anti-gun movie!*

Hard to believe, huh? Watch this picture today and tell me that you don't shudder at almost every frame. The way the boys casually take their rifles, sling them over their shoulders, and go hunting in the hills. The way the hero/bad kid tries to steal a gun and, quite naturally, gets sentenced to reform school, without anyone much worrying about root causes. The way the lovers die—he killing her out of love—because for them there's no way out. And the way *nobody mourns them!* The last words of the script imply relief that the sheriff and his men who have hunted them down are all right. In other words, the bad apples got what was coming to them, and they were going to have to sort it out in the afterlife.

Today we see it through a different prism. We see it as a depiction of what a terrible place this country was more than half a century ago, a country where—well, a country where people were left alone to play out their own destinies. And we can't have that, can we?

As the criminals' rights movement proceeded apace from the 1960s onward, "root causes" became more important than the crime, and the perpetrator became a public figure, an object of sympathy, while the victim moldered, quickly forgotten, in his grave.

Fundamental change!

We have unleashed an army of lawyers against you, whom you then put into elective office; an army of unelected regulators, who take the self-serving laws made by our fleet of ambulance-chasing tort shysters and proclaim and implement new and ever more onerous rules and strictures; an army of unfireable bureaucrats and permanent civil "servants" who now make more money than you, get better benefits than you do, and expect you to support them forever in the pasha styles to which they have become accustomed. Eventually, all these "sacred promises" will come due and do you think the Party of Take is ever going to vote itself a pay cut?

Please.

Every step we've taken since the baby boomer generation came of age during the blood and fire of 1968 has been taken in the name of individual freedom, but in reality all we have done—and all we intended to do—was to limit that individual freedom, to strip it out of your social institutions, your daily life, and your government. "A nation of laws, not men" we solemnly intoned during the Nixon impeachment hearings, but what you fools didn't realize was that what we meant to do henceforth was not to observe the Constitution's precepts of limited government and enumerated powers, but to greatly expand it in creative ways the Founders, those racists, never would have dreamed of. "A nation of laws, not men" may have sounded good, but what we really meant by it was to tie you down with laws, turn you into (in the words of the Vietnam era) a "pitiful helpless giant."

So look at yourself in the mirror:

You can't fight back in the many states in which you have an "affirmative duty" to retreat to a place of safety should one of our beloved predators come a-calling on you and your family.

You can't sue the state that let him loose.

You can't vote the bums out, because the new bums are even worse; as the Who, my dad's second-favorite rock band from the 1960s, right after the Rolling Stones, famously sang: "Meet the new boss, same as the old boss."

You can't buy the car you want.

You can't buy the light bulbs you want.

You want to add a bathroom? Permit. Build a new garage? Permit.

Fill in that swamp in the backyard—hah!

Pretty soon, you won't even be able to sell your house without a government permit.

If you run afoul of our lawyer-designed-and-operated tax code, backed by the enforcement brigades of the IRS, we'll nail you. And speaking of the IRS, just wait—hoo-AHH!—till you get a gander at the glorious new People's Health Care System we've designed for you, cradle-to-grave shared misery in the best socialist tradition, each jot and tittle backed up by oodles of new regulations to be overseen by scads of newly minted bureaucrats whose operating principle is simple: guilty until proven innocent. But guilty anyway. And all enforceable by your friends at the Internal Revenue Service. Kafka would be so proud.

In short, we've made the old adage come true: you can't fight City Hall.

In 1968, Andy Warhol famously said that "in the future, everyone will be famous for fifteen minutes." When we finally get our way, after "fundamental change" is fully effected, everyone will be a criminal for at least fifteen minutes. Except, of course, us.

And you know what happens to criminals.

Wiseguys and Dolls

As is well known, as they used to say in the old Soviet Union, the Democratic Party has been, practically from its inception, indistinguishable from a criminal enterprise, a profitable haven for thieves, embezzlers, drunks, plagiarists, gangsters, slavers, shysters, segregationists, seditionists, fellow travelers, manslaughterers, and even murderers. If you look under nearly every rock since Plymouth, you'll find a Democrat slithering around in the ooze. And yet, amazingly, as the proud party of slavery, segregation, secularism, and, when necessary, sedition, we've been able to pin some of the biggest scandals in American history, from Teapot Dome to the Depression to Watergate, on you guys. We are nothing if not resourceful.

Still, as a card-carrying member of the Party, I am damned proud of our record and will happily match it up against that of any great crime family, from the Borgias to the Bourbons to the Gambinos. In fact, whenever I'm attending a Democratic convention, thrilling to speeches and promises of the great things to come, it reminds me of nothing more than an event that happened way back in 1929, when a group of great and wise men gathered by the breakers in Atlantic City, New Jersey, and set America on a course for a century to come. They were men—sorry, ladies, no women allowed at the time, except for hookers—from all sorts of different backgrounds, a glorious mosaic of Christian, atheist, and Jew, who had a vision for the future of America. And, yes—they could!

I'm speaking, of course, of the Atlantic City Crime Conference of 1929, the event that put the "organized" in organized crime. Everybody who was anybody was there that May weekend. From Chicago: Al Capone (fresh off ordering the St. Valentine Day's Massacre), Jake "Greasy Thumb" Guzik, and Moses Annenberg, father of the late Walter Annenberg (yes, *that* Annenberg). From New York: Frank Costello, Lucky Luciano, Owney Madden, Joey Adonis, Meyer Lansky, Benny Siegel, and Arthur Flegenheimer, aka Dutch Schultz. From Philadelphia: Waxey Gordon and Nig Rosen. From Detroit: Abie Bernstein and his Purple Gang. From Cleveland: Moe Dalitz. From Kansas City: John Lazia, standing in for Harry Truman's boss, the Irish gangster Tom Pendergast.

Yes, there were giants on the earth in them days. Which got me to thinking about a miniseries I might want to pitch about a group of mobsters who take over an American political party and heroically not only lead it to victory but mostly manage to survive and stay out of jail. Talk about a triumph of the human spirit! A miniseries set not in old passé Atlantic City but in the new playground for the rich and criminal: Martha's Vineyard, Massachusetts.

Every net in this crazy town will lap it right up too, since all the network heads are, of course, Democrats, have summer houses on the Vineyard, and would love to see their ~~heroes~~ friends and neighbors on the little screen each week.

Naturally, I'm calling it *The Untouchables: This Time, It's Personal.*

Now, for you civilians out there, the way you pitch something here in Hollywood is by comparing it to something the exec already knows. No point in trying to sell it on its merits. Let's say we're doing a teen sex comedy/slasher film: "It's *Gidget Goes Hawaiian* meets *Friday the 13th*." Or an uplifting drama: "*The Nun's Story* meets *The Wrestler*." You get the idea. So my series, a story about a group of people who were only trying to help, albeit behind the business end of a gun, is basically "*The Godfather* meets *Erin Brockovich*." Meet our *dramatis personae:*

Don Vito Corleone (*Aaron Burr*)—the history of the Democrats started off with a bang—literally!—when Aaron Burr shot and killed Alexander Hamilton during a duel in 1804. But this was no ordinary duel: *Burr was* *the sitting Vice President of the United States under Thomas Jefferson at the time,* while Hamilton not only was one of the Founding Fathers, and a co-author of *The Federalist Papers,* but also the first Secretary of the Treasury. And did Burr suffer any kind of penalty for it? Of course not. Indicted for murder in both New York and New Jersey (the duel was in Weehawken) he skated in both states—a development that, happily, would become both predictable and habitual for us Democrats. For good measure, Burr was one of the founders of Tammany Hall, the gold standard in big-city, machine-politics corruption. No wonder he maintains such an honored place in our pantheon of heroes.

Richard F. "Boss" Croker *(Christopher Dodd)*—the very incarnation of the Irish panjandrums and poobahs who ran Tammany Hall (motto: "Stealing elections for the Democrats since 1797") from the end of Boss Tweed's reign through the heyday of sachems "Honest John" Kelly and "Silent Charlie" Murphy. Sure, you've never heard of Croker or any of the other great Tammany sachems, but then you'd never heard of Senator Dodd either until he moved his family from Connecticut—the state he "represented" in Congress—to Iowa in order for him to pursue a quixotic and wholly useless "presidential campaign" during the 2008 election. The Irish-born Croker beat a murder rap, ran New York City's Democratic machine with an iron fist, took bribes from all and sundry, amassed a huge fortune in his little tin box, and eventually retired to his castle in Ireland, one step ahead of the law. Dodd, the famous "Friend of Angelo," was exonerated by the Senate Ethics Committee (stop laughing) of any wrongdoing regarding Countrywide Mortgage or just about anything else, but for some mysterious reason chose not to run for re-election. Like Boss Croker, Dodd may well choose to end his days puttering around his own estate in the Ould Sod.

Happy Jack Mulraney *(Joseph P. Kennedy)*—the partially paralyzed, thoroughly psychotic leader of the Gopher Gang in Hell's Kitchen, which terrified the West Side of Manhattan with its bravado and its brutality, is one of our great role models. He had a dream, of when the poor West Side Irish of Hell's Kitchen would escape their lowly potato farmer origins and make their way up from crime to, well . . . getting into Har-

vard! Happy Jack may not have lived long enough to see his fantasy
become reality, but his amoral ruthlessness certainly made it possible
for the generations who came after him to realize his version of the
American Dream. The Patriarch, meanwhile, was Owney Madden's
bootlegging partner during Prohibition, ruthless political operative,
Hollywood mogul, chairman of the SEC, Ambassador to the Court of
St. James, unabashed admirer of Adolf Hitler, and philanderer extraor-
dinaire, who flaunted his relationship with Gloria Swanson in front of
his long-suffering wife and their children. Speaking of whom:

The Corleones *(the Kennedy Family)*—who better to portray them than
the children of the Patriarch?

Sonny Corleone—*Joe Junior,* the apple of his daddy's eye, bought the
farm during the Big One, so he can play the part as a younger guy.
Then we get the sainted *Jack Kennedy* to step in. After all, he managed
to squeeze in a couple of years as POTUS between trysts with Mar-
ilyn Monroe and party girl Judith Campbell, who split her recre-
ational bedroom time between JFK and Chicago mobster Sam
"Momo" Giancana, so memorably described by police as "a snarling,
sarcastic, ill-tempered, sadistic psychopath." Then, alas, they both
die in a hail of gunfire.

Fredo Corleone—that would be *Bobby,* affectionately known as "that little shit, Bobby." Poor Bobby could not get anything right, beginning his career as a liberal icon as Senator Joseph McCarthy's B-team
hatchet man, sitting at the right hand of the even more evil Roy
Cohn. As an aide to Arkansas senator John McClellan, Bobby took
part in the farcical Senate Labor Rackets Committee hearings of
1957–59, during which his father's old business associate Madden—
who as a resident of Bill Clinton's hometown of Hot Springs conveniently had McClellan in his pocket and on his payroll—was briefly
called and then dismissed. Once his brother was elected president,
Bobby coincidentally found himself, at thirty-five, Attorney General of the United States, where he could indulge his vendettas
against the very racketeers who had helped both his father and
brother, not to mention also illegally wiretapping Martin Luther
King, Jr., thus providing FBI director J. Edgar Hoover with count-

less hours of salacious listening pleasure. The runt of the litter, he had to deal with sloppy seconds in the girlfriend department, and was constantly heard to shout: "I'm smart!" Like Fredo, his life was ended with a bullet to the head, fired by a Palestinian in the opening salvo of the domestic front of the Arab-Israeli conflict.

Michael Corleone *(Ted Kennedy)*—no gangland function would be complete without a Dearly Departed. Forget the expulsion from Harvard. Forget Chappaquiddick. Forget the poor ex-wife. Forget even the unpleasantness at Palm Beach with William Kennedy Smith, where a classic Kennedy evening of fun ended with an unfortunate rape accusation. Like youngest son Michael, Edward Moore Kennedy sought to expiate a life in the rackets with the forgiveness of Holy Mother Church, but just when he thought he was out, the health care rackets kept dragging him back in.

Like any abortion-supporting true Catholic, Ted played Augustine of Hippo to his dear 104-year-old mother's Saint Monica; nearing his deathbed, Ted decided it was high time to get himself right with Jesus after all these years, so he went right to the top. Like Michael Corleone writing a big check in Rome, he penned an epistle to His Holiness, begging for absolution on the grounds that he'd always been a good liberal who fought for the poor, opposed the death penalty, and "*I also want you to know that even though I am ill, I'm committed to doing everything I can to achieve access to health care for everyone in my country.*"

Now that, you have to admit, is an instant classic of trying to have it both ways. We lefties may disdain foxholes, but when the end is nigh, we hop right in alongside Father Coughlin and Bishop Sheen and beg them to pray for us. And what thanks did Ted get? "Here in Rome, Ted Kennedy is a nobody," said a Vatican spokesman. "He's a legend with his own constituency." Just like Michael Corleone.

Carlos Marcello *(Bill Clinton)*—that would be Calogero Minacore to his friends, as played by William Jefferson Blythe III to *his* friends, should he actually have any. Marcello faked just about everything about himself, including his citizenship, on account of he wasn't one. A U.S. citizen, I mean. Born in Tunisia in 1910, he "emigrated" illegally to Louisiana with his parents a year later, became a petty criminal in the French Quarter, where he was unfavorably compared to Fagin in *Oliver Twist* by the local newspapers, but eventually rose to control the rackets in the oldest Mafia town in America. Together with Madden pal Frank Costello, Marcello became king of the slot machine rackets in the Big Easy.

Which makes our boy Billy Jeff Blythe III—aka Clinton—the perfect actor to play him, for like Marcello's, much of Clinton's background is either invented or obscured. "The Man from Hope" was indeed born in Hope, Arkansas, but he only lived there until he was four. For all practical purposes Bill Clinton is from Hot Springs— Tammany Hall South, the "retirement" home of Owney Madden, who moved there less than forty-eight hours after his rival and partner, Dutch Schultz, was shot to death in the Palace Chop House in Newark, New Jersey, on October 23, 1935. The largest illegal gambling town in America, "Bubbles" (as it's called locally) was also the home away from home of Al Capone, Madden's buddy and colleague, and a notorious hideout for mobsters on the lam from the law in places where there actually was a law. And who was Madden's nurse and assistant anesthesiologist in his final days? Why, none other than Virginia Kelley Clinton.

Little Billy sat at the great gangster's feet at Madden's favored hangout, the Southern Club and Grill on Central Avenue in Hot Springs, right there where the main street of Bubbles takes a turn to the northwest and passes kitty-corner from the Arlington Hotel, where Capone used to stay before Kevin Costner, or Eliot Ness, or the feds, or whoever, got after him. Clinton was best friends with the son of Madden's lawyer, Q. Byrum Hurst, Sr. (who did some jail time himself), and soaked up all kinds of good stuff there in the front room of the Southern, not only the atmosphere of the old Wigwam on 14th Street, but also the whatever-it-takes ethos of the wiseguys passing through—most of them illegal immigrants and all of them, I'm proud to say, card-carrying Democrats.

Clinton was the perfect Democratic candidate: a liberal masquerading as a "moderate," a draft-dodging Rhodes Scholar (if there's anything we liberals love more than a man not in uniform, it's a Big Brain like a Rhodes Scholar), and best of all, a Guilty White Southern Boy governor. We ran him against George Herbert Walker Bush. Enough said.

When Poppy barfed into the lap of the Japanese prime minister, we knew he could be had. And when he just sat there with his pet gargoyle, James A. Baker III, perched on his shoulder, as the news of the fall of the Berlin Wall came roaring over the wires—well, let's put it this way: he should have been standing on a White House balcony firing an automatic weapon into the air, like some kind of super-WASPy version of Tony Montana at the end of De Palma's *Scarface* instead of acting like he was late for his tee time. And so a guy most people had never heard of a year before became President of the United States—sound familiar?

Maerose Prizzi *(Nancy Pelosi)*—the femme fatale so memorably portrayed by Anjelica Huston in her daddy's movie *Prizzi's Honor,* finds a real-life counterpart in the lovely and talented Annunciata d'Alesandro Pelosi (net worth: $19 million). She's the daughter of "Old Tommy" d'Alesandro, whose "parking garage" connections forced him out of the Maryland gubernatorial race in 1953, and the sister of Franklin D. Roosevelt "Roosey" d'Alesandro, arrested in 1954 along with fifteen other youths, as *Time* magazine reported at the time, for "taking two girls, ages 13 and 11, on an all night joy ride and keeping them in a furnished flat for a week. He was acquitted of the rape charge, but out of the investigation of this case grew a perjury indictment against twenty-one-year-old Roosey." Nancy's mama, also named Annunciata, got into trouble that same year when she admitted on the witness stand to receiving $11,000 from a contractor named Dominic Piracci, who was convicted of conspiracy to defraud the city. Oddly enough, Piracci's daughter married Tommy d'Alesandro III, who later followed his father into the Baltimore mayoralty. Let's see . . . Italian . . . politically powerful family . . . skeletons in closet . . . check! All in the family.

Johnny Torrio *(Saul Alinsky)*—Remember Chicago in the 1920s? Well, neither do I. But thems whats knows the history of Democratic organized crime can tell you who this jackass was: the man who lost out to Al Capone. Torrio was a philosophical genius, the man who schooled later generations of Chicago gangsters in the ways of the world, i.e., community organizing. It was Torrio who "organized" the South Side, teaching his fellow mobsters the first and best rule of rubouts: take your opponent out in the primary, well before the general election. Accordingly, it was Torrio who contracted the elimination of Chicago gangland boss "Big Jim" Colosimo, paving the way for his gang's ascendancy in the Hyde Park neighborhood. Think of Torrio as a visionary, the guy who wrote the book on theory, but who didn't quite have the stones to put it into practice.

Casting Alinsky is perfect—he studied at the feet of Capone second banana Frank Nitti, so he certainly knows the territory.

The Terrible Gennas *(Rahm Emanuel, David Axelrod, Valerie Jarrett)*—the Windy City bad bellies, starring Rahm "the Dutchman" Emanuel, the son and nephew of Israeli Irgun and Stern Gang terrorists/freedom fighters; the red diaper baby David "Jake Lingle" Axelrod, the former *Chicago Tribune* "journalist" turned Daley Machine hack and campaign manager; and consummate Chi-Town fixer Valerie "Ma Barker" Jarrett. The Gennas were the triggermen for the old Chicago Combine, before it turned into the "Combination" (of Democrats and Republicans) that it is today. They took out Scarface Al's enemies *molto con brio,* but eventually learned the hard way the first lesson of gangland; that everybody except the Big Fella is expendable. Today, they are all buried in Mount Carmel Cemetery, right next to Dean O'Banion (Jack Ryan), one of the early opposition candidates for the Community Organizer-in-Chief, and the sworn enemy of—

Al Capone *(TBA)*—one fine day, a young man of great ambition and an utterly ruthless nature suddenly appeared in Chicago, as if from out of nowhere (okay, Brooklyn and the Five Points), where he was taken under the wing of the city's leading South Side thug. Quickly surpassing his mentor, he organized the community, developing productive relationships with union members, employee groups, and Democratic politicians, and treating himself to the best in clothes, transportation, whiskey, and cigars as he burnished his "man of the people" image. There was nothing, it seemed, he could not do . . .

Mounting a nationwide search for the perfect candidate.

GREAT MOMENTS IN
THE PEOPLE'S HISTORY

OCCASIONALLY, *FILM COMMENT* or *Cahiers du Cinéma* or some other fanboy mag will ask me about my youth, in an effort to explain to their readers just why I am the go-to guy for every B-list sequel kicking around this town. What made me the man I am today. So, in order to oblige them, I've scribbled down this little scenario, as part of my ongoing series of *Scènes de la vie du Dave* . . . Naturally, I speak of myself in the third person.

THE SCENE IS AN INSTITUTE for Social Research classroom on the Columbia University campus in New York City. The year is 1999.

Students chat, flirt. A few of them have cell phones; a couple have laptops. Half of them look hungover, and the other half like they just fell out of bed, which they probably did.

The CAMERA pans over their ranks, stopping to ogle the pretty girls in their fashionable low-riding blue jeans, finally finding our hero: DAVID KAHANE, an incredibly handsome young man of about twenty-two who looks like the love child of Adonis and Joan Baez. We notice, somewhat incongruously, a grand piano in one corner of the room. On the blackboard we see something scrawled in European handwriting:

"GREAT MOMENTS IN THE PEOPLE'S HISTORY."

The door opens and the classroom falls silent as PROF. KARL-GEORG VON U. ZU BENJAMIN-MARCUSE enters the classroom.

He is an imperious, august man in his early 100s, but there's still a spring in his step and his eyes burn with revolutionary fervor. Instead of speaking, he heads straight to the piano and sits down, his hands hovering over the keys. At once the apparently lazy, typical American college students shoot to their feet, and as he begins to play they break into a rousing chorus, in German, of the famous "Alabama Song" from *Mahagonny* by Kurt Weill and Bert Brecht, ending with the refrain, "Oh, don't ask why."

The music finishes, the students sit. The professor speaks in a German accent so thick he might as well be speaking German itself.

"Excellent. *Ja,* this is how it was in ze glory years, back when vee rose up as one against, how you say in English, the Man *oder, besser gesagt,* the Pigs, ha ha. Of which revolution am I speaking, *Kinder?*"

One pretty girl's hand shoots up immediately: "The Bavarian Council Republic of 1918?"

"Nein!" barks the old professor. For a centenarian, he still has quite a pair of lungs.

The class jock—an outstanding intramural ping-pong player—tries next: "The Spartacist Uprising and the Free Socialist Republic in Berlin?"

The professor slams his fist down on his desk. *"Überhaupt nicht!"* he thunders. "That was 1919, *du Dummkopf.*"

Dave ventures a guess: "The revolution of 1848?"

The professor snorts. "No. Even I am not that old. I am talking about the revolution of 1968. When I taught your fathers and mothers the very same thing I am about to teach you now, *und* zey went out into the streets and fought for the rights of *die Arbeiter und ze* working man, the laborers, the proletariat. A premature revolution, as it turned out. But now perhaps vee may begin once more to bring it to fruition, *ja?*"

At once, the class shouts back: *"Jawohl, Herr Professor Doktor!"* Enraptured, they listen attentively as the Great Man launches into his lecture:

"From the beginning of this sad, benighted country, the battle for the soul of America has been waged over one simple issue: the individual vs. the state. *König Georg* against this terrorist, how you call him, George Washington. You forsook the peace and security of a loving tyranny for the deep uncertainty of 'freedom.' *Und* yet, we cultured Europeans continue to hold out the red hand of friendship, fellowship, and understanding. After all, we call each other comrades and sometimes even comrades-in-arms; nothing would thrill our hearts more than to watch, with you, the serried ranks of goose-stepping soldiers, resplendent in their handsome uniforms, marching smartly on May Day for world peace."

[Scattered applause, murmurs of "right on," "all power to the people," etc.]

The ancient professor nods to his comely teaching assistant, who flicks on a PowerPoint presentation, which consists mostly of covers of the old German communist publication *Die Rote Fahne* (The Red Flag), accompanied by Soviet choral music sung by the Red Army Choir, as he provides the voice-over:

"And yet you, you fools . . . you continue to honor the lone wolf, the reluctant warrior, the yeoman farmer. *Warum*? Which would you rather be? A free-born Roman or Caligula? A young woman of marriageable age or Henry VIII? A French peasant or the Sun King? I *zink die Antwort* is clear."

"But what about the right to be left alone?" comes a question from the back of the room.

Professor von und zu Benjamin-Marcuse's head starts to rotate like Linda Blair's in *The Exorcist*. "Who said that?" he shouts. "I will have him shot!"

Immediately, all the principled young people turn and point out the miscreant, a strangely crew-cut kid who obviously doesn't belong in this group of radical freethinkers. "Your papers, please," the professor says to the hapless idiot. "What is your name?"

"Marlon Kurtz, sir," replies the kid.

The professor gives him the fish eye. "*Ja*, so, Kurtz, if that is your real name. You remind me of Greta Garbo: you *vant* to be alone. Forget such nonsense! We will *not* leave you alone. We are here to help you, correct you, *fix* what is wrong with you. That is what Progressivism is all about: you need our help and you *will* accept it. This is why we are known as, what do you call it? The Good Guys."

Amidst the applause, a hand goes up. Dave notices that it's that strangely sexy Myrna chick, who made her bones early in the semester by holing up in her dorm room at Barnard for nearly a month, existing on a starvation diet of Diet Coke, Oreos, and takeout sushi until the Episcopal Church withdrew its moral support from Israel. From that point on, she got straight As from all her professors, whether she showed up to class or not.

"Professor Ben, if you don't mind me calling you that, if the people united can never be defeated, how come they're always defeated, that there's always another revolution to be fought and won? I mean, do we just, like, suck, or what?"

The professor pretends to give her query a moment's thought. "You have an expression in your country, which goes something like this: everybody loves *ze Unterhund*, no?"

"*Ze Unterhund?*" asks Myrna. "You mean the underdog?"

"*Ja, ze Unterhund.* The 'bottom dog,' *so zu sagen.* We are the under-hound and we must stay the underhound. And who has been more the underhound throughout history than us—the mean, the nasty, the du-plicitous, the whiny, the weak, *und* the contentious? All together now, united, as one. *Und* if the side of the oppressor is the mastiff's powerful jaws, then we, proudly, are his hindquarters and underbelly, the reflec-tion of life, of the struggle, as it really is." A picture of a dog's rear end flashes on the screen. Nobody laughs.

"Consider our noble history . . ."

Inwardly, the entire class groans: now comes the dry, dusty part of the lecture, one that likely will start with the ancient Greeks and make its way slowly forward into the Middle Ages sometime tomorrow. This is going to be endless. But Professor Benjamin-Marcuse surprises them:

"As I was saying to *mein Freund* Howard Zinn just the other day, you know, Howard, there really is only one story when you look back on it. Only one story. The story of an oppressive majority, likely installed in power through electoral or biblical chicanery, some group that seized power unfairly, or inherited it or simply bought it and then has lorded it over the rest of us since then. Call them the ancient Greeks"—a small moan from the class—"or the Romans or Hitler or Eisenhower or *Nixon* . . ."

His voice trails off, and for a moment the class thinks he's having a heart attack. Solicitously Dave half-rises . . .

But the aged prof is all right. "Forgive you me. Anyhow, you get ze *Bild*. The entire course of human history is an unbroken line of oppression, a conspiracy, a monstrous plot. You had heroic socialist movements springing up all across your country—collectivists, spiritualists, proto-feminists, abolitionists, nudists, even the odd Mormonist—and what have you got to show for it? Al Gore in earth tones.

"You see, the big mistake, ze *big* mistake, we made in the past was imposing paternalistic hegemony; we were the Daddy party, *ja*. Now, at last, we realize that here in America you don't like your daddies . . . ah, but you love your mommies. So now we must present something completely different: Fascism, with Mommy's Face. And for this I need your help."

Suddenly, the old man sits down, near tears. It's as if his life's work is ebbing away before his eyes as he stares off into the middle distance, somewhere between Bonn and Bialystok.

In a flash Dave is by his side, consoling him and comforting him. In this moment, we can see what a natural leader Kahane is, and how much the other students admire him; he's clearly going places. Even Myrna shoots him an admiring glance.

"But, sir," says Dave, "look at all we've accomplished. We brought nudity and four-letter words into the cinema, we've made the all-American dad a figure of ridicule, we've liberated women to work forty hours a week so we could effectively halve their husbands' purchasing power and yet still tax their families at a higher rate to expand government and increase the power of the state. We cut the average size of the American family practically in half, which means fewer future workers to support the Social Security system, even as the population ages and the baby boomers start to emerge from the business end of the python and bankrupt the system. In order to make up for that, we're welcoming millions and millions of 'undocumented workers' into the Southwest over our porous Southern border, where they speak openly of *la Reconquista* even as we try to convince them to vote for Democrats and, once in a while, to pay some taxes instead of sending all their remittances home."

The old man turns to look at Dave's face, shining with the same true belief that he knew so well back in the 1930s. He obviously feels better now. *"Danke, mein Sohn,"* he murmurs. "You remind me of a young Bert Brecht . . ."

"Danke, Kamerad," replies Kahane in perfect unaccented German. "But there's so much more to fight for." Impassioned, he can feel the proud heritage of Columbia flowing through his veins: the campus unrest, the Battle of Morningside Heights, the takeover of Hamilton Hall, and the occupation of President Kirk's office in April of 1968. The other students are cheering. Myrna flashes a look at Dave that tells him he just shot to the top of the Lucky List.

"There's so much more to destroy. We have to hold Amerikkka to her highest ideals and, when she can't live up to them, take her down. We have to divide the land into warring factions of race and gender and class; we have to make blacks, women, Hispanics—everybody who's not white—look past the progress that has been made, forget that together we created modern America. We have to manipulate the electoral system, register vast numbers of fraudulent voters through seedling organizations around the country—call them acorns—unionize the public sector employees so they'll have the whip hand when dealing with the taxpayers. We have to put capitalism down and make sure it never gets up again—except, of course, when we're trying to sell our books and movies."

The class is cheering wildly now, and Dave knows how proud "Che" would be if he could see him now. On a roll, he continues—

"We have to attack the system, the government itself, eliminate the Electoral College so that a handful of cities and their Democratic machines can dominate the entire continental U.S., instead of giving a bunch of yahoos from Nowhere, Nebraska, an equal say in the important issues of the day. And, once we fully seize control, we have to expand the very government we just attacked, extending its reach into every aspect of people's lives, right down to, to . . ." He stops for a moment, searching for the craziest, most trivial thing he can think of. They'll never believe this:

". . . right down to which kinds of light bulbs they can use!"

Rejuvenated, Professor Benjamin-Marcuse leaps to his feet and kicks up his heels. "And why, class? Why must we do this? Why?"

As one, they shout: "Oh, don't ask why!"

The professor pounds the piano, like the mad Clare Quilty at the end of *Lolita*. The class rises and begins to dance. It's a terrible and wonderful bacchanalia that lasts until, like Electra, they finally collapse exhausted on the floor. Only the professor is still standing; amazingly, he looks at least seventy years younger than when we first saw him.

"So, now perhaps vee may begin to see," the professor is saying, "that *ze viskey bar* in our song is just a symbol. It stands for *revolution*."

He nods to his TA, who fires up the PowerPoint once more—

"1848." A picture of Richard Wagner flashes on the screen . . .

"1918." Kaiser Wilhelm abdicates the throne as Russia is officially declared a Soviet Republic . . .

"1938." The *Time* magazine cover featuring Adolf Hitler as Man of the Year . . .

"1968." Riots in the streets of America and Europe, as Soviet tanks roll into Prague . . .

The PowerPoint goes dark. Among the students, a realization begins to sink in . . . *all the years end with the number eight* . . .

"But Professor," says Dave, "it's already 1999. A new millennium may be about to begin, but we've missed our chance. What are we to do?"

The professor smiles, and goes to the blackboard. He picks up a piece of chalk and writes down a number, which he conceals behind his back as he turns to his charges.

"Hope," he says, stepping aside. "And change."

Now everybody can see the date: 2008.

Higher Education

or The Way to Rot a Society's Brain Is Through the Emotions of Its Children

As a famous and highly remunerated Hollywood screenwriter, I am nothing if not all about subtext. Subtext is what we pros call that underlying layer of meaning with which we underpin our scripts and novels—the thing we call the "story" as opposed to what you proles refer to as the "plot." So let me straighten you out right now on the crucial difference between the two, so we're all on the same same page going forward.

In *The Godfather* and its two sequels, the plot is this:

Vito Corleone sees his mother killed in Sicily, escapes, flees to Manhattan as a kid, meets a couple of characters who will later play important roles in the movie . . . steals a rug, opens an olive oil business, blah, blah, blah. Plot—*blecchhh*.

Story: immigrant boy tries to save family in brave new world, condemns his children to eternal hellfire.

There—simple, wasn't it?

Same goes for our society. We've kept you clowns focused on the plot while the story sailed right over your heads. You thought you were watching *Thelma and Louise*, a travelogue chick pic about two hotties on a road trip from Louisiana (not Texas!) to Arizona. Meanwhile, we understood that the movie we were watching was about two wounded birds, both with a wing down, who had to play out their hatred for men by driving their pink Cadillac off the edge of the Grand Freakin' Canyon. Made sense to us.

Which is why you may have noticed that I've been implicitly celebrating our educational achievements in the foregoing chapters, because without the universities we could never have come this far this fast. Whether it was Cloward & Piven, or the Free Speech Movement at U.C.–Berkeley, or the armed takeover of the Cornell University campus, we have had so many proud moments in higher education over the last half-century that I hardly know where to begin in celebrating them. But I think all right-thinking people have to agree that the basis for our current cult of nihilism began with the "critical theory" of the Frankfurt School.

No, the Frankfurt School has nothing to do with the space behind the Green Monster at Fenway Park where they teach the vendors how to soak those Fenway Franks in water until they're good and soggy and then stick them in one of those cheesy buns that look like a chunk of Wonder Bread sliced down the middle and immediately come apart in your fingers, especially when you spill beer all over them. Instead, it's a reference to a group of revolutionary geniuses, the cream of German philosophical society, who had made international reputations for themselves at the University of Frankfurt and then, when the Nazis took power, fled to the United States, where they were welcomed into the highest levels of our educational establishment.

Unfortunately for you wingnuts, the Frankfurt scholars—Theodor Adorno, Erich Fromm, Wilhelm Reich, Max Horkheimer, and a bunch of other people you've never heard of, like Jürgen Habermas, and some you might have, such as Herbert Marcuse—sprang from a hard-core Marxist-Leninist ideology that called for an unremitting, all-out assault on pretty much every Western value and institution. Like Marx, they regarded religion as the opiate of the masses, and most temporal authority they viewed as equally negotiable. As Marx said: *"Religious distress is at the same time the expression of real distress and the protest against real distress. Religion is the sigh of the oppressed creature, the heart of a heartless world, just as it is the spirit of a spiritless situation. It is the opium of the people. The abolition of religion as the illusory happiness of the people is required for their real happiness. The demand to give up the illusion about its condition is the demand to give up a condition which needs illusions."* That's telling 'em, baby!

The slogan "Question authority!" is one of their legacies. At the *Institut für Sozialforschung* they made their Marxism explicit and after they came to America, where they landed at Columbia University, they continued their work of social revolution masquerading as intellectual inquiry, thus lighting the way forward as we seized the institutions in the 1960s and began sucking the life out of them in earnest once we'd received our doctorates and couldn't fake being students anymore.

Oddly enough for a bunch of academic bigdomes, "critical theory" means pretty much what it says: an attack on just about everything, including the family—the "authoritarian personality," i.e., Dad—the patriarchal society, social institutions, religions, the whole nine megillas. Critical theory saw itself in opposition to "traditional theory," which was basically everything in human history that had come before it, and the amazing thing was that so many people were so filled with hatred and loathing for their own culture that they actually bought into it.

Want a taste? Here's Marcuse:

> Freedom of enterprise was from the beginning not altogether a blessing. As the liberty to work or to starve, it spelled toil, insecurity, and fear for the vast majority of the population. If the individual were no longer compelled to prove himself on the market, as a free economic subject, the disappearance of this freedom would be one of the greatest achievements of civilization.

Let's try a little Horkheimer on for size:

> Although most people never overcome the habit of berating the world for their difficulties, those who are too weak to make a stand against reality have no choice but to obliterate themselves by identifying with it. They are never rationally reconciled to civilization. Instead, they bow to it, secretly accepting the identity of reason and domination, of civilization and the ideal, however much they may shrug their shoulders. Well-informed cynicism is only another mode of conformity.

And, my personal favorite, from Adorno:

> A German is someone who cannot tell a lie without believing it himself.

This being academe, "critical theory" got all wrapped up in talk of Kant's phenomenology and Hegel's dialectic, and the finer points of Marxism-Leninism—academics love to chew the fat about things like this and do it from today until a week from next Tuesday without hardly drawing a breath—but at root it was (and I say this proudly) essentially a Comintern-directed assault on the Western democracies. I mean, if you're going to be a follower of Marx, study at the Marx-Engels Institute in Moscow, go head-to-head with the other important socialist ideologies of the day—the Italian *Fascisti* and the National Socialist German Workers Party of Adolf Hitler and Alfred Rosenberg—you might as well go whole hog.

See, here's the part you reactionaries never grokked, which is why we've been able to pin Hitler on you for more than a half-century: Weimar Republic Germany had not one but two socialist movements battling for supremacy on the left—the communists, led intellectually, among others, by the Frankfurt School, and Hitler's Nazis. They didn't call it the National Socialist German Workers Party for nothing. They *both* opposed not only the tottering republic, but also the Junker establishment that had controlled Germany since Bismarck—it's easy to forget that Germany only became a unified country in 1871. Their battle in the universities and in the streets, redshirts against brownshirts, was the semifinals in the larger struggle against Western democracies, with the winner taking on the real war—the war for the soul of the twentieth century and beyond.

Hitler and his cohort may have been to the right of the communists, but they were in no sense "on the right." Hitler had fought in World War I, was gassed, and was awarded the Iron Cross, but he *hated* the aristocracy as only an Austrian peasant whose father was very likely the result of an incestuous union in the backwoods of Linz could. Born in Braunau am Inn, Hitler could look across the river and see Germany and, like many of the leaders in World War II, he was not really "from" the country he led. After all, Stalin wasn't Russian, he was Georgian, and Winston Churchill's mother, Jennie Jerome, was from Rochester, New York. But there's no patriot like an immigrant patriot.

Get it? No matter which side had won the battle for Germany, the *ancien régime* was going to be stood up against the wall and shot anyway, and a country with no long-standing institutions besides the Catholic Church in the south and the Lutheran Church in the north could not long withstand the battering it took. In the end, as we know, the Nazis took Germany, the Marxists took Russia (for a brief period after World War I, Catholic Bavaria became a Marxist state), and that was pretty much that. As further proof of their brothers-under-the-skin bond, Hitler and Stalin stunned the world—and certainly stunned the ranks of the American fellow travelers living and plotting in Greenwich Village!—with the Molotov-Ribbentrop Pact of 1939, which gave both sides the license to seize everything in the middle, from Finland and the Baltics to Poland and Romania. Hitler, of course, blew the pact away with Operation Barbarossa, his ill-fated invasion of the heroic Rodina in June of 1941, but that's another movie, as we say in Hollywood.

Still, just think: had Germany gone communist instead of National Socialist—and kept its brave, avant-garde theorists at home in their cold-water flats in Prenzlauer Berg and Schwabing—we could have been decades, maybe even a century, from where we are now, critically theoretically speaking. We could well be living in a very different country today, one in which old-fashioned virtues like God and Country were not under open attack, where sexuality was fascistically fixed and not progressively fluid, and where education was about different academic disciplines instead of indoctrination and social revolution.

Which brings me to my main point: you've gotta watch what's going on at the campuses, in the high schools and the primary grades too, right down to the playgrounds. When the German parents saw all those clean-cut, blue-eyed blonds marching around with their arms in the air when they weren't merrily tossing books onto bonfires, right then and there they should have known something was up. The National Socialists appealed to disparate groups, including the street-fighting thugs of Röhm's SA and the fresh-faced boys and girls from the *Gymnasia* (roughly akin to our middle school and high school combined, but for smart kids) and the universities. There's no revolutionary like a college kid, fired up with unearned anger and blinded by utter ignorance, that's for sure. And today some of them are my best friends!

And not just the college kids—given the blazing success of Head

Start, mandatory preschool for everyone! It's never too early to start the summer indoctrination camps. We'll outlaw home schooling, which everyone knows produces only fascist Christian gun nuts, squeeze out the Catholic schools, whose very existence in this country is an affront to the divine separation of church and state, so beautifully articulated absolutely nowhere in the Constitution, and herd *all* the little beggars into government schools.

This happy state of affairs, of course, was only a gleam in my daddy's eye when he and his fellow boomers marched smartly off to college instead of off to war in the 1960s. Dorms were still segregated then—by sex, I mean—and cohabiting off campus, if not actually illegal, was considered something very naughty indeed. You had a hard time checking into a hotel room unless you were married, or could fake it convincingly, and there was as brisk a trade in phony wedding rings as there was in fake draft cards, not that I've ever seen either of those things, real or fake.

Although "Che" and "Uncle Joe" and the rest of the gang may not have been heading for Vietnam, they were still spoiling for a fight and down for the struggle. If those who went to Nam were not our crowd, dear, if you know what I mean—the regular Joes, the guys who were ticketed for gas station attendant before Uncle Sam punched them a new number, the suckers going over there for a year, to kill some commies for Christ and then come back and marry their high school sweetheart—those who went to Berkeley and Columbia were made of finer, if not sterner, stuff. It was *on*.

The amazing thing was their professors joined them at the barricades. It was like the communists and the National Socialists: far from being natural enemies, they took one look at each other and realized that, ultimately, they were on the same side. Sure, there was that little matter of grades and such, but that was quickly disposed of via pass/fail. Classrooms became venues for sit-ins instead of Shakespeare. The assault on the Patriarchy began, as the Canon of Western Civilization—basically, all those boring old books, paintings, scientific discoveries, and musical masterpieces by dead white punks like Dickens, Leonardo, Newton, and Beethoven—were swept into the ash cans of history, to be replaced with . . . well, nothing, really, except a bunch of transient agitprop, which our side somehow got people to take seriously. Today that agitprop, the counterintuitive claptrap about race, gender, and class that we have force-fed your children like geese heading for the *foie gras* farm, is now basically the Law of the Land. It makes a fella proud.

What a time it was, and not only here. We all had missed the revolutions of 1848, although Dad told me that he had professors who certainly talked as if they had been right there on the barricades with Richard Wagner, but all of them could celebrate the Morningside Heights direct action, and cheer on their coevals in France, where the student riots of May of 1968 nearly brought down de Gaulle. Elsewhere in Europe, students got some serious hands-on experience in revolution, via such exemplars as Danny Cohn-Bendit and the Baader-Meinhof group in Germany. The immortal icon of a million T-shirts, Che Guevara, was one of our heroes, along with Carlos the Jackal, as were the Weathermen, of course, and the kidnappers of Patty Hearst, although that little episode ended tragically for everybody but Patty, who eventually married her bodyguard. We were on a roll, all right.

Naturally I'm unbelievably grateful to the trailblazers of my father's generation—we stand on the shoulders of giants—but if I do say so myself we have brought the vision of the heroic Frankfurt School communists to a fuller realization than even they could have hoped or dreamed. And it didn't require outright revolution or, ugh, actual bloodshed. By the time I got to Columbia, all of the principal issues had been as settled as the settled science of global warming, or climate change, or whatever we're going to call it tomorrow, and so it was given to us now to put them into practice. By the time we left school, we were a well-trained cadre of destruction, ready to seize upon any agent of change, no matter how idiotic, and know that our friends in academe and the media would help us sell it to a distracted and demoralized American public.

And you bought it. Hook, line, and stinkbomb. Because we understood the first rule or two of sales, which are a) there's a sucker born every minute, and b) the sucker only buys what he's already disposed to buy. Had we tried to sell you this load of arrant codswallop in the 1950s or even the early 1960s, you would have called the cops on us. But timing is everything . . .

For we are nothing if not incrementalists. This is where you always make your fatal mistake. It is the age-old struggle between strategy and tactics, between the drive on Berlin and the Bridge at Remagen. Since we don't have real jobs—surely, teaching at Harvard and working in the State Department, or having a Rhodes Scholar show on MSNBC doesn't qualify as a "real job" by anybody's standard, certainly not by those standards you in farmer/factory worker flyover country consider "real"—we have plenty of time to plot and plan strategy, while you lot consider the odd electoral victory here and there as proof of your superior moral and popular virtue. To which my dad, "Che," and I say: hah!

How well I remember the traumatic evening of the election of 1984, even though I was only seven years old. What misery! I can still see the horrified faces of "Che" and "Uncle Joe" and their guests that evening, whom they had invited for their Walter Mondale Presidential Victory Party and Plato's Retreat South Mixer at our modest home in Hallandale, Florida, not far from the racetrack. As the first returns came in, and it was clear that the Amiable Dunce was going to swamp the Full Norwegian in a way not seen since the hated Tricky Dick clobbered the first real progressive since Woody Wilson—that would be George McGovern—the grown-ups were disconsolate. I mean, suicide was mentioned, and not in the usual good way. You would have thought that Liebknecht had been shot again, and that Red Rosa Luxemburg had just gotten fished out of the Landwehr canal! It was like the end of *die Welt*: a historic wipeout from which the forces of good would never recover. Well . . .

You know the rest of the story:

We always recover. And how we did it was simple.

We turned fat old Tip O'Neill's tiresome bromide about how "all politics is local" right on its head. Instead of going door-to-door like some cheap Chicago alderman with a basketful of promises and his hand out, we took advantage of our increasing majorities among academics and journalists and began to focus everyone's attention on Washington, D.C. Okay, so your alderman was a crook, your mayor a corrupt idiot, your governor headed to the hoosegow. And, of course, they were all Democrats. So what? We convinced you that the only place such problems could really be solved was the **District of Columbia**.

And that, my friends, was all it took. That's where we revolutionar-

ies manqué built upon the efforts of Tammany Hall and the Chicago
Machine and the Red Brigades and the various People's Liberation
Whatzits: by gradually narrowing the focus of everything in the country to Washington and Washington alone, we were able to reduce the
United States from a giant, continental-sized country to the 68.3 square
miles of the District of Columbia, a place so special that for centuries
many of the laws that the fifty states had to follow didn't even apply
there, where the Congress controlled the city government, where the
taxis charged by the zone instead of with a meter, so that congressmen
could get from their apartments to their favorite saloons and bordellos
to Capitol Hill all for one low price, whereas the tourists got soaked
crossing Constitution Avenue. By nationalizing the media, by turning
the Washington bureaus into the only game that mattered, we laid open
the way for nationalizing everything. And we couldn't have done it
without the seminal destabilization of the cultural norms and "verities"
by our elite colleges and universities.

Because Derrida and Foucault and all the other guys whose names
neither I nor Rush Limbaugh can pronounce were right: "reality" is a
construct, a game, and the "text" is meaningless (as we'll see in our discussion of the Constitution in Part Two) except insofar as we give it
meaning. There is no concrete right or wrong, just an infinite number of
shades of gray; the truth is not a rock, but only one mirror in a wilderness of them. Your faith, your culture, your country are nothing more
than an illusion, of which we are here to disabuse you. It's not like it was
back in the 1960s, when the professoriat could expect at least some benighted fools or "students of principle" to resist the deconstructionist
matrix; not only was my generation open to their progressive ideas,
they were already there, in embryo, implanted by our parents and the
state-run grade schools, ready to be brought into full flower. We could
move from home to the classroom to the dorm room to our first off-
campus apartment without ever encountering a single voice of opposition—a voice that, were it even to be heard, would surely be that of an
ignorant, unlettered, racist bigot, most likely from the South.

And this is our view of you, our *Weltanschauung* as the Germans say
(a word I learned in my Hegel classes): that if you are not with us you are
against us. There can be no agreement, no bipartisanship, no middle

ground. When you reach across the aisle, you'd better be prepared to cross it, irrevocably, or else you can expect to lose at least your hand and probably your entire arm. The only kind of bipartisanship we desire is the same kind that animated the cowboy, Reagan, in his unfortunately successful campaign to bring down our beloved Soviet Union: "We win, they lose."

And unless you stop us pretty quickly, that's the only kind of bipartisanship you're going to get.

The Enemy Within

All of the battles of the 1960s, the cracked skulls, the bloody noses, the brief jail time, the joints that had to go unsmoked while we got the tear gas out of our eyes and our lungs, would not have been worth it if we hadn't achieved our main objective, which was seizing the Democratic Party and turning it into a wholly owned subsidiary of the international revolutionary movement. And while we took a beating in the election of 1968, when Tricky crushed our war hero, George McGovern, we didn't really care, since we knew the real victory had already been won. We had seized the levers of power and, with our huge cohort, would not easily give them up again—certainly not in our lifetime.

I've mentioned before how easy it all was, although it may not have seemed that way at the time to stalwarts like "Che" and his comrades. But once through the test of blood and iron, victory was pretty much inevitable, and for one simple reason: the generation that had survived the Great Depression and had won the Big One just didn't have the strength or the heart to fight us anymore. After all, as we kept reminding them: we are your children. And who wants to see his kid's head busted up by some pig cop wielding a truncheon? We bled for your sins.

Aside from Kent State, which caught us completely by surprise, we were fairly secure in the knowledge that, in the end, you would not turn your weapons on us. (And Kent State, of course, was not generational warfare but intragenerational: the shooters were the kids too dumb to get into Kent State.) "The whole world is watching," we shouted, and the cameras dutifully showed up, to lovingly record every chipped tooth.

There was one other thing at work, the congenital flaw in the very idea of "western civilization," which was this: deep down, the hegemonistic white male patriarchy has always been fascinated by the imminence of its own destruction. It's as if some primitive self-defense gene got bred out of your species along the way, and the culture that gave the pristine, green world almost all of its polluting technology can no longer wait to see the whole thing collapse. You're suffused with self-loathing; you know you had it too easy, that you don't really deserve all this so-called "goodness," that your lives are a lie and that the country you imagine you inhabit is nothing more than an illusion.

Or maybe that's just us, projecting again. Still, you remind those few of us who had a proper upbringing of Wotan at the end of Wagner's *Ring* cycle, helplessly watching as Valhalla burns, and knowing that it was the only possible outcome. Original sin is a useless concept, unless we are using it against you.

Which brings me to our ultimate strategy.

Next to Alinsky's famous treatise, and its predecessor, *Reveille for Radicals*, perhaps the greatest tactical manual ever written comes from the tag team of Cloward & Piven, who in a famous article in 1966 (!) for the left-wing magazine *The Nation* outlined both a strategy for bringing down the United States—to overwhelm the system by placing impossible but "morally" indisputable demands upon it—and the tactics with which to implement it.

For those of you who don't read *The Nation*, which is nearly every man, woman, and child in the nation, living, dead, and yet unborn, it describes itself as the oldest continuously published weekly in the U.S., dating back to its founding in 1865, when it supported the antislavery, Union side in the Civil War, which was probably the first and last "patriotic" moment in its history. Since then, it has evolved into an unabashed pro-communist, pro-Soviet, anti-American journal of liberal elite opinion. Of course, that doesn't mean it has ever been factually right about anything. Indeed, *The Nation* kicked off its storied inability to miss plain facts when it published in 1868 an article by John William De Forest, a novelist and Civil War veteran from Connecticut, who began the search for the Great White Whale of American letters in the title of his *Nation* essay: "The Great American Novel." (*Moby-Dick*, the actual Great American Novel, was published in 1851.) Oh, well . . .

Truth be told, *The Nation* isn't even really much of a magazine, more like a newspaper pretending to be a very short book. I used to gaze upon it in wonder as a kid, when I flipped through the yellowing pages of the lovingly collected back issues looking for racy pictures and never finding any. It's a cut above those mimeographed things I've heard they used to have back in the old days, but not by much. And yet, for some odd reason, people seem to take it seriously, the way they do another openly subversive publication, *The New York Review of Books*, which somehow never seems to be about the books it's ostensibly reviewing but instead acts as a kind of official compendium of whatever lunatic ideas we have floating around inside our heads every two weeks.

Cloward & Piven—or, to give these unsung heroes their full names, Richard Cloward and Frances Fox Piven—articulated their simple but brutally effective road map for subversion in an article entitled "The Weight of the Poor: A Strategy to End Poverty." Well, you know when you see a colon that you are in the presence of two bigdomed academics, and in fact you are because, oddly enough, both Cloward and Piven were sociologists at Columbia University's School of Social Work. Oh, and did I mention they were both political activists as well? And Democrats?

Columbia being the American refuge of our sterling forebears, the Frankfurt School sappers, it's no surprise that the recipe for municipal meltdown was cooked up in Morningside Heights, continuing that institution's grand tradition of cultural subversion and really bad sports teams. Under the guise of "helping the poor"—luckily, as atheists, we have forgotten, if indeed we ever knew, or else totally rejected, Jesus's pessimistic observation that the poor will always be with us—Dick and Frankie cooked up a doozy of a destabilization program, one that, behind its smiley face, was a live hand grenade rolled down the aisle of the Great Society and straight into its beating black heart.

For Democrats in the Johnson era had a big problem. It may be hard for you to credit this today, but back in the mid-1960s, Lyndon Baines Johnson was as loathed a figure as there was in American politics. He was everything Jack Kennedy was not: ugly, heavy, uncouth, and from Texas. In the tragic aftermath of the Kennedy assassination, when Saint Jack was struck down in his prime by the FBI stooge/right-wing hired hand of the Hunt family and the Cuban mafia, Lee Harvey Oswald— okay, so he was a card-carrying communist who had defected to the Soviet Union, so sue me—progressives found it impossible to accept that this big slob, who won a Silver Star during World War II by tagging along on a grand total of one airborne mission, could actually be President of the United States. He picked beagles up by their ears, flashed his appendectomy scars, and gave interviews while sitting on the john, for crying out loud. Worst of all, he sent the kids of my father's generation to fight and die in Vietnam. "Hey, hey, LBJ, how many kids did you kill today?" went the *chanson du jour*. Sure, he won election in his own right in a landslide in 1964, but that was only because he a) was succeeding Kennedy, b) hadn't escalated the Vietnam War yet, and c) convinced the voters that a guy you clowns probably think of as a good and honorable and principled conservative named Barry Goldwater was in reality a crazed lunatic who wanted to nuke little girls plucking daisies in a field.

The point being—and one that you should keep in mind, as we shall see—that even back in the day, when the Democrats owned both Congress and the presidency, the old circular firing squad was in effect as the Roosevelt coalition began to fracture. On one side there were the racist Southern rednecks, who would soon defect to their natural home, the Party of Lincoln, as blacks switched their party affiliation the other way en masse, and the racist urban ethnics, who would soon defect to their . . . well, okay, they mostly didn't defect except when they became "Reagan Democrats." On the other hand, you had the Frankfurt School types, the intellectual *francs-tireurs* who made it their mission to bring down the country that had saved many of them from the Holocaust, the Ivy League chin-pullers, and, increasingly, the media, which began to see its mission not just of natural opposition to whichever party was in power, but to actually advocate for the Left, as if they were the lawyers that so many reporters wished they could have been.

Yes, the far-left progressives despised Johnson. As a card-carrying group of intellectuals, we hate people who talk with Southern or Midwestern hillbilly accents, preferring the plummy tones of the mid-Atlantic, if not the downright honk of the Lower East Side and the bray of Boston. We're the ones who are always lecturing you lot never to judge a book by its cover—that would be profiling!—but rest assured that we judge you that way all the time. Why, with one look and just a brief snatch of conversation I can probably peg your politics in an instant, so don't try to fool me. We egalitarians are nothing if not snobs.

And since the Left despised Johnson, they grabbed hold of an important principle, one articulated by Alinsky in the famous tactical Rule No. 4—*make the enemy live up to their own book of rules*—and given practical shape by Cloward & Piven. Which was this: make the Great Society live up to its book of rules (in this case, regarding social services) and then simply overwhelm the system with supplicants until it collapses under its own weight. And then you can start building a *really* Great Society. The "strategy to end poverty" turned out to be essentially the same strategy perfected by our beloved Soviet Union: to bring down the rich to the level of the poor and make everyone equally miserable.

Unless, of course, you're one of the Big Boys. You see, in our mindless but joyous destructive rage, we progressives love the idea of wrecking everything, just as long as it doesn't wreck anything for us. Pop used to regale me with his tales of life in the glorious U.S.S.R. during his student days, the happiest of his life. It was a time of comradeship and vodka, of beautiful Russian girls and more vodka, of Marxism-Leninism and still more vodka. Naturally the peasants had nothing, but for the *nomenklatura*—and as a fellow traveler from the U.S. he was very well taken care of, once the KGB had cleared his bona fides during an interview in Room 101 of the Lubyanka—everything was hunky-dory, including beer for breakfast, the finest Cuban cigars, and caviar for every meal. If most of the Chicken Kiev and Beef Stroganoff consisted of mystery meat in sauces of uncertain provenance, at least the Russian girls were pretty and willing, and if you didn't die of dysentery by accidentally drinking the tap water, which is more or less the way Tchaikovsky checked out, you were okay. And if you weren't, there was always yet more vodka. Now we know how the Soviet Union lasted so long: everybody was plastered!

Now, I can hear you saying, *"Hey holy cow Dave why would Democrats want to destabilize the Democratic Party I mean isn't that a little like saying that you can't be both a capitalist and a communist at the same time? What gives?"*

Well, first of all, smart guy, you can too be a radical leftist/

progressive and a capitalist simultaneously: just look at George Soros. Or me, for that matter. Or lots of my friends. We devote our lives to the guilty cause of wealth accumulation so we can then turn around and destabilize the very system that allowed us to make vast fortunes—okay, so in my case, my fortune is nowhere near as vast as George's, but then I went into the arts instead of specializing in undermining the currencies of entire nations. So, in order to alleviate our intense pangs of shame while we buy a new Mercedes for cash, fund the Center for American Progress, and donate to the Democratic Party, we turn our self-loathing outward, onto society itself. I realize that most of you, like me, no longer believe in the fantasy of "heaven" and "hell" and "God" and "Satan," but there's a reason that Uncle Saul hailed Lucifer as the very first radical in *Rules for Radicals*. Satan had a good thing—no, a great thing—going in heaven but, like us, his children, he just couldn't control his urge to wreck it. And so he did, winding up in a burning lake of fire, wondering what fresh hell was this, and vowing revenge on you-know-who:

> *So stretcht out huge in length the Arch-fiend lay*
> *Chain'd on the burning Lake, nor ever thence*
> *Had ris'n or heav'd his head, but that the will*
> *And high permission of all-ruling Heaven*
> *Left him at large to his own dark designs,*
> *That with reiterated crimes he might*
> *Heap on himself damnation, while he sought*
> *Evil to others, and enrag'd might see*
> *How all his malice serv'd but to bring forth*
> *Infinite goodness, grace and mercy shewn*
> *On Man by him seduc't, but on himself*
> *Treble confusion, wrath and vengeance pour'd.*

Sounds pretty good to me, almost as nice as Hàllandale in the summer, but you get the picture. If dissent is the highest form of patriotism—and it always is when one of your guys is in power—then good ol' Satan has got to be reckoned a patriot.

And, when you've got a political party sitting right there in front of you, its "internal contradictions" (as we commies used to say) glaringly evident, what's a true patriot to do except to try and take it over, the way the Bolshies co-opted Kerensky, and then take the new, improved Zombie Party into the fight, knowing that most people would think it was just good ol' Fred, looking a little under the weather, instead of Fred the Undead, wandering the world like Caine in *Kung Fu* and looking for fresh, innocent brains to munch on.

As I said earlier, think of us as cultural suicide bombers, which is why we are always in such a hurry to get into the temple, the church, the pizza parlor, even the mosque, and pull the pin on our exploding vests. (We think of ourselves as Samson in the temple, wreaking havoc and revenge on Delilah and the Philistines.) We know that, eventually, you'll get wise to us and we'll be back in the wilderness, beyond the pale, until a new, idealistic generation comes along, one that burns with anger at the structural injustices of the world and harbors a fierce desire to fix things. (Suckers!) One that is susceptible to our sweet nothings, our whispers, our blandishments, our temptation. For who, after all, does not see himself as the hero of his own movie? That old American impulse, rooting for the underdog, can be so easily turned against you, and used to lure your children into the swamp of moral relativism.

Demolish Detroit? Done! Take over as much of so-called private industry as we can get our hands on? Done! Weaken the nation's defenses? Done! Urge that "if you see something, say something" to help fight "terrorism," and then whipsaw you with racial profiling and a hate crime when you point the finger of suspicion at a member of one of our protected demographics? Done! So much to wreck, so little time. Think of our leadership as kamikaze pilots who know the American big guns are trained on them and have to finish their task of Fundamental Change before the voters permanently retire them.

And so, just a couple of years after C&P unveiled their brilliant strategy to "cure poverty"—by collapsing the system and forcing the government to guarantee an annual income, more or less just for existing—the free radicals took over the party, and America has never been the same. Which, of course, was the whole point all along. Here were some of their recommendations; note the use of military terminology:

- The offensive organizes previously unorganized groups **eligi**ble for government **benefits** but not currently receiving **all** they can.
- The offensive **seeks** to identify new beneficiaries and/or create new benefits.
- The overarching aim is always to impose new stresses on target systems, with the ultimate goal of forcing their collapse.

Well, it couldn't be clearer than that, could it? And yet, few dared call them out on it. After all, they were from *Columbia University*, where **no idea** is too ridiculous to be taken seriously by progressives, argued, and, ultimately, implemented. You fools keep falling for this act, assuming bona fides on our part—it's *Columbia University!*—and that's just the way we like it. Keep seeing us as we wish you to see us (we're sort of like **Dracula** in that regard) and not as we really are. Ignore your intuition. **Discard the plain evidence of your senses as you first contemplate, and then adopt, our nostrums.**

And then look back over the wreckage of your country since 1968 and tell me none of it happened.

The Jake Lingle Society
or How We Seized the "Narrative"

If you really want to see the face of your sworn enemy, just turn on the television. From the minute you wake up in the morning to the moment you finally fall asleep to the flickering glare of your flat screen, you are being bombarded by a worldview that, to put it mildly, has almost nothing in common with your own. Should perchance you be one of those trusting types who get their news from "newspapers," you will encounter a similar cognitive dysfunction, as the world they describe increasingly bears no resemblance to the one you have known and lived in for years.

Sure, those happy-talk newsreaders look like a swell bunch of guys and gals, but while you're sitting there shivering in your underheated living rooms, reading this book, they're living the high life in corporate headquarters in New York, Los Angeles, and Atlanta, homogenizing all of the disparate news of the day into a smooth, processed blend of disinformation that basically boils down to this: we know better than you.

'Twas not ever thus. Once upon a time, and a very long time ago it was too, there was no such thing as the "media." At the nation's birth, the "media" was a loose aggregation of independent publishers, writers, polemicists, and pamphleteers, each one going at the others and, collectively, at the government. Didn't matter which government. Whatever it was, they could find something about it they didn't like, and they weren't afraid to speak their mind, even if it sometimes, or often, landed them in the hoosegow. For the colonists and early Americans were of one mind about one thing: that the freedom of speech, especially political speech, had to be paramount, lest tyranny reassert itself. And when in 1735 a German immigrant named Johann Peter Zenger beat the rap of "seditious libel" when he printed a series of anonymous blistering attacks on the sitting governor of New York, William Crosby, he struck the founding blow for what would later become the First Amendment. Crosby tried to shut down the paper and, under the law of the time, had a clear right to do so. But, in an early example of jury nullification, Zenger's lawyer mounted a spirited defense of the right to free speech, essentially adopting John Milton's argument in the *Areopagitica*, that libel was in the eye of the beholder, and was thus subject to disputation: "Wholesome meats to a vitiated stomach differ little or nothing from unwholesome; and best books to a naughty mind are not inapplicable to occasions of evil."

The early Americans, in other words, understood that journalism— which was not and should not be a "licensed" profession—was a full-body contact sport, and not only would there be tears, there would be blood as well. Truth was to be proven in combat, not by assertion or fiat or governmental edict, and if you couldn't take the heat, well then, get out of Hell's Kitchen. It's no accident that the journalists of the early twentieth century, when the modern media first began to take shape in all its institutional glory, more often than not came from the same levels of society as actors, gangsters, whores, cops, and the clergy. They not only wrote about the people, they actually knew them. They *were* the people.

As the Bill of Rights was being written, the dead white men you wingnuts so sexistly and racistly call the "Founding Fathers" understood the importance of freedom of speech and of the press. They had a bellyful of top-down dictatorship and they realized, to use a cliché that was once one of our favorites, that "sunlight is the best disinfectant." Let a thousand flowers bloom, as Mao famously said, even though, in fact, he wasn't one of the "Founding Fathers," no matter what we teach your kids in school today. They knew it wasn't going to be pretty—if you think some of the invective being hurled around these days is tough, you should get a load of the things Adams said about Jefferson and vice versa, and they at least were on the same side vis-à-vis Good King George. And of course we

Democrats unleashed an absolute Hurricane Katrina of obloquy and op-
probrium upon the first Republican president, your guy Lincoln, and
hammered away at him until one of our number, an actor, finally killed
him. But I'm getting ahead of my story.

As the twentieth century progressed, a still largely decentralized nation was festooned with local radio stations, each with its own quirks,
multiple daily newspapers fiercely competing with one another for
scoops and circulation, and locally owned and operated television stations. It was gloriously anarchic, often unethical, and very definitely engaged in for a profit, but it probably got us collectively a lot closer to the
truth than is possible today—unless, of course, you get your news from
the Web, the closest thing we currently have to the freebooting days of
The Front Page. It wasn't perfect, but despite its many and manifold
flaws, it often somehow staggered its way from the bar to the truth.

Naturally, we couldn't have that.

So, as part of our Long March Through the Institutions—the
Maoist rhetoric was, of course, deliberate—we put seizing media high
up on our to-do list. Control of the press and airwaves had obviously
been one of the heroic Soviet Union's principal activities and so being
natural Soviet sympathizers we glommed right on to their plans. As the
Progressive movement arose in the early part of the twentieth century,
the beachheads were established by bona fide bonzes like Walter Lippmann, a veteran of Woodrow Wilson's fascist-loving administration, to
organize a little something in 1922 he liked to call *Public Opinion*, in
which he famously called for opinions to be "organized *for* the press if
they are to be sound, not *by* the press, as is the case today." Now *that's*
what I call the state-controlled media!

To cover our bets, we leftists also co-opted, recruited, and infiltrated
our own cadre of sappers disguised as "independent journalists" into the
national conversation, men like I. F. Stone, who peddled the image of a
crusty curmudgeon, when in fact he was collaborating with the Soviets,
as the Venona cables unfortunately proved when they were finally re-
leased.

In between the bigdomes and "men of the people," however, lay another rich field to plow—that stratum of reporter animated by nothing
more than his own greed. While you can motivate a traitor with ideol-

ogy (we call those guys "suckers"), and sex (the "honey trap"), the most effective tool is simple money. Because while ideology can flag—especially once you get a load of our real faces, our skulls beneath the smiling skin—and lust eventually wears off and must be replaced, no one ever gets tired of money, nor loses his need for it.

So say hello to the patron saint of American journalists everywhere, Jake Lingle.

For those of you unfamiliar with the ineffable Jake, he was a *Chicago Tribune* legman—not a reporter-writer, but the kind of guy who back in the Roaring Twenties kept his ear to the ground, phoning in tips to the news desk. Jake's beat was, purely coincidentally, the criminal rackets of Chicago, and a very handsome living he made from covering them too. Oh, not from the *Tribune*—the newspaper paid him only $65 a week, yet somehow he had an annual income of around sixty grand, enough for him to blow wads of cash on regular visits to the track, wear a diamond-studded belt buckle, stash the wife and kids away on the West Side of Chicago, where he had grown up, while living himself on the twenty-seventh floor of the Stevens Hotel on Michigan Avenue across from Grant Park. (Today, it's the Chicago Hilton and Towers.) No, Jake's handsome lifestyle came from the other side of the street— the part of town where Al Capone lived. And Jake was ripping off Capone.

For Jake, you see, was one of those reporters who played both ends of the perfecta, funneling tips and tidbits as a day job, and keeping the criminals and gangsters who then, as now, ran Chicago, informed on matters of mutual interest. The fact that the police commissioner, William F. Russell, was Jake's boyhood buddy from "the Valley" didn't hurt. In the newsroom, nobody liked Jake Lingle, considering him high-handed and stuck-up, but they damn sure admired his swag; no one was ever quite able to pin down how Jake came by his money (which was never enough) and his expensive lifestyle, but it's likely that Jake tipped off Capone to various police activities while at the same time helping to roll up minor gangland goombahs to make the cops look good. Which is why few mourned when, one fine day in 1930, somebody put a .38 slug in the back of Jake's head as he was crossing under Michigan Avenue. Sure, Colonel McCormick, the petty tyrant who owned the *Tribune,* loudly proclaimed Jake's innocence as he mounted a hunt for the killer (who turned out to be Leo Brothers, a dime-a-dozen gunsel hired from St. Louis): "The *Tribune* cannot be under suspicion. It is a preposterous thing even to discuss," declared the Colonel.

Eventually, the truth came out and the Lingle case was a huge black eye for the *Trib* and for Chicago journalism. Amazingly, Bill Russell resigned the day after the murder, and later it came out that the commish was financially involved with Lingle in at least one investment account, which may account for his sudden attack of ethics.

It was a nice racket while it lasted. And, in one way or another, it lasts to this day. Only this time, the state has replaced the gangsters, Georgetown cocktail parties have replaced the whorehouses of 22nd Street in Chicago (now Cermak Road, in honor of the mayor who took a bullet for FDR in 1933), and television face time to hawk your new book containing "exclusive" information you gathered on your employer's time and should have published in his pages, not yours, has replaced overt payoffs and fancy hotel suites that came complete with the chorus girl of your choice.

Imagine this heroic scenario: You're a reporter for a major metropolitan daily—say, the *Chicago Tribune*, of all places—and you rise through the ranks until you become—oh, I don't know—City Hall bureau chief. Inclined to the idealistic Left from birth—just for the hell of it, let's posit that you were born on the Lower East Side of Manhattan and your mother worked for a hard-left daily newspaper in Manhattan—you had naturally gravitated into journalism as an agent of social change. But now you're bored—you're interacting with Da Mayor every day and seeing various wiseguys what got sent by other wiseguys making a fortune off the city. Realizing that politics, not journalism, is where the main chance lies, you cross the street and start working for the kinds of politicians you used to cover, eventually starting your own campaign consulting firm (after all, you've got a hell of a journalistic Rolodex). And not just the politicians you covered, but those politicians who fit your idea of what a candidate should be, i.e., one who embodies the "social justice" ideals that you imbibed along with your mother's milk. Which more or less gives the lie to your former "journalistic neutrality," but so what? Now that your cards are on the table, you've got bigger fish to fry: a presidential campaign.

And what do you know—after a perfect storm capsizes the other side, you're ready to make your move. You've got a candidate that, a few years ago, nobody ever even heard of, one whose past is completely shrouded in secrecy, its only known "facts" those the candidate himself has shared with us in not one but two "autobiographies." And so, deftly, you maneuver this candidate through the Democratic primaries, your media buddies supporting you every step of the way, never once asking a serious or pertinent question, attacking the opposition candidates—first the other progressives, then a hapless old troglodyte suffering from advanced stages of Keating Five Disease, along with delayed Stockholm Syndrome (an overwhelming desire to please your media captors)—and the next thing you know, it's Inauguration Day! After which half your buddies in the media who were "covering" the campaign suddenly wind up with snazzy digs in the White House and the EOB, where every night they pull out the fifth of whiskey from the bottom drawers of their desks and drink a toast to Jake of sainted memory.

Nah, never happen. And besides, given that I'm a Hollywood guy, *the preceding is a work of fiction and any resemblance to persons living or dead is entirely coincidental.*

But you see where a latter-day Jake Lingle could possibly go, if he caught all the right breaks, stayed atop all the right waves, and never had to look at himself in the mirror. Throw in the exalted status reporters briefly enjoyed after Woodward and Bernstein took down Nixon and you can understood why journalism schools enjoyed record-breaking enrollments through the 1980s and 1990s—everybody wanted a piece of the action.

We have spent years indoctrinating fine young minds at some of our best schools, creating a new social class of "journalist" who is so imbued with the proper way of looking at the world that he or she literally cannot see another side to the argument (which is the whole point of our educational system in the first place: to encourage "correct" thinking).

And look at the results: we've gotten an entire generation of journalists to frame every issue through the structuralist lens of race, class, ethnicity, and gender (which is what we used to call sex before sex became so commonplace that it's more titillating to think about having gender these days than it is to think about having sex). It doesn't matter what the news event: once past the actual report of the event, the press can be counted on now to move the story to the next level, to interpret it in the media's own alternative universe of bias, discrimination, glass ceilings, and unicorns. Admit that you're no longer surprised when you read a headline or a Chyron like this:

Two Swedes charged in plot to bomb airliner.

The first you think of is a couple of big blond guys who look like Dolph Lundgren, or maybe a guy and gal who looks like a member of the Swedish bikini team. What you don't think of—of course you wouldn't, you filthy racist—are a couple of Arabs from North Africa, who had been living in Sweden as asylum-seekers while they merrily colluded with al-Qaeda and surfed the jihadi beheading videos on the Internet and exchanged messages of spiritual guidance and consolation with an imam in Yemen.

So sensitive are the members of the American Fourth Estate to the slightest hint of racism—which, under the current definition consists of the very act of noticing that someone is of a different race than you— that they have utterly altered what we used to consider reality: that Sweden was a country, like most European nation-states, of cousins who shared a common language, culture, history, and gene pool. It was not a racist cliché to assume that many Swedes were, in fact, tall, blond, and good-looking, it was a fact. But now the definition of ethnicity has been changed, in part to reflect that all the European countries are undergoing a demographic and immigration-driven hollowing-out, and that what we used to think of as being quintessentially "British," "Italian," or even "German" will no longer be true in the future, if it even still is, and that henceforth you will be blinded to the demographic changes going on across the pond and right here at home. And the media leads the way.

That's why charges of racism fly so freely today, nearly a half-century after Dr. King's great speech on the Mall in Washington. A sports coach, in the heat of the moment, calls a fan shouting insults a "fat Mexican" and he is fired, even though the fan may well have been a) fat and b) a Mexican. It's racism! Anyone opposing the policies of a black elected official can automatically be deemed guilty of racism, no matter what the merits of the disagreement, or even the facts. And henceforth, all Swedes are presumed to have no distinguishing shared physical characteristics at all, and you'd best wrap your mind around this brave new world if you know what's good for you. The media, like the generals, loves to fight the last war, and it's clear from a close reading of *The New York Times* that for decades its editors have been waking up every day and wondering whether it's 1943, with the Holocaust still raging—although they are, like the *bien-pensants* everywhere, vehemently anti-Israel, go figure; or 1963, with Bull Connor (a Democrat, of course!) turning fire hoses on black people. Today journalists will not rest until they root out every last vestige of racism and hate in America, even if they have to invent them.

Indeed, we are witnessing another perfect storm, a mighty nor'easter of "corrupt" (we prefer the term "opportunistic," as in George Washington Plunkitt's famous aphorism about "honest graft"—"I seen my opportunities and I took 'em") journalists salivating at the prospect of getting to cover the only beat that matters anymore, which is the Washington beat, more accurately the White House beat, and politicians only too willing to dangle the carrot of "access" in exchange for, well, "obedience."

For here is the dirty little secret of most reporters—deep down, they wish they were something else. Anything else. Like real writers. Political consultants. President of the United States. Like sportswriters, they spend so much time hanging around people who are actually doing something—like running a baseball team—that they begin to imagine that they could do it equally well, if not better (and thus Rotisserie League baseball was born). Worse, as reporters began to get face time on the Sunday shows, and then on the cable networks, they began to take themselves more and more seriously. Today, they are no longer reporters, they're "journalists," no longer grubby little men in cheap suits and battered fedoras with a tattered "press" pass in the hatband, but players, men and women whose Opinions Matter. Indeed, half the cable talk shows in the evening now consist of one talking head interviewing another talking head, usually a colleague on the same network: a perfect circle of jerks.

And no journalists, of course, are worse than that special blend of lickspittle and sycophant, of plotter and Polonius, known as the Washington Correspondent. Nursing their deeply held grudges against the world, convinced that they could be doing a better job running the

country than the idiots in charge, keenly aware of the constantly shift-
ing balances of power in the Medici court, at which they fancy themselves courtiers but are treated like jesters, they now proudly take their
places on panels opposite politicians, their received wisdom greeted as
blindingly original thinking, their Pulitzer Prizes handed back and forth
among the same group of people as if they were Ghastly Gifts at a recy-
cling party. It's probably only a matter of time before one of them de-
clares his or her candidacy, receives the plaudits of the minitudes in the
briefing room—and then is astonished to find that he has absolutely no
constituency outside of the newsroom. But until that day comes, the illusion will persist.

Even worse, Gaia forbid, some of them want to be screenwriters.

In the early days of Hollywood, most of the "scenarists" (as we were
called back then) were in fact moonlighting reporters from the big-city
dailies. "Schmucks with Underwoods" (typewriters, to those of you under
ninety), as one studio chief famously called the ink-stained wretches. Indeed, when Ben Hecht was summoned by Herman Mankiewicz westward
from Chicago to work on a movie, the cable read: "Millions are to be
grabbed out here and your only competition is idiots." Once word got out,
reporters flocked to the City of the Angels, eager to get at some of that
moolah, and they've been doing it ever since. Even—especially—those
losers who stayed put on the east side of the Potomac, in the city most definitely not of the angels, Washington, D.C.

To the untrained eye, what we lefty American media types and our
ink-stained comrades everywhere do may look like storytelling, and in a
manner of speaking it is. The stories written by our trained media seals
have characters, events, incidents, action; most important, though, is the
fact that our stories, like fables and fairy tales everywhere, have *narrative*.
A framework of good guys and bad guys; archetypes and stereotypes. A
shorthand for our audiences, so that instead of wasting time on establish-
ing characters we can get right to the morality play/propaganda point, all
the while disguising it as "news" or "entertainment." The "narrative" is
like a continuing serial or soap opera, which our audiences can drop in
and out of, secure in the knowledge that they know what's going on.
Thus urban minorities = good; white ethnics = bad. Corporate chieftains
= bad; union leaders = good. Brave Hollywood screenwriters speaking

truth to %$#BUSH@#$!!! = good, Limbaugh/Hannity/O'Reilly = bad. It really is that simple and, as the most recent presidential election returns showed, that effective.

Which brings me to the heart and soul of our "narrative," the key proposition that until recently we were too skittish to actually articulate clearly in front of the American people. For decades, even centuries, we've been afraid that some backwoodsman Natty Bumppo type would hear the words that are about to come out of my word processor and soon out of the mouths of our outliers and sic the Last of the Mohicans on us—or, if not Chingachgook himself, then Horatio Alger, or Jack Armstrong or any of the other all-American boys you used to look up to, heroes who made their own way in the world, and who inspired others to do so. Hell, once upon a time there were even a few reporters like that. The great Henry Morton Stanley—the Welshman who uttered the famous words "Dr. Livingstone, I presume"—was acting as a reporter for the *New York Herald* when he braved the dangers of Darkest Africa to find the good doctor by the shores of Lake Tanganyika in 1871. Imagine Howard Fineman doing that!

On the other hand, it's easy to imagine Fineman or any of the other wizened, bookish, non–Ernie Pyle types who now make up the nation's press corps actually uttering these words: "socialism = good, capitalism = bad." As Mark Levin might shout: "There, I said it!"

From FDR on, we tested that meme on America, hoping against hope that one day the time would be right for you to accept it. Roosevelt reached out to the "little guy" in those Fireside Chats, all the while staying up nights thinking of ways to screw him. Social Security, the Mother of All Ponzi Schemes, began to chip away at the Bumpponian tradition of self-reliance. The regulatory agencies began to snake their tentacles across the land, coming first in the guise of benefactors (the Tennessee Valley Authority bringing electricity to the Walker Percy hillbillies) and then as the commissars of the new regime. In Hollywood, we embraced our Soviet allies in movies like *Mission to Moscow,* and battled the House Un-American Activities Committee in the pages of the press, and on radio and television. We tarnished Tail Gunner Joe McCarthy's name forever, made him—without any historical justification—the bad guy responsible for the Hollywood "black list," even though it was the studio moguls who did that, not politicians—and whitewashed Bobby Kennedy's relationship with the Wisconsin drunk, er, senator. Hell, we even got a Pulitzer Prize for one of the great fellow travelers, Walter Duranty, who did his level best in the pages of—where else?—*The New York Times* to conceal the so-called crimes of Joseph Stalin from the American people.

And then in 1944, with the world war still raging, there was the "Second Bill of Rights," proposed by Roosevelt in his State of the Union address. At the time he made the speech, FDR had already violated an unwritten constitutional rule, one that limited the chief executive to no more than two consecutive terms in the White House. It had been good enough for George Washington, good enough for Thomas Jefferson, but it wasn't good enough for the Indispensable Man, Roosevelt; later that same year he ran for and won his fourth presidential election, although he died a few months after his inauguration. But with the outcome of the war very much in doubt—D-Day was still months away—Roosevelt might have had his legacy on his mind as he proposed the following new "Economic Bill of Rights":

- The right to a useful and remunerative job in the industries or shops or farms or mines of the nation.
- The right to earn enough to provide adequate food and clothing and recreation.
- The right of every farmer to raise and sell his products at a return which will give him and his family a decent living.
- The right of every businessman, large and small, to trade in an atmosphere of freedom from unfair competition and domination by monopolies at home or abroad.
- The right of every family to a decent home.
- The right to adequate medical care and the opportunity to achieve and enjoy good health.
- The right to adequate protection from the economic fears of old age, sickness, accident, and unemployment.
- The right to a good education.

"All of these rights spell security," the President said. "And after this war is won we must be prepared to move forward, in the implementation of these rights, to new goals of human happiness and well-being.

America's own rightful place in the world depends in large part upon how fully these and similar rights have been carried into practice for our citizens."

Well, those were fighting words to the men and women of my grandfather's generation, the perfect articulation of the Progressive Agenda and something we've been fight, fight, fighting for ever since. And it all sounds pretty familiar, doesn't it? And who could be against good jobs, putting food on your family (as &%@!BUSH!&$! said), a nice place to live, health care, and education? Who could possibly be against social "security"? Where all this security was going to come from, FDR didn't say. But we, who know the secret code, sure did: from the t-a-x-e-s of the s-u-c-k-e-r-s. In one swift judo move, the President flipped the entire history of the American republic on its head; a system that was set up to reward risk was now to be repurposed toward ensuring "security." A system that, like the men who would soon be storming Omaha Beach, did not have time to mourn a comrade felled by the creative destruction of the Hidden Hand, would now be repositioned to look backward. The last shall be first, the meek shall inherit the earth—and the productive class shall pay for it.

Despite, as Marx might say, all the "internal contradictions" inherent in our little fairy tales, we somehow got you to believe them, which is why you're on the verge of selling out more than two centuries of your hard-won patrimony for a mess of pottage while you murmur nervously, like Oliver Twist, *Please, sir, may I have some more?* "We Are All Socialists Now" proclaimed *Newsweek*, in a cover story co-written by Evan Thomas, who totally coincidentally is the grandson of the six-time Socialist candidate for president, Norman Thomas, and if that doesn't say it all, I don't know what does.

"You know, Billy, we blew it," says Captain America (Peter Fonda) to Dennis Hopper at the end of *Easy Rider.* And so you did. For a time there, you had both houses of Congress, the presidency, and a majority of the governorships and you blew it. You can bet that *we* won't be making that mistake on our way to "fundamentally changing" what used to be your country. You should have nuked us when you had the chance.

Now, however, our buddies in the press are in trouble. Major newspapers are suffering steep circulation drops or even going out of business entirely, the advertising market has all but evaporated, and free circulation is pretty much the only option left. "Mainstream" news shows on major networks are shriveling. Much more interesting ways of framing and commenting on the news have appeared, for free, on the Internet, and there is always talk radio to turn to when your side has finally had a bellyful of being lectured by our side over the breakfast table. Life in the media bubble has made the members of the Mainstream Media so crazy that they no longer can distinguish fact from fiction and fantasy from reality, and yet they keep on pushing it, like a small child who's been taught that if he just keeps on shouting he'll eventually get what he wants. Only it's not working anymore, and this is something that is really distressing us.

Which is, of course, the reason we need a return of the Fairness Doctrine.

This Internet thing was all well and good when it was our people out in front of it, but lately I've noticed that you wingnuts have started making a comeback and, worse, are actually developing a following. Some sort of governmental regulation is clearly called for here, because the last thing that we want is another loose aggregation of pamphleteers springing up as they did in the mid-eighteenth century, rabble-rousing, destabilizing, creating the conditions for revolution. We've already co-opted your Declaration of Independence with our own form of oligarchy, and are well on the way to having you question, along with us, just about every clause in the Constitution, including the emanations of penumbras, until you no long believe a single deconstructionist word in it.

But we know it's a race against time. The very fact that I'm writing these words ought to clue you in to the desperation we now feel. To have had everything in our grasp, only to watch it slowly slip away as an aroused citizenry casts off its TV-induced torpor and begins to reengage with its own culture, is just about our worst nightmare. Which is why we'll keep on frantically trying to fool you with outright misstatements and bald lies, with *The Real Housewives of Toledo, Ohio* and other mind-numbing, ratiocination-destroying, time-wasting circuses and, when all else fails and you've finally tumbled to all the tedious ins and outs of our scam, to pleas—to demands—to continue to tolerate us for your own good.

That's more than Jake Lingle got. Jake wanted to be several things at once, none of them likely to happen on a legman's salary. He wanted to be rich. He wanted to have his counsel listened to at the upper levels of the Florentine court that was Capone's Chicago. He wanted to be around the hard men with guns, the men who got their way not through force of argument but through the cold blue steel of a Colt .38 Detective Special, men for whom the thought of violence inspired no counterthought of consequences. Men who *acted* instead of bloviated.

And then, on that fateful day in the underpass, he met one. Thank Gaia, that will never happen to us.

SUMMARY NOTES ON HOW TO TAKE DOWN A NATION

For Four Eyes Only

So my agent called me the other day and said she's putting me up for the newest James Bond movie and would I come up with a "take" so I can go in and pitch. Of course I said sure, because if there's one thing I know, it's James Bond movies. I've been watching them since I'm a kid, caught up with all the old ones on Netflix, and actually have a friend who's a friend of the guy who wrote three of the best of them, which by Hollywood's way of measuring these things means that I practically wrote them myself.

Coming up with a "take" is what we highly paid writers do out here, which translated into laymen's speak means we work for free until the studio, against its better judgment, decides to actually hire us, and even though we're not supposed to do this, we do it anyway because beggars can't be choosers, and when you're a writer out here O brother are you ever a beggar.

So I thought about it for five minutes and came up with my take, which I'm now going to test on you before I go over to wherever the ghost of MGM is located these days and pitch it to some fresh-faced young executive who's never even heard of Roger Moore, much less Ian Fleming. I'm calling it *For Four Eyes Only: This Time, It's Personal*.

Every Bond film has a killer pre-titles sequence, an exciting but, plot-wise, irrelevant four or five minutes' worth of nonstop action. Then come the titles, complete with catchy song, then comes the movie proper: Bond gets the assignment from M, heads off to some exotic locale, beds a bird or two or six, gets into some seriously life-threatening hot water, turns the tables, kills the villain, conquers the leading lady, and we go out on a trademark Bond quip, preferably a sexual double-entendre. That's it!

Exciting Pre-Titles Action Sequence. We open in Washington, D.C., where a lame-duck President of the United States has just received some very bad news. It seems that the *entire U.S. economy has collapsed overnight*, the stock market is plunging, houses are worth less than a loaf of bread, except in Los Angeles, where every house still costs at least a million bucks, and the Mexican peso is laughing at the dollar. Condition red!

The president, a hapless idiot I'm calling George Walker, is in a swivet. Looking like he's making a hostage video, he goes into the Rose Garden, stares into the cameras and says that, effective immediately, he's transferring the sum of *one billion dollars* to a shadowy European financier who's threatening to destabilize the planet with "fundamental change."

The president is interrupted by a snickering press corps. He looks down at the notes he's written on the palm of his left hand, then corrects himself. The sum of *one trillion dollars*, payable in cash, securities, super-saver coupons, and cereal box tops before sundown, or else . . . as we CUT TO—

James Bond (Haley Joel Osment), lying on Rehoboth Beach, a lovely on each arm. His next-generation PDA, which he's cleverly hidden in his swim trunks, starts vibrating. "Why, James," asks one of the beach bunnies, "are you getting a call or are you just glad to see us?"

Bond leaps into action, then a bunch of cool stuff happens and somehow in a flash he's grappling with a horde of Ninja assassins in San Francisco, all of whom he kills in the most imaginative ways possible, but which I'll have to think of later. He enters a room from which an ominous, Central Europeanly accented voice has been heard calling him "Meester Bondt," but when he breaks through the Krell-steel doors there's nothing there but a pair of reading glasses, a tuft of white cat fur, and some old French newspaper clippings about an obscure insider trading scandal . . .

Act One: London. Bond flirts with Moneypenny (Geena Davis), sees M (Harvey Fierstein in drag), and is informed that the world is not enough, that you only live twice, and that tomorrow never dies. Bond stops off to see Q (Crispin Glover), gets some cool new weapons that I'll have to think up later, then heads for someplace glamorous, ditto, where he meets a girl, plays a few rounds of baccarat, wins big, sleeps with the girl, who wakes up dead. During his interrogation for her murder he's miraculously busted out of police headquarters by a mysterious Beautiful Woman/Bond Girl who pulls up in a Testarossa. As they drive along the Corniche, they're suddenly chased by a squad of deadly Mini Coopers. The Bond Girl, however, is too much for them, and one by one they go plunging off the cliffs, screaming, to their deaths. Only the driver of the last Mini Cooper survives long enough to be interrogated, but when Bond asks him whom he's working for, the man gets a terrified look on his face, curses Bond in a funny foreign language that mystifies even the multilingual Bond Girl—but which Bond seems to recognize—and chokes himself to death with his bare hands.

Bond and the Bond Girl make love. When Bond wakes up, he finds himself strapped to the bed, naked and looking not at the girl, but at:

GYÖRGY SCHWARTZ. Holding a white cat and chuckling ominously.

BOND: Ut-wo expecto du moi to duo?
BOND GIRL (amazed): Shames, I didn't know you spoke Esperanto.

If Schwartz is surprised by Bond's fluent command of Esperanto, he doesn't let on. Instead he replies:

SCHWARTZ: Expecto ich tuo to die-o.

(All Esperanto will, of course, be subtitled.)

Act Two: As we writers know, this is the boring part—seventy–eighty pages of car chases, explosions, deaths of minor characters. You civilians call this part of the film "the movie."

Act Three: Varna, Bulgaria. As usual, Bond awakens in bed. The Bond Girl is beside him once more. By now, though, she's in love with him, so she's no longer working for Schwartz; her heart belongs to the man she calls, in her delightfully piquant former Yugoslavian accent, "Shames."

"Shames," she says, "he's going to kill us. So make love to me, like it was the last time."

FADE OUT and FADE IN

"I know," says Bond, lighting up a cigarette and then remembering it's no longer politically correct to smoke. Steeling himself for the torturous ordeal he knows is coming, he stubs it out on his manly torso, singeing his chest hair. The Bond Girl falls in love with him all over again.

"Nada vas me mein selbst thru went have," said an ominous voice. It's Schwartz, dressed as Harvey Fierstein as M in Act One. Suddenly it's all terribly clear . . .

At this point, we think that Schwartz is going to kill Bond and that will be that. After all, that's what any real-world super-villain would do. But since this is a movie, we now need the obligatory scene in which he gets to *explain himself.*

Accordingly, he tosses a dossier at Bond and the Bond Girl. Bond glances through it, smiles a cruel little smile—

BOND (in English): You're a Hungarian Jew . . .
SCHWARTZ: Mm-hmm.
BOND: . . . who escaped the Holocaust . . .
SCHWARTZ: Mm-hmm.
BOND: . . . by posing as a Christian.
SCHWARTZ (switching to English): Right.
BOND: And you watched lots of people get shipped off to the death camps.
SCHWARTZ: Right. I was fourteen years old. And I would say that that's when my character was made.
BOND: In what way?
SCHWARTZ: That one should think ahead. One should understand that—and anticipate events and when, when one is threatened. It was a tremendous threat of evil. I mean, it was a—a very personal threat of evil.
BOND: My understanding is that you went out with this protector of yours who swore that you were his adopted godson.

SCHWARTZ: Yes. Yes.

BOND: Went out, in fact, and helped in the confiscation of property from the Jews.

SCHWARTZ: Yes. That's right. Yes.

BOND: I mean, that's—that sounds like an experience that would send lots of people to the psychiatric couch for many, many years. Was it difficult?

SCHWARTZ: Not, not at all. Not at all. Maybe as a child you don't . . . you don't see the connection. But it was—it created no—no problem at all.

BOND: No feeling of guilt?

SCHWARTZ: No.

BOND: For example, that, "I'm Jewish, and here I am, watching these people go. I could just as easily be these, I should be there." None of that?

SCHWARTZ: Well, of course . . . I could be on the other side or I could be the one from whom the thing is being taken away. But there was no sense that I shouldn't be there, because that was—well, actually, in a funny way, it's just like in the markets—that is I weren't there—of course, I wasn't doing it, but somebody else would—would—would be taking it away anyhow. And it was the—whether I was there or not, I was only a spectator, the property was being taken away. So the—I had no role in taking away that property. So I had no sense of guilt.

Is that dialogue great or what? The scene continues:

BOND (in perfect Esperanto): Permesso zu smoke-o?

SCHWARTZ: Naturalmento, Bondo-san.

Bond reaches into his jacket pocket and fishes out the GLASSES we saw in the first scene. In a bit of absolutely gratuitous near-nudity, the Bond Girl takes them to ~~Blofeld~~ ~~Soros~~ Schwartz and puts them on him: they fit perfectly!

Bond jumps out of bed, wrestles with Schwartz, the two of them go crashing through a window and land on the deck of a speedboat with its motor running, killing the guy who was going to help Schwartz escape.

The boat careers about the Black Sea, or whatever it's called, as Schwartz and Bond grapple manfully with each other, but—I forgot to tell you—Schwartz has injected Bond with some sort of slow-acting poison and he gradually becomes weaker until it looks like the final curtain when all of a sudden he quips:

BOND: Me dankt dass Christmas kommen only once-o per jahr-o—

At which Schwartz suddenly starts laughing so hysterically that Bond is able to muster just enough strength to KICK HIM OVER THE SIDE OF THE BOAT and into the mouths of some hungry sharks that he'd been keeping as pets in an earlier scene that I haven't written yet.

I'm telling you, you can't make this stuff up.

The Future Is Now

By now, our nature should be pretty clear to you as well as our intentions. I mean, surely you can't be as stupid as you look and act. Surely there must be some innate animal cunning behind that doofus exterior, some angle you're playing concealed behind the Potemkin Village of your silly Midwestern accents and seemingly trusting natures. My friends and I pretend to like you, pretend to accept your "wholesome, all-American virtues" as the norm, but at root we think you're a bunch of racist schmucks, at once foolish and sinister, dedicated to resisting the brave new world we have planned and almost ready for you.

This is how we have framed the argument and, thus, framed you as well. Because it is inconceivable for us to view any set of facts or circumstances other than through our Marxist prism of race and class, we naturally assume that's the way you see things too. So what if you don't?—By our lights, you're guilty as charged!

But this cocksure certainty that we have all the answers, as supplied by Marx, Engels, Lenin, Derrida, Foucault, Marcuse, and Evan Thomas, is also our Achilles' heel. This, as David Mamet might say, is how you're going to get Capone. Not by pulling a gun when we pull a knife, or by putting one of ours in the morgue after we've delivered one of you to the tender mercies of a single-payer health care system. Well, okay, that too; you can't win if you won't fight, and we've grown a little rusty since our salad days back in 1968.

Still, it's hard for us to imagine that you can possibly see it any other way than our way, which is why our most useful of Useful Idiots duly, dutifully, and habitually hammer you on the op-ed pages of our major dailies. As you can tell, I am the smartest, most accomplished, and by far the best writer among my leftist tribe and yet even I, the Great Kahane, am having a hard time fully grasping that the real reason you're resisting our Huxleian new world order is not that you're a bunch of resentful white boys who cannot accept the inevitable course of cultural change, but that you *actually believe the American promise is given to everyone.* That unlike us, you don't see race first and foremost. That you don't see external traits as voting blocs. That you believe in the free will of the individual and not, unlike us, in the coercive power of the state.

No wonder we hate you. You actually want this great experiment to work. In fact, unlike us, you're invested in its success.

I realize that it's hard to accept that someone would deliberately set out to wreck the United States of America, but don't look at me like my side is the first one to try it. Putting aside for the moment the incidental difference that they were actually hostile foreign powers and not your fellow citizens, the Germans and the Japanese certainly intended to flush Amerikkka down the Axis drain, swept away to the clang of the Iron Cross in the morning glory of the Rising Sun. But their error lay in thinking that, somehow, they could defeat a country protected by two oceans, a mighty arsenal that could turn its manufacturing infrastructure practically on a dime, to retool from making passenger cars to making Pershing tanks, a country that (unlike the Germans, who couldn't even cross the English Channel) could project its power and might overseas, could send its Flying Fortresses to fill the skies above Hamburg and Tokyo, and to rain death down upon them. Big whoops.

The Soviets, Gaia bless them, had a better idea. They knew better than to tangle with the States, which is why you never saw the numerically superior Red Army ever try to scoot through the Fulda Gap into Germany. With all their missiles and space technology, the Soviets were smart enough—and had a big enough inferiority complex—not to tangle with the U.S. militarily, except around the edges. Sure, their ships and our ships played chicken on the high seas a lot, and we fought proxy wars all over the globe, letting the funny little brown people kill each other, doing the work Americans and Russians wouldn't do.

But the Soviets' real genius was in working to take down the U.S. from the inside, and to that end their intelligence agencies, the KGB and the GRU (military intelligence), waged a long, fierce war in the shadows to destabilize America. They had spies everywhere, littered throughout the State Department—Alger Hiss, take a bow!—and working on stealing nuclear secrets—Julius and Ethel Rosenberg, George Koval, come on down! They sent their agents into industrial plants, ensconced them in newspapers and magazines (say hello, "independent journalist" Izzy Stone!), and put them on the air. They had operatives whose only job was assuring the American people that there were no Soviet agents, that McCarthy was a hallucinating crackpot, that J. Edgar Hoover was a drag queen.

Now this may all strike you like "the Devil's greatest trick" stuff and in a way it is. When the Soviet Union finally came crashing down in 1991, the silence on our side (aside from a few stifled sobs) was deafening. We couldn't wrap our minds around the fact that the central reason for our entire existence, the thing that we had loved and cherished and nurtured and tried so desperately to transplant had suddenly vanished—outlawed, even!—and we were left to figure out what had gone wrong.

As usual, there was only one possible conclusion: communism just hadn't been given a proper go. Besides, Russia was a lousy place for the experiment; as everybody knew, Germany was supposed to have been the Mother Ship of the worldwide communist revolution, and if it hadn't been for that loathsome Hitler fellow, it might have been. Sure, we managed to revive blatantly "socialist" parties in all the Western democracies after the war, not only in Germany but in Britain and France and Italy, but it wasn't really the same. All that hard work propping up a country where they couldn't even make a functioning elevator really depressed us, and we had a long hangover about it. Luckily, you were all so busy celebrating the "End of History" that we had time to rethink and regroup, and now here we are.

"End of History" my pet rat's patootie. You had us on the ropes and now look—like the demon spirits in the movie *Poltergeist*, we're baaa-aaacck! We're back in Russia, where the renamed KGB is doing its level best to deliver the Rodina back into the hands of either the Czars or old dead Lenin himself. We're back in South America, where the banana republics retain their distressing tendency to turn into banana dictatorships pretty much every time some *caudillo* slips on a banana peel and decides to deal with the humiliation by organizing firing squads. As long as the Castro bros, or their heirs and assigns, are still functioning in Cuba we'll have a presence in the Caribbean, and of course we never left China, which has a zillion-man army and a bunch of really good computer nerds at its beck and call for the day when push finally comes to shove and the Kuomintang needs beachfront property in Honolulu.

But America—this land is your land, this land is my land. She is the big prize, the shining city on the hill. She is the thing that history's first rebel, Lucifer, saw at the bottom of the lake of fire. Forget Adam and Eve and the rest of humanity; we don't really care about them. But if we can bring the mountain to Mohammed, so to speak, the struggle will have been worth it, the Long March a success.

For it doesn't matter if we succeed in making our pathetic system work. We know it won't. What does matter, though, is that we reduce you to our level, to show the universe that Satan is at last the master of God, and that the true meaning of equality is misery.

To that end, a joke from the old country:

It seems there were two farmers, Ivan and Mikhail, living side by side and equally poor, probably thanks to the crimes of the *kulaks*, thankfully eliminated by Comrade Stalin through the simple Soviet expedient of starving them and shooting them. As that Uncle Joe famously said: You can't make an omelet without breaking a few eggs, and the Soviet Union in the 1930s was some kind of socialist soufflé, let me tell you.

Anyway, Ivan and Mikhail have everything in common. They sleep on straw pallets, have dirt floors in their rude homes, and their wives pull the plows in between delivering babies in the fields. Then, one day, something terrible happens. Ivan gets a cow (don't ask me how—it's a fable). Almost immediately, his life totally changes. No longer does Irina, his wife, have to pull the plow. They have milk and cheese. They breed the cow and suddenly they have meat. On the black market, they sell one or two of the calves and manage to hoard a little money (for which they should have been shot, but that's another story). The transformation is amazing.

Ivan is thrilled. Mikhail is devastated. All their lives, they have been equal, the way good Soviet Men should be. They had nothing, and nothing is what they shared equally. You could not have asked for a purer expression of true communism. As Mikhail watches Ivan's lot improve, he seethes. He complains to the local soviet, but there's nothing they can do, because even in the U.S.S.R., it's not against the law to have a cow. Mikhail briefly considers reporting his friend to the Cheka, but finally decides against it; after all, he's not a bad man, just a poor man.

Finally, in utter desperation, he does something he'd almost forgotten how to do. He prays. One night while his wife, Ludmilla, is sleeping, reaching back into a long-suppressed wellspring of Russian Orthodox religiosity, he gets down on his knees and beseeches God: "Please help me. Ivan and I have always been equal. And yet now, for some unfathomable reason, you have smiled upon my neighbor and he has prospered. I have always tried to be a faithful communist, and though I have fallen short of my duties to the state through human failings, I have never failed to believe and respect the fundamental teachings of Marxism-Leninism. All my life I have striven to be a good atheist and not believe in you. But now, I humbly come to you directly. Please, God, please hear my prayer. Please make us equal again."

For a moment, all is silent. Then, to his utter amazement, a voice emerges out of the clouds, a voice that only he can hear. "Mikhail," says God, "your prayers have been answered. You shall be made equal again."

Mikhail leaps to his feet in disbelief. A look of transfigured radiance plays across his noble Slavic peasant features. He cannot believe his good fortune. "Oh good!" he exclaims. "You're going to kill Ivan's cow!"

That sound you hear is us sharpening our long knives.

The War Against God

As you know, we progressives have no use whatsoever for false gods, especially "God Himself." For decades, we have waged a war against the imaginary deity you have enshrined in your national motto, "In God We Trust," and on your currency, and even in your Supreme Court—a blatant violation of the separation of Church and State, about which we constantly remind you. There was a time, even in the last century, when the clear majority of you pretty much subscribed to the same basic Christian religious principles, and welcomed a small minority of Jews. Everybody got along pretty well, or thought they did, notwithstanding the occasional outburst of religious intolerance, or even downright animus. The Know-Nothings of the nineteenth century, the Ku Klux Klan (as anti-Catholic as it was anti-black), the lynching of Jews like Bobby Franks in the Deep South—these things were seen as the aberration, not the norm. You condemned such atrocities and didn't consider them indictments of your entire society. You didn't assume that a single flaw in your moral fabric would thereby rend the entire tapestry. And then we came along.

Don't get me wrong—we're perfectly capable of co-opting "men of the cloth," and from time to time you'll even find us paying lip service to "religious values," as long as you understand that we don't really mean any of it. Whether we're renegade Catholic priests turned social warriors, double-lived evangelical Protestant ministers involved in one form of sexual excess or another, or garden-variety, self-described "Jewish atheists" who flirt with Buddhism, our hearts belong to secular progressivism, which is, let's face it, our religion of choice.

Sure, you'll find plenty of us men of the left among the mainline Protestant churches and Reform synagogues, and the Catholic bishops are always ready to throw a monkey wrench into everybody's understanding of just where the papists stand when they simultaneously applaud radical environmentalism (minus the murder and arson part, of course), demand universal health care, and then excommunicate the brave progressive "Catholic" politicians who disagree with them about the most sacred teaching in the Church of Progressivism—a woman's right to choose to terminate an inconvenient pregnancy at any time and for any reason. Since we seek to exploit the "slippery slope" every time we attack you, we are not about to let it happen to us, which is why we take such a hard line on abortion.

Still, these religious "leftists" are really not part of our movement, although they function perfectly well as useful idiots and human shields; why, there's even an organization called Americans United for the Separation of Church and State, which we regularly trot out to show that we don't hate all religion, just real religions—except, of course, Islam, because unlike you Christians, they actually take their religious instruction seriously and a fella could get hurt if he gets in the way. In any case, we're perfectly happy to watch the mainline Protestant churches turn into (in Ann Coulter's memorable phrase) "gay dating services" or, as I prefer to think of them, "privately funded public homeless shelters." Popes we are inherently suspicious of, especially with their ludicrous pretension to "infallibility" in matters of faith and morals—the fact that they are blind to our version of the Theory of (Moral) Relativity tells you all you need to know about their bigotry and closed-mindedness, and as for the Muslims, well . . . see above.

In any case, we already have our Apostle Saul, and this is perhaps his most important commandment. Learn it, live it, love it:

Make the enemy live up to their own book of rules.

Thus spake the Great Alinsky in Rule No. 4 in the "Tactics" section of *Rules for Radicals*. At first glance, it doesn't seem to mean much, other than a broad exhortation to try and hold your opponent's feet to the flames of his own best ideals. But, with true insidious genius, it's so much more than that.

Remember: we think like lawyers. Deep down inside, we all wish we were lawyers. We use lawyers the way a soldier uses his weapon, both offensively and defensively. When you think of a lawyer, what do you think of? Somebody like the old Perry Mason, a truth-seeking defense attorney whose job was to serve Justice. Or DA Ben Stone on *Law and Order*, a truth-seeking prosecutor whose job was to serve Justice. However fictionalized, it was men like these who originally defined the concept in the public's mind—not the shifty weasels who actually populate the profession and certainly not the kinds of lawyers we have on our side. Our lawyers are not there to defend anybody, except in dire necessity. No, our lawyers are there to *take you down*.

One of the lawyer's favorite clichés is the old *falsus in unum* dictum, which is not, as you perhaps may suspect, a line from the old Latin Mass but a principle that states that testimony that is false in one particular may be considered entirely false. Naturally, it partially depends on the detail, and whether the falsehood was uttered deliberately or inadvertently, but the point is that those caveats no longer matter for our purposes. For just as we have hijacked almost everything that properly belongs in the court of public opinion, and have demanded that you view any given issue, whether social or personal, as if it were being discussed in a court of law, so have we wormed our cant and jargon into your discourse, and made you accept that rules designed for the artificial and stylized combat of the courtroom are now applicable in daily life.

Thus, the brilliance of *falsus in unum,* for it can be used to preemptively invalidate just about every argument in your arsenal. Because the chink in your armor is called "hypocrisy." And who among us has not, at some time, been guilty of that?

By accepting the validity of our premise—that you *must* practice what you preach—we have won the argument before it has even begun. "You can kill them with this," writes Alinsky, "for they can no more obey their own rules than the Christian church can live up to Christianity." Here we truly see the hand of the Master for, of course, there is no single "Christian church." Only a non-Christian like Alinsky could imagine such a thing, but it is a lovely way to tar one of the world's two largest faiths—the other being our beloved Islam—with the atheist's brush, and we are about nothing if not the cheap shot. For the first mistake you make—declaring that you're on the nonprogressive side—is also your last, because from that moment on you must either be perfect, or you are nothing. Hoist with your own petard, whatever a petard is!

Have you cheated on your wife? Have you drunk to excess? Cheated on your taxes? Spoken out in favor of morality yet secretly viewed pornography? Then you, sir or madam, are a hypocrite and nothing you say will henceforth be seriously entertained. By your own actions you have invalidated your own argument, because you have made the fatal error of professing to stand for a set of abstract "moral" principles, whereas we stand for nothing at all.

Yes, sir, you can say a lot about the Left—that we're godless, malevolent, scheming, ambitious, amoral power-seekers who bend or break any rule in order to get what we want—and not only would you be right, but we'd accept those terms as the compliments they so obviously are. There is no law, even one we passed ourselves, that we will not seek to ignore, change, or subvert if it serves our larger goal. Heck, just ask the good Democratic solons of Massachusetts who, faced with the possibility that John F. Kerry might win the presidency in 2004 and therefore be replaced in the U.S. Senate by a Republican, changed the law to take such an appointment out of the hands of the governor (then a Republican) and instead replace the missing senator a few months later in a special election, with the seat vacant in the meantime. Five years later, after the death of the Lion of Chappaquiddick, and desperately needing another secure vote to pass the "health care" plan, they simply repealed the law and allowed the governor to immediately appoint a hack to the seat until the duly ordained election rolled around.

Similarly, when the stench of corruption surrounding then incumbent, now former New Jersey senator Robert Torricelli became too ripe even for the Garden State to bear, the organized crime entity known as the New Jersey Democratic Party just replaced him as their candidate with the husk of a superannuated prior senator shortly before the election, in clear violation of the plain language of the New Jersey constitution and election laws. So . . . you wanna make something out of it?

Surely, you object, these actions in themselves constitute rank hypocrisy. And if your side tried to pull stunts like these, you'd be right. But this is what I'm trying to get you to understand: *when we do it, it cannot, by definition, be hypocrisy*, since for us there is no such thing. For us the means always justify the ends, since the end—the "greatest good for the greatest number"—is also our unlimited, untrammeled power: *by any means necessary* is our movement's slogan. And—in the unlikely event

you raise an objection—all we have to do is merely find one single example of your side doing something remotely analogous and—*voilà!*—
the objection is dismissed, usually with the glib observation that both
sides are equally guilty.

Let me put it another way.

Your side believes in Universal Truths. Here's one you probably subscribe to now. It's from your own Declaration of Independence: "We
hold these truths to be self-evident, that all men are created equal, that
they are endowed by their Creator with certain unalienable Rights, that
among these are Life, Liberty and the Pursuit of Happiness." And yet it
is but the work of a morally equivalent moment to render them meaningless, since they were contradicted the moment they were written by
the Peculiar Institution of slavery, and are accordingly not worth the
parchment they were inscribed upon.

See how easy it is. This simple principle enables us to invalidate any
aspect of your culture at any time we choose. Your country—the one
we're fundamentally changing, in case you hadn't noticed—is an almost
laughable target-rich environment, which is why we are incapable of
being appeased. We will not stop, we will not falter, and we will not fail
until we have brought the America of Jefferson and Jackson to its knees,
forced it to confess its Original Sins, and then blow its brains out.

Our side, on the other hand, believes in *personal* truths. Our Long
March has found a natural terminus in the groves of academe where we
have diligently labored to remove cultural certainties, to deconstruct
cultural norms, separate the text itself from its plain meaning. With
Foucault and Derrida as our models, and applying the principles of
Fromm and Adorno, we have managed to render multiple generations
of college students incapable of reading "The Night Before Christmas"
without applying Critical Theory to it, turning it into gibberish and
their brains into contortionate mush.

Did I mention that "judgmental" is the dirtiest word in our vocabulary?

I like to call what we're doing "the Elevation of the Singular to the
Universal." As is our wont, we have turned normal logical thought
processes upside down, opting for the counterintuitive and then trying
to sell it to you as normative. A weird sort of perversion of Christian
theology, it goes like this:

To avoid the tyranny of the majority—even though "majority rule" is the bedrock of the political process—we must have instead the tyranny of the minority. The existence of one exception to the norm invalidates the norm. The exception, in other words, not only proves the rule, it becomes the rule.

Consider something noncontroversial . . . oh, let's say abortion. By positing the merest existence of wire coat hangers and back alley scrapers at any time in our past, we have automatically arrived at one of the arguments for legalized abortion, since even one death at the hands of these social outlaws is unconscionable, and in our fertile imaginations there is not merely one such "provider" lurking in the shadows, but an army of them, ready to emerge at the stroke of a pen, to wreak their depredations upon the legions of women who are the daily victims of rape and incest.

Or, if abortion is not controversial enough for you, let's try race, always one of our favorites. You're not going to like what I'm about to say here, and in fact I think it may be a tad politically incorrect myself, but since this—as Barbara Bush said to Katie, or Barbwah, or Oprah, or somebody—is just between friends, let's talk about race.

The civil rights movement was, for the men and women of "Che's" generation, the be-all and end-all of their existence, their alpha and their omega. It was the case they committed their young lives to, as lawyers, journalists, poll workers, you name it. It was a great moral moment whose time had come, and so what if the bad guys in the South were, can you believe it, *Southern Democrats* (not to mention recalcitrant Democrats in certain precincts up north, in Boston and elsewhere, but they'd have to wait their turn). You might have thought that, since we're Democrats ourselves, that might have been an obstacle to our seizing the moral high ground on this issue, but we had gone to school on the HUAC hearings and the Hollywood blacklist, and we realized that it was but a simple matter, a mere judo flip, to pin the tail not on the donkey but on the elephant. So we turned Bull Connor and his gang into *premature Republicans* (along the lines of my grandfather's generation's *premature anti-fascists*), rewrote the history books as needed, and went on our merry way. We had to go to the mat on the civil rights issue, which meant we had to eliminate anybody or anything that got in our way, because we saw, as others didn't, how important it was. Not because it was the right and moral thing to do. Not because it forced Amerikkka to live up to her highest ideals—hell, we all agreed on that.

Because it was the wedge that would allow us to destroy every other institution in the country. I know this is going to be hard for you to accept, even those of you on my side, but bear with me.

You see, in their own revanchist, racist way, those demonized Southern Democrats, senators like Robert KKK Byrd and Albert Arnold Gore, Sr.—father of Albert Arnold Gore, Jr., and grandfather of Albert Arnold Gore III, the Hillbilly Dynasty!—and "Sleepin' " Sam Ervin— actually had a point about "states' rights," otherwise known as that pesky Tenth Amendment. Although they were wrong on the particulars, they were right on the general principles, which was that once you start undermining the bedrock foundations of the country—once you undermine *only one*—then there's no stopping you; excuse me, I mean "us." From that moment on, everything is on the table, and any opposition, no matter how principled, can be dismissed by comparing it to opposition to the civil rights movement. A movement that had begun to rectify the specific Original Sin of the Constitution—the three-fifths compromise (without which there never would have been a Constitution) and all that flowed from it, from the Missouri Compromise to the *Dred Scott* decision to the Civil War itself—could be co-opted and transformed into a weapon against the nation itself:

Gay marriage? Just like the civil rights movement.

Universal health care? Just like the civil rights movement.

Cap and trade? Just like the civil rights movement.

Illegal immigration? Just like the civil rights movement.

Women in combat? Just like the civil rights movement.

The Real Housewives of Beverly Hills? Just like the civil rights movement.

Okay, just kidding about that last one. Everybody knows there are no real housewives in Beverly Hills.

Still, you see how easy that was? And race was the key to it all. It was the heart plug of the Harkonnens in *Dune*, the chain we could always yank, because—no matter how much racial progress was made—it was always yankable. And all we ever had to do was simply point to the Constitution, your original sin, and defy you to live up to all its implications, penumbras, emanations, and effervescences. Indeed, we can spin this train of argument out nearly *ad infinitum*, until we create a "moral universe" in which there is no morality whatsoever, except what we dictate. By positing the existence of rare or even imaginary creatures, we can bring down all of your society's defenses with the merest intellectual sleight-of-brain. And there is nothing you can do about it. Except, of course, come over to our side.

Let me tell you where all your troubles started. Where you could have stopped us had you decided to fight, but where our willing accomplices in the Supreme Court overruled the will of the people and their duly elected representatives, in two little decisions we like to call *Engel v. Vitale* and *Abington Township School District v. Schempp*, which under the guise of the all-purpose Establishment Clause effectively moved the ball from the Christian court, regarding establishment of one religious sect over all others—where do you think the word "antidisestablishmentarianism" comes from?—to the atheist court. Suddenly the argument was no longer about which version of Christianity, if any, was to be state-ordained or -supported (many of the original colonies had established churches, which laws lasted well past the adoption of the Constitution, such as the Congregational Church, the official state religion in Connecticut until 1818 and in now-heathen Massachusetts until 1833). The notion that the Constitution requires a "wall of separation" between the state and religion is a load of hogwash that derives from Jefferson's 1802 letter to the Danbury Baptists, when said Danbury Baptists were suffering from being a nonestablished, and therefore suspect, religion in Congregationalist Connecticut. Here's the pertinent paragraph, penned by the very first Democratic President of the United States, which has caused so much mischief for so long:

> Believing with you that religion is a matter which lies solely between Man & his God, that he owes account to none other for his faith or his worship, that the legitimate powers of government reach actions only, & not opinions, I contemplate with sovereign reverence that act of the whole American people which declared that their legislature should "make no law respecting an establishment of religion, or prohibiting the free exercise thereof," thus

building a wall of separation between Church & State. Adhering to this expression of the supreme will of the nation in behalf of the rights of conscience, I shall see with sincere satisfaction the progress of those sentiments which tend to restore to man all his natural rights, convinced he has no natural right in opposition to his social duties.

And then along came Madalyn. If we had patron saints, she would certainly be one of them.

Since the sainted Madalyn Murray O'Hair, the Presbyterian-turned-warrior-against-"God," arrived on the scene and began to break the stranglehold that religious superstition had on the body politic, we have waged unremitting warfare against your culture, missing nary an opportunity to hamstring you.

What a magnificent legacy Ms. O'Hair has left us. Why, all you have to do is think about how things were in the public schools of the United States (hint: Racism! Sexism! Homophobia! Senior smoking rooms!) in the bad old days before the historic *Murray v. Curlett* lawsuit that culminated in the 1963 Supreme Court decision, decided by an 8–1 vote, which forever banned school prayer and the reading of Bible verses in the nation's public schools.

You wingnuts have been carping about this ever since—it was one of the reasons that, back in my dad's youth, people wanted to impeach the chief justice, Earl Warren—but by now, if you just put aside your irrational rancor, you see what a good idea it has proven to be. Just think back to those postwar high schools, with all those clean-cut kids and the romantic rebels with their DA haircuts and muscle cars. Think back to the music of the period, to the way the girls looked in their bobby-sox, the way the boys looked in the V-necked sweaters. Horrible, right?

Now look at high schools today. Without wasting a lot of time invoking "God," we can devote more time and money to metal detectors, to self-esteem classes, to lectures from cops about the dangers of drugs and weapons. Instead of hectoring their "charges," as if there were some sort of inherent power imbalance between students and teachers, we now have teachers in our urban jungles cowering in fear from their "students," assaulted, beaten up, threatened. We have teachers' unions that can now devote themselves entirely to their real purpose, which is making sure that the teacher will never get fired (a small price to pay for having to endure the level of hostilities in the inner cities that a still-racist society engenders). With "God" no longer in the classroom, the old taboos have flown out the window along with discipline, morals, and learning. If you'd wanted to destroy the public schools in the U.S., you couldn't have found a better tip of the spear than Madalyn Murray O'Hair, which is why she enjoys such an honored place in our pantheon of heroes today. It matters little to us that Ms. O'Hair met an especially unfortunate, if dramatically satisfying, end at the hands of a member of her organization, American Atheists. In 1996, she and two members of her family were kidnapped, robbed, tortured, and hacked into small pieces by one of her followers, a man named David Roland Waters, who had previously embezzled $54,000 from the organization. Waters later died in prison.

And you know what the best part is? As a lifelong committed atheist, she probably didn't feel a thing as Waters was torturing her, other than a few brief moments of physical pain as he severed her limbs and decapitated her. As we all know, psychological pain is far worse than physical pain, so I can state with a certainty that she was never troubled by the notion that there might be a life after death, that there might be some ludicrous "Supreme Being" awaiting her, there to sit in judgment of her stewardship of her life.

No, there would be no judgmental Big Fella with a clipboard, ready to ask her a bunch of unpleasant questions about her time on earth, asking her to justify why she had changed the very relationship the vast majority of Americans had once enjoyed as part of their compact with the government; that, in exchange for paying their property taxes and consigning their children to its tender mercies, the government would respect the larger culture and not seek to interfere with it or replace it with something alien. That both elements of the First Amendment's mention of religion would be equally respected: "Congress shall make no law respecting an establishment of religion, or prohibiting the free exercise thereof."

He would not be there, going over her rap sheet, why she went through husbands and lovers, why she had tried to defect to the Soviet

Union at its embassy in Paris (at just about the same time that another American atheist, Lee Harvey Oswald, was defecting to the Soviets as well), only to be turned away by the Russians. She wouldn't have had to worry that He might bring up the little unpleasantness involving her assault on some Baltimore police officers who were trying to restore a runaway girl (who was seeing Madalyn's son, Bill), and why she sued NASA when the Apollo 8 astronauts read from the Book of Genesis as they orbited the moon, and why she functioned as pornographer Larry Flynt's speechwriter during his 1984 presidential campaign.

No, none of that would have been going through her mind as she died alongside her illegitimate son, Jon, and her granddaughter, Robin, serenely confident that nothing but darkness awaited her and that, if her body was ever found it would ultimately be identified by the serial number on her prosthetic hip. What a relief and a comfort the absence of a "Supreme Being" must have been to her in those final, triumphant moments.

No need to fear His powers of moral suasion, His threats against our way of life, or even the lurking fear of punishment that may or may not come only after the lights have long since gone out. When we look in the mirror, we see God, and that is good enough for us. It ought to be good enough for Him too.

Our Secret Weapon: Political Correctness

From Woodrow Wilson to Franklin D. Roosevelt to Jimmy Carter to Bill Clinton to Barack Hussein Obama, those of us on the Left have steadily eroded your American notions of freedom, individual responsibility, civic autonomy, and free will, all in the name of protecting you from the terrors of the night. Think of us as Maria Ouspenskaya in one of the old *Wolfman* movies, warning a shivering Lon Chaney, Jr., about the evils that dwell just beyond the edge of the forest. And then stop believing in those evils.

From a nation of free men and women, who once crossed the Great Plains in prairie schooners, conquered the Rockies, sent whaling ships around the world, and rose to defend freedom wherever and whenever it was threatened by people like—well, like us—you have become a nation of sheep, cowering disarmed and unmanned in your homes, worrying about the children. Which you don't have any of, since we have also convinced you that having kids is selfish, that we're destroying the planet with our very presence, that we have to reduce our "carbon footprint" (how I laugh every time I hear those words, since we are carbon-based life forms), and, my own personal favorite, that it would be a crime to bring children into a world as horrid as this one.

We have taught you to mistrust art by coarsening it and cheapening it, by offering you vulgar substitutes for what once were your staples, supplanting Shakespeare with vulgar reality shows as popular entertainment. (Not that there's anything wrong with that! After all, the Bard was plenty vulgar in his time.) Even better, we have gotten you to despise it, as our Critical Theory legions swept across your shores and taught your children to mistrust the wellsprings of their own nation and culture. Beethoven, when queried about the meaning of his piano sonata Op. 31, No. 2, replied, "read Shakespeare's *Tempest*." But, of course, you won't—because most of you no longer can.

One of the reasons Shakespeare no longer means anything to you is that he is no longer politically correct. Yes, that's right! In the process of making you hate your own culture, which we may shorthand here as "old, dead, white male culture"—so you just know how socially unjust that must be—we've also rendered it "politically incorrect" for you to celebrate it or, soon enough, even to indulge in it. And here you thought that Ray Bradbury's famous book *Fahrenheit 451*—not to be confused with our hero Michael Moore's anti-Bush propaganda movie—was a work of fiction. But make no mistake about it: books will be burned, reading matter will be restricted, and speech will no longer be protected. It must be so.

Why? Simple. For us to be able to control you sheep, the last thing we can permit is your ability to think for yourself. If Walter Lippmann thought that the public opinion ought to be organized for the press rather than by the press, he was only dimly glimpsing the way forward, for he understood that some opinions should simply not be allowed to exist. There is no such thing as "free speech"—that was always a Founding Father chimera, an Enlightenment fantasy, a brief moment in time when the oceans kept Fortress America safe from the taste of our conformist lash—and it's high time you understood that. There is only "acceptable speech" and "unacceptable speech," and as you can imagine the latter is simply, well, unacceptable.

Political correctness is, to put it bluntly, fascism of the mind, our way of ostensibly protecting you from your own worst instincts, but really protecting ourselves from the consequences of your inadvertently articulating the truth. Of all the Master's inventions, it is among the most brilliant.

By imposing the scourge of "political correctness" upon your discourse, we have robbed you of the ability to speak—and thus to think—freely. You must now weigh every word you say against an imaginary standard of offense that constantly shifts. No matter how stupid or uneducated the individual, you must watch what you say, even to consigning unto purdah perfectly good English words that somehow might be misinterpreted by an idiot. In the guise of "compassion," one of our favorite words, we have essentially deprived you of your own language, and replaced it with one more to our liking. One, in other words, in which you can't criticize us. For, as John Milton noted in the *Areopagitica,* freedom of speech goes hand in hand with freedom of thought and, indeed, with all other freedoms: when you cannot call your tongue your own, then truly you possess nothing.

Political correctness did not simply happen. It was not born out of some popular mandate, or out of the collective unconscious, striving to rectify a past wrong. We made it happen. It came to you in the guise of a good thing—who could object to inoffensiveness? To an unhostile workplace? A nonthreatening atmosphere? A nonhurtful culture? Everything we do always seems so reasonable, does it not? And you bought it. It never occurred to you, so browbeaten had you become, that there is plenty to object to about inoffensiveness. Vigorous, bold, and, yes, offensive speech has been a hallmark of the American discourse since the frontier days. It used to be a staple of your political discourse as well. You used to be man and woman enough to take it and like it and give it back tenfold. That used to be a point of pride with you. And yet we have convinced you that our way—the way of the weasel, the whiner, the tort lawyer, the talking head; the way of Ellsworth Toohey in *The Fountainhead*—should be your way as well. Now self-censorship has tiptoed into your life, a vice cloaked as a virtue, just the way the Master drew it up on the blackboard so long ago, if you don't mind me injecting a little anachronism in my pursuit of a cheap sports metaphor, for soon enough sports metaphors will be just about the only ones you'll be able to understand.

Imagine if I told you that you and your family were being attacked in your home by a gang of vicious thugs. These thugs had broken down your door and had driven you to the farthest back bedroom, where even now you are cowering in fear. Your youngest child is whimpering in terror, your wife is having a nervous breakdown, and your teenage daughter does not at all like the way several of the thuggees have been looking at her.

Now imagine that, amazingly for the kind of guy you are, the room in which you have taken refuge is, in fact, an armory. You don't know how all those weapons got in there, and Gaia forbid that you would ever use one of them, but there they are, locked and loaded and ready to do some serious damage to the home invaders. There's your ancient ancestor's harquebus, a muzzle-loader from the First Revolutionary War, a Colt 1911 .45 semiautomatic pistol, a BAR, an M1, a grenade-launcher, a Thompson submachine gun, a Barrett .50 caliber—good Lord, man, you have enough weaponry and firepower to hold off an army!

As the fists pound on the door and the axe begins to splinter the wood, your wife and kids are crying out to you to grab a weapon or two and at least fight back, if not actually put an end to the danger.

But no. Your nerve fails you. You cannot overcome some still, small, scared voice within you that says it is better to die on your knees than to stand and fight on your feet. You look at the guns, realize that they could possibly save you, and still you don't pick one up. Because to do so would be . . . wrong.

And so you die. This is what "political correctness" will do to you if you leave it unchecked and unchallenged.

If that seems a little extravagant a claim for what is, after all, just being nice to people, think again. I can't emphasize this point enough: PC is fascism for the mind, a way of imprisoning you in an irrational and vulnerable land of what seems like happy talk and sweet thoughts, but is in reality the most vicious *Stalag* you can possibly imagine. For once you have accepted the premise of PC-speak—that there are some things you not only can't say but can't even *think*—then you have capitulated in our assault upon you and, except for the terms of surrender, the war is over.

First, let's look at what PC purports to be, the way it's sold to you as being reasonable, tolerant, and above all, fair:

Political correctness posits that any form of speech that stereotypes, insults, or hurts other people ought to be refrained from, especially if there's another way of saying whatever it was that you wished to say. And who could be against that? Hurting other people is something we learn not to do in kindergarten, just like Robert Fulghum, who learned all he needed to know there and even wrote a bestseller about it, and so our natural instinct—ours, I said, not yours, you racist, redneck bigots—is to ameliorate our speech, so that, in the immortal words of Rodney King, we can all just get along.

"Here he goes," I can hear you thinking, "telling us that we ought to start using racial epithets and stuff, to free our minds and express ourselves, and then when we do the Left can just laugh and point and call us bigoted redneck racists all over again, because we've just proved that everything they say about us is true." But that's not it at all—that's what we want you to think. What it really is, is a way for us to control not only your speech, in clear violation of the First Amendment (something for which we have very little use, insofar as you are concerned, and plan to eviscerate once your final defeat is assured, all in the name of fairness), but your very patterns of thought. You and I speak different languages and although the words might be the same, the meanings usually are not. For example, you thought it was a joke, fiction, a nightmare, when Orwell predicted the kind of society we wish to impose on you, a regime that tells you War is Peace and Weakness is Strength and that we have always been at war with Eastasia, but for us it was a bridge to the twenty-first century, a road map for peace and a passport to your oblivion. After all, what was Newspeak except an early form of PC?

For example: when you hear the word Freedom, you think freedom for everybody; when we hear it, we think: freedom is the absence of you. When you use the word Peace, you are thinking that it applies universally: a blessed time when there is no conflict, all men are brothers, and the lion lies down with the lamb. But, like our Islamic brothers, when we hear it, we are thinking that it applies specifically to a blessed time when there is no conflict, when all men are brothers and the lion lies down alone because *there are no lambs*; like you, they have been devoured. End of conflict, arrival of peace.

Political correctness, in other words, is appeasement by another name.

Surely you have heard the chants that have been rising from the East for more than thirty years. "Death to the Great Satan! Death to America!" There was a time when those imprecations might have been fighting words, words and threats against which you would have taken up arms. When someone said he wished you dead you took him at his word, and prepared yourself accordingly. No longer. That would be belligerent. That would be rude. That would be insensitive.

Accordingly, we have invested more effort in this one single aspect of American life over the past twenty-five years than in anything else we do. Our trained seals in the media—by now, most of them superbly schooled in the dogmas of PC as a result of their expensive Ivy League educations—have done yeoman's work in this regard, first censoring their own copy and speech, and then extending their proscriptions about what does and does not constitute valid public discourse to you. Go back to television programs as late as the mid-1980s and you will be astonished at the amount of "offensive" material that everybody seemingly had no problem with whatsoever. But gradually, the edges were chipped away and made smooth; the goalposts were constantly shifted, until we are now at that gloriously teleological point at which "offensiveness" is entirely in the eye and ear of the putative offendee, and an accusation is tantamount to a conviction. Because after all, unless you have walked a mile in the other man's shoes . . . blah blah blah.

Political correctness has become the water we swim in and the air we breathe. That's why it's both amazing and disconcerting when someone prominent—someone we always thought of as *one of us*—suddenly has a Damascene moment as the bonds of illusions are cast from his eyes. Here, for example, is the great David Mamet, someone whose plays always received the most glowing reviews from our pet drama critics (and you know who you are!). Someone whose freewheeling and pungent celebration of the Anglo-Saxon roots of the English language bespoke a man of iconoclastic taste and temperament, like us. Someone whose loyalty to the Cause of Peace and Freedom and Tolerance could never be questioned. Until one day in 2008, he had to go and write this:

> I took the liberal view for many decades, but I believe I have changed my mind. . . . [My wife and I] were riding along and listening to NPR. I felt my facial muscles tightening, and the words beginning to form in my mind: *"Shut the fuck up?"* she prompted. And her terse, elegant summation, as always, awakened me to a deeper truth . . . This is, to me, the synthesis of this worldview with which I now found myself disenchanted: that everything is always wrong.

Needless to say, that was the end of Mamet in our pantheon of heroes and it's no surprise to me that his entire oeuvre is currently under-

going a reassessment from some of our finest revisionist drama critics
(and you know who you are!). Which is why, by the way, we have always been mistrustful of artists and writers and their ilk. My father still
gets misty-eyed when he thinks back to the Stalinist purges in the Soviet
Union during the 1930s and 1940s, a time when the Leader and Teacher
could have meddlesome priests, writers, poets, and composers stood up
against a wall and shot whenever he felt like it. Because Uncle Joe (not
my Uncle Joe, the guy he was named after) understood that real artists
are the most dangerous people on the planet, because their art leads
them to the one place that a dictator can never really reach—the people's hearts.

As my atheist father taught me, we live in an age of science, and
Marxism-Leninism was nothing if not scientific. We even had fancy
phrases to gussy it up, phrases like "dictatorship of the proletariat" and
"dialectical materialism." There was no trouble in our River City that
we couldn't handle at the point of a Kalashnikov, and even though we
gave some of our chimps just enough of a free rein to make them appear
independent, the others knew the leash was short, and it could end in a
cigarette, a blindfold, and a bullet if they didn't toe the party line.

This is why every real writer I know, every real composer, every real
artist—as opposed to the "brave" and "courageous" trough-feeders who
are supported largely by grants from the National Endowment for the
Arts, or live by floating from the Iowa Writers' Workshop to the
MacDowell Colony to Yaddo to the Bread Loaf Conference to, for all I
know, the Meatloaf Conference, where they study and debate the
meaning of Jim Steinman's lyrics—doesn't just play a rebel at the
Poseur's Conference, but actually is one. If you are a real artist you, like
Luther, *kann nicht anders.* You can do nothing else but be who you are.
And how does that self-knowledge come about?

By examining the mysteries of the human heart. All of our bloody
dialectical materialism and scientific socialism went out the window
when the Hungarians opened the border with Austria to let the poor but
(we thought) ideologically reliable East Germans out during that dreadful, sorrowful summer of 1989, and when the first unretaliated chink
was taken out of the Berlin Wall later that fall. It was a real shock to the
system, let me tell you, although our faith in it remains basically un-

shaken. And so the Anti-Fascist Protection Barrier fell—not just to our astonishment, but to the utter and complete mystification of our useful idiots and fellow travelers in the West, including the CIA and the entire U.S. State Department. What a tragedy it was; we had become the enemy you loved and suddenly we were gone . . . underground once more, our usual habitat since the early days. And all of your diplomatic and intelligence agencies could not predict an event that even a minor writer such as that rotter, Solzhenitsyn, would have deemed too obvious to write down as a short story.

Why? Political correctness. It would have been an "insult" to the Soviets not to have treated them as the Other Superpower, part of the First World. It would have hurt their feelings and their Slavic pride. You looked at their ranks of missiles on May Day, the tottering geezers atop the Lenin Mausoleum, and you said to yourselves: these are people we can work with. When what you should have done—what nobody did until the loathsome Reagan—was give them the back of your hand, tell them to stop acting like spoiled children and come back to the bargaining table when they were serious. And by the time they actually were serious, when a desperate Gorby, trying to save his own bright red commie tush, could look at the balance sheet and realize the jig was up, it was too late and our carefully constructed, scientific edifice of Marxism-Leninism simply collapsed and vanished overnight.

Naturally, our side took a great deal of ribbing from you reactionaries about this, some of it even dripping with contempt, which is something we're not used to having directed our way. So it was to preempt this very contempt that we were forced to invent political correctness—a kind of retroactive snatch of victory from the jaws of defeat—to weasel out of our long and loudly expressed passion for the First Amendment and instead begin to subtly discern distinctions, nuances, in the whole idea of "free speech." Up popped campus speech codes, featuring the great, grand Boogeyman of them all, "hate speech."

You really have to hand it to us for this one. For decades, we've been the ones railing against your side in the vilest terms imaginable, charging you with every crime, real and imaginary, under the sun and flinging a barrage of four-letter words, personal insults, even racial insults at you. But that was okay. Why? Because *you deserved them.* Because they were all true, and as you know there's nothing we enjoy more than speaking truth to power. But you so much as think of returning such sentiments to us in kind and we'll have the hate speech lawyers on you like, well, lawyers on you. You are not allowed to notice, or in any way signify that you have noticed, any differences of sex, race, creed, color, or sexual orientation. You are not allowed to comment on our choice of words, our lack of logic, or in any wise make us feel bad ourselves. You are not allowed to comment on our hairy women, our capon men, our fey little NPR voices, our lack of physical coordination, our total inability with any piece of mechanical equipment, our lack of military service, our pathological fear of firearms and our utter incapability with them. You are not allowed to impute to us any actions that are anything less than ameliorative or benign; you are never either to imply or infer that we have ever acted out of base or ignoble motives. And you are never, ever allowed to question our patriotism.

In our pursuit of unbounded hedonism (which is what we call freedom) we were forced to gradually start restricting what could and could not be said and written about our activities, and if that meant we were suddenly out of love with the First Amendment, tough. After all, we had been taking a blowtorch and a pair of pliers to the "free expression" clause regarding religion for decades, and so it was a relatively simple matter to turn our baleful glare on freedom of speech and of the press. So long, old friends! Under your sheltering embrace, we had introduced pornography to mainstream American culture, and convinced judges and juries that nude dancing (not that there's anything wrong with that!) was protected under the First Amendment, as John Adams would have no doubt agreed. But that job was long since finished, and so "freedom" now had to go.

In short, there's nothing that we won't throw overboard, or under the bus, when it suits our purposes—which are always and everywhere focused on power. Not just power for us, but our power over you. For what good is power if there is no enemy to acknowledge it? Until I got well and truly into this racket, I used to idly wonder, in between working on my Rosa Luxemburg coloring book and my official Supreme Soviet action figures, featuring Konstantin Chernenko and Leonid Brezhnev, why the great potentates of olden days would force their defeated enemies to prostrate themselves before them, just before they struck off their heads. Then one day "Uncle Joe" took me to a production of Verdi's *Aida* at the Metropolitan Opera (or maybe it was the kids' version, at the Little Red School House, I forget), and when I saw Radames lording it over Amonasro and parading him before the King of Egypt, well . . . that was a moment.

So you misread our motives at your own peril. No matter what we say it's about—civil rights, free speech, ecdysiasm—in the end it's always about power, and part of our pleasure must and does lie in your discomfiture.

And thus, once more, political correctness. PC is the grease that causes the wheels of your destruction to move inexorably forward, as it strips you of your words, and then of your thoughts, and then of your dignity, and, finally, of your humanity. Once you have accepted its central premise—that other people have the right to tell you what you may think—you're done.

And the rest is, as they say, commentary.

"Fairness" and "Tolerance"

As discussed earlier, we progressives have abandoned God's command-ments as the relics of the judgmental, pre-deconstructionist, patriarchal culture they so obviously are. We reject your father-knows-best fascism in all its manifestations, and this most definitely includes those silly rules that Moses allegedly brought down from Mount Sinai, the better to found a monstrous conspiracy known as "monotheism" and thus make our lives difficult thousands of years later.

Okay, not exactly abandoned them, but edited them, replaced them with a couple of simple rules that have served us well, if only as protec-tive coloring, in our war against you. Just as a yellow dog who knows he's about to be seriously eviscerated by a bigger, meaner canine rolls over on his back and shows his belly and his balls—his most vulnerable bits, as it were—in the hopes that the Big Dog will take that as a sign of surrender and thus spare him, so have we perfected the art of pretending to surrender when, every so often, you finally rouse yourselves to call us out over one trivial provocation or another, all the while planning and plotting to live and stab you in the back another day.

Yes, I know this makes us sound like the cowards we are, but that's exactly why you find it so hard to fight us. *You can't hit a girl*. And, basi-cally, we're all girls—not that there's anything wrong with that. "You're a lonely, ugly arsehole, and you must accept it," says Tony to Colin in Richard Curtis's brilliant script for *Love Actually*. "Never. I am Colin, God of sex," replies his friend. And you know—he was right! As long as you buy into our transparently phony posturing and premises—because you *want* to believe, because not to do so would be rude or, worse, bigoted in some fashion—we have you at our underdog mercy. *We* are the gods of sex, and you are the lonely, ugly arseholes, instead of vice versa.

One of the reasons we pretended to be horrified by what happened on 9/11—why we had to endure all those tedious candlelight vigils outside the Capitol, feigning horror at the senseless loss of life, when deep down we were secretly thinking: *We deserved it! Hit us, Berber, one more time*—was that, as usual, we had to conceal our true feelings so that we wouldn't let the mask slip, and reveal how much we despise you and your unwarranted, overbearing, tiresome pride in your own country. This is what we have done to your culture: where once real men used to take it outside and settle it like, well, like real men, today we whine, we cry, and, if all else fails, we sue. Think of us as Bernie Bernbaum in the Coen brothers' greatest film, *Miller's Crossing*, falling on his knees in sheer crocodile-tear cowardice and begging the Irish gangster, played by Gabriel Byrne, for his life. "Look in your heart, Tom!" he cries and whines and whinges and weeps and well . . . to his everlasting regret, Tom lets him go. Like the aliens in *Independence Day*, we're using your own weapons—your strength, your decency, your sense of fair play, and your laughable compassion—against you.

Because while you wingnuts are busy getting bogged down in the house-to-house fighting of *Rahmbo v. El Rushbo*, or whichever clownish side show we have managed to distract you with this month, the larger point of what's happening to you is sailing right over your fat heads. You're letting yourselves get bogged down in minutiae—when you should really be seeing the Birnam Wood behind Dunsinane's trees. For, in the end, our Cold Civil War against you conservatives and your institutions is not really about personalities, or even policies: it's about *principles*. Meanwhile, you would rather discuss policies.

And what—besides Blame America First—are those principles? What are our greatest commandments? Not being congenitally Christian, we of course reject the message of Jesus, who boiled the patriarchal laws of Moses down to two nifty aphorisms: Love God and Love Thy Neighbor as Thyself. When you get right down to it, that's pretty much all Christianity is, if you leave out the racism, sexism, homophobia, school prayer, cucumber sandwiches, dancing with your maiden aunts at weddings, drinking at funerals, and, of course, the Spanish Inquisition.

Our strictures, however, have a much more positive spin than the dreary List of Don'ts inscribed upon Moses's tablets, and they're much more modern than Jesus's goody-two-shoes bromides. You probably already know what they are, but in case you don't, here we go:

Fairness and Tolerance.

Sure, they're not in any Bible, Torah, or Koran that I know about, and naturally, being an atheist and all, I'm hard-pressed to cite a scriptural reference for any of them, except for maybe *The Prophet* by Khalil Gibran, which was all the rage in my dad's day. You don't want to know how many times he scored with a few lines from this Age of Aquarius precursor written by a Lebanese Maronite Christian who was raised in Beantown's South End. Suckers!

And what do we mean by Fairness and Tolerance? Not, of course, what you think. As should be clear by now, we never use a word with a uniform meaning that's clear to both sides when we can use one with a double meaning, one of which is invisible and inaudible to you. As Churchill said of Britain and America, the Left and the Right in America today are two nations separated by a common language. We dwell on a one-way street, in which the traffic goes the way we say it goes, and it is no small measure of our success over the past half-century or so that you have never been able to figure that out.

Take Fairness. Sounds unexceptionable, right? That's exactly what we want you to think. Who could possibly be against Fairness, except for maybe Ayn Rand and the *Atlas Shrugged* kooks. In our view, everything in modern America is unfair if it results in the slightest disparity in income, lifestyle, job description, or the availability of Chicken McNuggets at your local fast food place—which we'll soon be shuttering in the interests of the People's Health, no further need to call 911. And we are more than willing to sacrifice everything you have in pursuit of this social justice.

Sure, it will make you mad for a while as we "looters" systematically sack your homes, smash your pianos, and turn over your spare rooms to the wretched of the earth, but after a while you'll come to accept it, and even embrace it. Shared misery—what could be fairer? *Vsya vlast sovyetam*: "All power to the Soviets!" If I were you, I'd get used to wrapping my lips around that particular phrase, because if we have our way you're going to be shouting it at rallies in Times Square, Pershing Square, Union Square, and from the balcony of the Drake Hotel if you know what's good for you.

I realize that, to you, "fairness" means treating all people equally, giving everyone the same chance, putting aside the old prejudices in favor of a color-blind society. To us, though, it means exactly the opposite. Just as, in Islam, "peace" means one thing to the formerly and thankfully no longer "Christian"—what are you going to do with all those empty cathedrals?—world and quite another to the *ummah*, so does "fairness" have a separate but equal resonance. To us, "fairness" simply means we win, you lose, no matter what the rules of the game. Are we perchance in the minority in Congress? Very well then, simple fairness dictates that you let us wield inordinate influence, all out of proportion to our numbers; otherwise, we will simply roll over onto our backs and show you our belly until you accommodate us. And in those joyous happy days when we have lied, wheedled, and cajoled our way to power, and have been by some miracle of obfuscation voted into the electoral majority by the American people who would far rather be watching *Dancing with the Stars* on their giant flat screen TVs than having to think about politics, well then "fairness" means what it used to mean back when men were men and tort lawyers got punched in the face in the back alleys behind bars, took it and liked it, lest they get the crap beaten out of them again and again until they stopped threatening to financially beggar a man with whom they had some slight disagreement.

And so to Tolerance.

For decades, we have been provoking you, goading you, mocking you, denigrating you, challenging your faith in God and country and yourselves—while at the same time demanding that you tolerate us. For us, there is no greater virtue than tolerance, since our definition of it means accepting not the best of a group with whom you may differ, but the worst.

Remember that, for us, there is no goal but your destruction, and tolerance is perhaps our favorite weapon, especially when blended with incrementalism. At the beginning of our effort to break down your society we, quite reasonably, noted the disparity between your professed beliefs and how you actually lived your lives, how you treated other people. What happened next was a bit of an intellectual trick, but once we fooled you with it—well, the results are evident all around you.

Understanding that human beings are naturally clannish and suspicious of outsiders, we had to get you to accept two mutually exclusive propositions and keep them both in your mind simultaneously, rather like the White Queen's being able to believe six impossible things before breakfast in *Alice in Wonderland*. On the one hand, you had to believe that there were absolutely no differences among racial or ethnic groups, that we were all part of the Brotherhood of Man—it said so, right there in your Declaration of Independence!—and that welcoming everyone to, and absorbing them into, your society would make absolutely no difference to the proper functioning of your democracy.

And the best part was—it didn't! Think about the raw power of the American Experiment: an Anglo-Protestant country, less than a century after its founding, swallowed up whole nations of starving Germans and Irishmen, fleeing Italian peasants from Calabria and Sicily, millions of *shtetl* Jews from the Slavic Pale, and not only survived but prospered. Passing through the hard times of Hester Street and Hell's Kitchen, these groups fought their way into American society, became cops, lawyers, doctors, artists, musicians, performers, writers, and scientists—became as "American" as any nativist, thanks to the most excellent among them, who realized they were fighting not only for themselves, but for the whole group, and that their success reflected well not only on them, but on all the others, including the wastrels, gangsters, murderers, bums, layabouts, and the less successful lawyers. So we had to switch to Plan B.

Plan B posited that there were, in fact, vast differences among ethnic groups, especially the ones that had not fared so well under the yoke and the lash of Intolerant America. Why, just look at the Chinese: forced into coolie ghettos as they worked on the railroads, forbidden to marry "white" women, kicked out of the country when they were no longer needed for cheap labor, and forbidden to return for many years under the Chinese Exclusion Act. According to our theory, the Chinese and the other East Asians shouldn't have stood a Chinaman's chance of succeeding in America . . .

Oops! Wrong example. Let's try another one. We cast our eyes around, looking for the best victim we could possibly find. We searched through the serried ranks of the poor and dispossessed among all the peoples of the world until our gaze at last settled upon . . . black people. And suddenly we could see the Promised Land of Affirmative Action emerging from the fog and haze ahead, like Shangri-La.

Amazing to think they had been here all this time, right under our noses but, being Democrats, we had been turning those selfsame noses up at them, which is probably why we missed them. We don't call the Democratic Party the party of Slavery, Segregation, Secularism, and Sedition for nothing—it's a title we've proudly earned practically since the day the party was founded as (what else?) the Anti-Federalist party, skulking under the name Democratic-Republicans, like that was going to fool anybody. Yes, you read that right: although the history is a little complicated, we modern Democrats basically are the descendants of the men who opposed the party of George Washington (the Ronald Reagan of his day) and, especially, John Adams (the George H. W. Bush of his day), not to mention John Quincy Adams (the George W. Bush of his day).

Being a party with its strongest roots in the Old South, Democrats back then were fervently in favor of slavery, and opposed all efforts to modify or end it. I don't want to bore you with the involved and complex history that resulted in the three-fifths compromise in the Constitution (in which black slaves were counted as three-fifths of a human being for apportionment purposes, lest the slaveholding South wield political power all out of proportion to its eligible voters), the Missouri Compromise of 1820 (which regulated the admission of new slave states into the Union along geographical lines), and the Kansas-Nebraska Act of 1854, which repealed the Missouri Compromise and opened up slavery for a vote in new territories (which sent Bloody Kansas into paroxysms of violence). No wonder we're always advocating compromise! It was in response to the violence that the modern Republican Party was founded that same year in Ripon, Wisconsin, making it its mission to oppose the slavery-loving Democratic Party at each and every turn. Six years later, they elected the first Republican President, Abraham Lincoln, whom we still have to pretend to like. So when South Carolina fired upon Fort Sumter to start the Civil War, it was in effect a war declared by Democrats on Republicans, and from that moment on the strife has not lessened, and black people have been caught in the middle ever since. You didn't hear much "tolerance" noise out of us in those days.

In the meantime, we fought a rearguard action against civil rights. We formed the Ku Klux Klan, to suppress Republican voter turnout and fight not only against civil rights for blacks, but, later, against Jews and Catholics as well. We had cheered the *Dred Scott* decision in 1857, when Chief Justice Roger Taney—a Democrat, appointed by a Democrat, Andrew Jackson—described black people as "an inferior order and altogether unfit to associate with the white race" and ruled that, being private property, they had no civil rights. When *Plessy v. Ferguson* came along in 1896, we cheered again when the Supreme Court upheld the constitutionality of "separate but equal," endorsing the Louisiana court's ruling.

African-Americans found few friends among the Democrats of the Solid South, where Democratic politicians such as George Wallace, the governor of Alabama; Lester Maddox, the governor of Georgia; and Orval Faubus, the governor of Arkansas, led the charge against them. In 1954, in the wake of the historic *Brown v. Board of Education* Supreme Court decision that overturned *Plessy,* Governor Faubus deployed the Arkansas National Guard to prevent the integration of Little Rock Central High School, only to be outgunned by his Commander in Chief, the Republican president Dwight D. Eisenhower. As a Democrat, Lyndon Johnson fought for the Civil Rights Act of 1964, but the Republicans supported it in much higher percentages than the Democrats. And who, you ask, led the filibuster against it? Why, none other than Albert Arnold Gore, Sr., a close friend and confidant of Armand Hammer, one of the Soviet Union's best and most effective agents against the U.S. during his long lifetime. And Senator "Sleepin' " Sam Ervin, later elevated to hero status by the Left for his pursuit of Richard Nixon during Watergate. And the late Exalted Cyclops of the Ku Klux Klan himself, the longest-serving senator in American history, the king of West Virginia pork, Robert "White Niggers" Byrd. What a swell crowd, and really something for all us progressives to be proud of!

And then, something magical happened. We made all y'all forget our racist past by the simple expedient of not only erasing it, but tossing all previous accomplishments of our newly adopted Victim Groups down the memory hole too. Gone was the Democrats' irremediably racist past—hey! Sorry about that!—and in its place came the Party of Compassion, looking at its colored brothers in all their pathetic inability to do anything at all without a bunch of us guilty white liberals assisting them, and then helpfully improving their lives as we brought the formidable powers of our Ivy League training to bear on the Negro Problem.

We are nothing if not all or nothing; full-throttle is how we roll in Progressiveland. Where once we hunted black people down, strung them up on trees, returned them with all the power of the state to their slave masters, and kept them riding in the back of the bus, we now showered them with our tender mercies. It began during the selfsame civil rights movements that Robert Byrd, Sleepin' Sam, and Albert Arnold Gore, Sr., had tried to stop, when Northern liberal Democrats headed below the Mason-Dixon Line to confront their Southern brethren. Suddenly, the personal was not only political, it was regional, and FDR's coalition began to break apart as Bull Connor battled Michael Schwerner and Andrew Goodman for the soul of Yawnapatawpha County, or wherever.

Then came our best trick of all: some disaffected Southern Democrats began to switch parties. It began when Strom Thurmond, the governor of South Carolina (that pesky state again) ran for President in 1948 on the Dixiecrat ticket, garnered more than a million votes, won several states, and collected thirty-nine electoral votes; later, elected as a senator on the Democratic ticket, he switched parties and became a lifelong Republican, as did such other stalwarts as Trent Lott . . . and Ben Nighthorse Campbell, and . . .

I dunno exactly, there must have been millions of them, but even if it was only a few, not counting crazy Arlen Specter, it meant that we were now able to write off the whole Southern wing of the party—you know, the one that had been in existence since, oh, Thomas Jefferson, and therefore claim that the Southern Democrats had really been *premature Republicans*! And that, ladies and gentlemen, is how you jettison your entire racist past in one easy lesson. It's so easy an amoral, sociopathic child could do it!

The next step was to strip African-Americans of all the accomplishments of their storied past. For us, you see, the world begins anew whenever we get involved with it, and it could not be that black Americans had ever achieved anything notable in our racist society. Without our help—impossible!

So out the window went black achievement. Sure, we managed to contain some of it in the February ghetto known as "Black History Month," where it could be presented through the prism of "stolen patrimony." The leftist media always needs a narrative frame in which to present its propaganda, and in this case by segregating the rich history of African-American accomplishment in the New World for the past half-millennium, we can pitch it as "the stuff white America doesn't want you to know about your own history," when in fact *we're* the ones who don't want you to know. But I'll never tell!

And so we merrily sorted through Black History's five hundred years, keeping Crispus Attucks—after all, he was one of the First Black Victims—but short-selling Austin Dabney, a slave in Georgia who took up arms against the British during the Revolution and, for his bravery, was rewarded with his own land and a federal pension at a time when blacks were forbidden to own property. We kept W. E. B. Du Bois, the scion of a prominent mixed-race family in Great Barrington, Massachusetts, who founded the NAACP, became a communist, and eventually returned to Africa, dying in Ghana at the age of ninety-five, and jettisoned Booker T. Washington, the bastard child of a white slaveholder and a black slave woman, who pulled himself *Up from Slavery,* dined with a Republican President, Teddy Roosevelt, in the White House (in an event that infuriated the Southern Democrats), and founded the Tuskegee Institute in Alabama, where he eventually worked himself to death in his lifelong struggle to better black America through education and hard work. We kept Michael Jackson, a self-mutilated child molester of whom it was once said that "only in America could a poor black boy grow up to be a rich white woman," and disappeared Scott Joplin, one of the most important figures in the history of American popular music, and the man who not only invented ragtime but memorialized the meeting between Booker T. and T.R. in an opera, now alas lost, called *A Guest of Honor.* Joplin invented or adumbrated every single strand of what evolved into American popular music of the twentieth century, and it is certainly safe to say that without him there would have been no Michael Jackson—which I suppose is the only bad thing you can say about a man born to a freed slave, educated in the bordellos of the Mississippi River, and who forged a synthesis of African and European musical strains to create something unique: the voice of modern America.

Ella Fitzgerald and Louis Armstrong, Jesse Owens, James Baldwin and Richard Wright and Frederick Douglass . . . That just begins to call the honor roll of black achievement in America, which of course is as long and glorious as any other group's, and was accomplished under unmatched strictures. And they did it all without *us*. And I can hear you now: In a rational world, *that* would be our focus, wouldn't ya think?

With a history like that, it's a wonder the black community tolerates us at all.

That's the stuff your bunch likes to talk about, all part of your mindless celebration of American history in general. But that would be judgmental—cheering only the best. What we want you to do is accept the worst—not the heroes but the criminals, not the men and women of all races and classes who helped create the country you live in today, but the men and women who have done everything in their power, whether through malice, indolence, indisposition, or hostility, to ruin it. Tolerance no longer asks you not to judge a man by the color of his skin; in fact, it does precisely the opposite—it *requires* you to notice the color of his skin and if he's doing anything illegal or destructive to ignore his actions. That is the real meaning of the word "tolerance" today.

As you can see, we've flipped it, which is always part of our arsenal against you. No sooner have we gotten you to accept a premise—which may in itself be innocuous or, on rare occasions, actually beneficial to everybody—than we start twisting it, revisiting it, modulating it, until by the time we're finished it bears almost no resemblance to what it originally started out as, except in the most superficial way. And by the time you've figured this out, by the time you timorously raise your hand to lodge a small, tiny really, practically infinitesimal objection, it's way too late. Once you've accepted the premise, you're all ours.

Let's take a sprint through the recent past to see how this works. Remember back in the 1950s, before women entered both college and the

workforce in such large numbers that today they constitute the majority of college students (boys are the coeds now) and dominate many
fields, including journalism? When Dad put on his hat, went off to
work, and Mom stayed at home with the kids, the breadwinner and the
homemaker working together in partnership, the children getting the
benefit of maternal love and attention, and learning to respect their father for the sacrifices he made in order to provide for his family? Remember that?

Well, neither do I, and as far as I'm concerned it's probably just one
of those phony cultural myths your side derived from television shows
like *Leave It to Beaver*. But there certainly must be some reason why, half
a century ago, a single man could earn enough money to support a wife
and multiple children (not just one designer kid), build or buy a house
in the suburbs, like Scarsdale and Pelham and Cleveland Heights and
Dearborn and Berkeley and Encino. There must be a reason why, after
women went into the workforce in a big way in the 1970s, two incomes
suddenly became the equivalent of one, four kids became two kids, divorce soared, and, after *Roe v. Wade* in 1973, two kids became one kid became no kids.

There must be a reason why crime rates were at historic lows, why
kids could play outside during the summer from just after breakfast
until the street lights came on, why they felt perfectly safe riding their
bikes all over town, taking the subway from Queens to Harlem and back
again and hitching rides on the cable cars in San Francisco and hanging
off the sides, just for laughs. There must be a reason why boys didn't
punch girls, why real men didn't curse in public, why wives wore dresses
and even gloves, why men wouldn't think to appear in the workplace
without a suit or at least a jacket and tie (and this was before the word
"workplace" was even invented!), why there were not multiple lawsuits
after every water cooler joke. But to ask these questions would be
"reactionary"—that's some word, isn't it, and one of our favorites, right
up there with "revanchist"—and even racist, somehow. Don't ask me
how; we'd find a way, probably in consultation with the *New York Times*
op-ed writers.

I know the answer we'd give you if you were dumb enough to make
these assertions in public anymore: what about the civil rights move-

ment? It's the answer we always give every time one of you wingnuts starts getting all weepy for the Good Old Days (which, as we all know, were hell on earth, not that there's anything wrong with that), and begin to reminisce how you shoulda seen the Atlantic Ocean back then, it was some sight. The civil rights movement is the ultimate trump card for all of you longing for the Garden of Eden you remember Amerikkka being during the Eisenhower administration. And it's such a simple syllogism that even a Young Pioneer could do it in his sleep.

1. Fact: the Civil Rights Act didn't happen until 1964.
2. Premise: therefore, this was an evil country until 1964.
3. Faulty conclusion: ergo, nothing that America did or was until 1964 could possibly be any good, as long as this one monstrous wrong remained unrighted.

To which, of course, you lot nod your heads and stroke your beards and suddenly shout: My God, Mildred! Don't you see we've been living a lie all these years! Let's kill ourselves in expiation of the sins of our fathers.

And that's it. You're done! No nuance, no looking at history—heck, not even an acknowledgment that Martin Luther King, Jr., was a registered Republican (as most black people were up to the 1960s). At one stroke, and no matter the merits of the actual facts, we have reframed the argument on our terms, made America's entire history hostage to the legacy of slavery, and cut the legs out from under you, our opponents. And the genius of it is, the argument isn't even about the civil rights movement—about which no one would disagree! The discussion is over, the science is settled, the voters have spoken, and now it's on to Chicago and let's win in November. *Falsus in unum,* and all that jazz.

This all-purpose reproach allows us to trash just about every icon and institution in the United States. We've turned the all-American dad into a doofus figure of fun. We've gotten you to loathe stay-at-home moms, celebrate pregnant teenagers, cheer on their abortions, and sue the doctors when they botch them. We've convinced you that kids are smarter than their parents; the poor are more virtuous than the rich; and that all cultures are equal. We demanded that you tolerate it—and you

did! Chesterton, or some other religious nut, may have said that tolerance is the only virtue left to the man who no longer believes in anything, but so what? Tolerance is the only virtue you need while we
cannibalize your culture, and when we're finished, well, you won't need
it anymore.

And so it has fallen to us to right the wrongs of the past two thousand years of the Common Era—thank Gaia that superstitious "A.D."
nonsense is a thing of the past, and we didn't even have to sue anybody
to get rid of it—by legislating and suing you out of existence. By tying
you down with a million petty regulations until everything you do, say,
or even think will be subject to prophylactic reflection before you do,
say, or think it. We've won. And now you're about to experience the
consequences of how much we dislike you.

Herbert Marcuse was right in *Repressive Tolerance*: the only thing we
can't tolerate is you.

Your Last Warning

Back in the good old days of the Soviet Union, before Mother Russia was brought down by the machinations of that cowboy Reagan, the naïveté of Gorbachev, and the duplicity of certain elements within the society—just as Hitler and the Nazis had their myth of *der Dolchstoss*, the "stab in the back" by the Junkers and aristocrats and Jews and communists and whoever else caused Germany to lose World War I, so do we have ours—there was something called the Brezhnev Doctrine. Doctrines, of course, come and go—when was the last time you heard anybody talking about enforcing the Monroe Doctrine, much less the Nixon Doctrine or, Gaia forbid, the Bush Doctrine?—but the Brezhnev Doctrine was fun while it lasted and deserves to be brought back again, which is what we're doing socially, if not politically.

The Brezhnev Doctrine stated that once a country goes communist, it can never become noncommunist again. You will immediately see that this doctrine is very similar to Islamic belief, which holds that one may freely accept Islam but never un-accept it, and that Muslim lands must always remain Muslim. Of course, Spain pretty much rendered that theory moot when, after a battle that had gone on for nearly eight hundred years, Ferdinand and Isabella finally kicked the Moors out in 1492, right along with the Jews, and packed Columbus off for Puerto Rico or wherever for good measure. Which is one of the reasons al-Qaeda is still ticked off.

Quoth Brezhnev: *"When forces that are hostile to socialism try to turn the development of some socialist country towards capitalism, it becomes not only a problem of the country concerned, but a common problem and concern of all socialist countries."* In other words, not only is the rule that once you go red you can never go back to bed, but that other free and peace-loving socialist duchies have the obligation to invade you, crush you, and kill your family, more or less. What's not to like?

We have our own version of the Brezhnev Doctrine, which states that once a university has gone leftist it can never return to the center, much less swing to the right. Once a state has flipped from red to blue, we will write letters to the editor of *The New York Times* until the day we die to keep it that way. And once the country has elected its first out-of-the-closet socialist, that will be the end of the dispute between capitalism and communism. No backsliding, in other words. Like that wacky party that ran Mexico for a million years, the Permanent Revolutionary Party, we are the permanent revolution, always fight, fight, fighting—fighting for you forever.

Which is why we're here to stay. Because, my friends, we are in the endgame now, the place where the rubber meets the road, where the you-know-what hits the thingummybob. Since the days of the sainted Marx—who, fittingly, died a stateless person in London in 1883—we have been awaiting this day, like some primitive tribe in the Hindu Kush of *The Man Who Would Be King*, enduring one false *moshiach* and failed Messiah after another in the hopes of finally encountering the god who cannot bleed.

To that end, as you may have noticed, we have fanned out across this great land of ours, moving like locusts from one state to another, gradually annexing you, turning you from red to blue (you have to love the way we flipped the color schemes a few years back, pinning our beloved red on you while we grabbed the more American blue). Our MO is simple: we effectively demolish a state by turning its government into a gangster cabal, flouting its laws with impunity, raising taxes that beggar the diminishing productive part of the populace, infiltrating our cadres of "community organizers"—Alinskyite Marxists operating under the protective coloration of, well, people of color—into your local corporations and institutions, and assiduously pursuing such radical endeavors as the "Secretary of State" project, which ensures that no matter what kind of financial, legal, or electoral trouble we get into while taking over your state, there is always someone Up There (in the state capital) to bail us out or grease the way.

Here's the Lefty Two-Step:

1) Take over a state politically. Back in the heyday of gangland, the genius of those original "undocumented immigrants" was that they could see what native Americans (no, not Indians) couldn't: that, if you set your mind to it, you could easily take over the rackets, not just in a neighborhood or even a city, but in an entire state. Why think small when you could think big? Gangsters like Madden and Luciano and Lansky were interested in money and booze and babes, sure, but more than that they were interested in *power*. They were the *descamisados* of Evita's Argentina, the dispossessed, the short, funny-looking guys who spoke with foreign accents, sweated profusely, used axle grease on their hair, spilled orange juice on their ties, or else shoved grapefruits into their girlfriends' faces. Most of them were illegals and some of them, in the days when you clowns actually enforced your racist immigration laws, even got deported. But still they soldiered on in their noble mission: to fleece as many "real Americans" as possible (which most definitely included members of their own ethnic groups and African-Americans too), take out their enemies, avoid the law as much as possible, hire the best shysters they could afford when they couldn't, and try to die in their beds in the good old U.S.A. if they could. Precious few succeeded (Madden was one), but you have to admire their moxie.

Today, we stalwart men of the Left—their spiritual and in some cases literal descendants—eschew such small beer. Why settle for a state when you can take over an entire country, with the media cheering you every step of the way? And that was just what we did in the "historic" election of 2008. Our aces combo of New York red diaper babies and Chicago red diaper babies and a compliant, complicit media managed to pull the wool over the eyes of the electorate just long enough to overcome even the formidable Clinton Machine (too fat, too sassy, too pant-suited) and the aforementioned hapless troglodyte who, now that he lost, is once again back in the good graces of the Democrat-Media Complex.

Those old thugs showed the way forward in New York, New Jersey, Arkansas, and Nevada, but since JFK unionized the federal workforce, our path has been much easier. We've long had the unions on our side, of course, but with the decline of the labor movement, after the victories over the steel industry and the auto industry, both of which are pretty much now defunct, we needed a boost and boy did Jack ever give it to us. Along with the Little Wagner Act, it allowed us to tap a great natural resource, which was those people who are dependent on tax dollars—taken from you chumps—for their livelihood. Sure, we understand that when the Party of Take becomes bigger than the Party of Give, the whole scheme will eventually collapse, but hey—Social Security's still hanging on, isn't it? By putting state and federal employee unions' muscle and money behind our campaigns we start with a huge advantage over the "normal" Americans on your side.

2) Take over a state culturally. Our promise of Utopia will naturally attract like-minded—I almost said "simple-minded"—folks to the state, if they're not there already. (Memo: pick states on the coasts with great natural beauty—you know, places where people actually want to live—instead of those Dust Bowl flyover places. The Pacific Northwest, California, New York, and New England were great places to start.) And for the first decades, things will be just great. California, for example, was settled by gold miners, prospectors, claim-jumpers, bankers, railroad tycoons, hoteliers, seamen, farmers, Dust Bowl Joads, real estate speculators, religious cultists, and various kooks, but by the 1950s they had all more or less blended into a homogenous, conservative Republican sort of place, the kind of state that would give birth to Richard Nixon and shelter Ronald Reagan. (You can see how awful it was.) It was a can-do kind of place that created the breadbasket of America in the Central Valley, created my beloved motion picture industry, built roads and dams and cities and fabulous bridges, enforced its laws, didn't whine, didn't bitch, didn't moan.

And then we showed up. And the rest is history. Today, California is a can't-do kind of place, zillions in debt, overrun by "undocumented immigrants" (all part of our plan!), dispirited, helpless, in thrall to its state employee unions and certain to be devoured by something that hasn't even registered on most folks' radar yet: the enormous, gargantuan, and really big, way underfunded CalPERS, the California Public Employees' Retirement System, which eventually will bankrupt the state as the last few private industry workers give up and set sail in a small dinghy from Catalina to the South Seas as they attempt to replicate *Kon-Tiki* in reverse.

Take New Hampshire. I mean, here you are, the last rational New England state, proudly waving your "Live Free or Die" banner, exulting in your status as a tax haven as your fellow, once proud Yankees succumbed to our baleful blandishments, when all of a sudden—whoops!—you discover that hordes of overtaxed "Massholes" just figured out that most places in the Granite State are within driving distance of Boston. The next thing you know, the electoral balance has tipped and what was once the lone outpost of sanity between Maine and Vermont is now just another welfare state.

Or take Florida. Florida has lots of things you wingnuts like: lax gun control laws, no state income tax. So what do we—who advocate strict control of your Second Amendment rights and who never met a tax we didn't want to raise (although paying it ourselves is another story)—do? We moved to Florida! Florida shouldn't have even been close in the election of 2000, but it sure was, and as we keep flooding in from our failed states up north, you can bet on two things happening: gun laws will get tighter, which means there will be more gun violence, not less; and some sort of income tax will be introduced, most likely as first "temporary" (as it was in Connecticut), to deal with some financial crisis or another, but you know what happens to "temporary" taxes. And that will be the end of Florida.

Thus, states that once formed a kind of bulwark against our encroachment gradually succumb to the *Reconquista*. Colorado has pretty much flipped, New Mexico is gone, and even Arizona is pretty shaky. But in states such as Idaho and Utah, the California refugees will at first give thanks for their deliverance but soon enough will start nibbling around the edges, querying, whinging, whining, and otherwise causing trouble, as the process of social disintegration begins once more. Eventually, like the transcontinental railroad, we'll meet in the middle, the Californians and the New Englanders, and someone—I hope it's me—will drive the Golden Spike and our conquest of the United States will be complete. And all without firing a shot, if you don't count the Slivovitz we drink after every success.

And on the happy day of the Last Trump, secular/socialist division, when we finally completely and utterly defeat you, we will most likely let just enough of you live to frighten our children with the bugbear of revanchism. Until then, we aim to keep you in a perpetual state of war, our version of the Islamic *dar al-Harb*, the world of war, as opposed to the *dar al-Islam*, the realm of the true believers. That's one of the reasons the word "fight" pops up in all our candidates' speeches. We want you losers to know that we are a bunch of fighters, symbolically speaking, and that we'll take our virtual fight to the beaches and streams and rivers and strands of every fancy vacation spot on the planet while our surrogates in the universities snipe at you from the op-ed pages and our lapdog reporters run heroic photographs of us wearing Speedos and windsurfing off Nantucket. As John F. Kennedy almost said in his one and only inaugural address, we are willing to pay any price, bear any burden, meet any hardship, support any friend, oppose any foe in order to ensure the survival and the success of socialism.

Here endeth the lesson. Now, what are you going to do about it?

DAVE: Okay, where were we?

MAX: The President has been kidnapped by Somalian pirates who brazenly sailed up the Potomac River, swarmed a couple of Coast Guard gunboats, and made off with the Chief Executive and most of the White House crown jewels. I don't know if I buy it.

DAVE: Why not?

MAX: The White House doesn't have any crown jewels.

DAVE: Details. You think anybody else knows that except you? Anyway, they're—here's the best part—holding him and the First Family hostage on an island just ninety miles from the Florida coast—

MAX: Most people call that "Cuba"—

DAVE: Right . . . in a special prison that *he himself ordered built*—

MAX: I suppose that's what your side calls "irony."

DAVE: Righteous payback. And the ticking clock is—

MAX: Explain "ticking clock" for our readers.

DAVE: You know, the bomb with the red and blue wires and the LED readout that lets the audience know exactly how much time is left before the thing goes off and blows our heroes—

MAX:—or the hostage kids—

DAVE:—sky-high. Anyway, the ticking clock is . . . What is the ticking clock?

Well, that's always one of the sticking points. What is the urgency of the situation? Me, I feel urgency all the time, the fierce urgency of *now*.

We've waited so long to grasp the levers of power again that it's only natural that we want what we want—and we are nothing if not needy—right away. Yes, I know we're supposed to take the long view, bide our time, strike when our opponents are most vulnerable, but can you blame me for a little excitement? And it's only a movie!

But this "ticking clock" thing—Maximus and I go way back on this one. As kids, I was so jealous of his grace, looks, and athletic prowess that I was always playing tricks on him, not just tripping him up on the playground but in life. If he got sweet on some girl, I'd start rumors about him and some other babe. If he was in the school play, I'd show up and sneeze loudly during his speeches. Nothing serious, just little practical jokes. But there was something about him, I dunno . . . his inner peace, his moral center . . . that I just had to knock off-kilter, to make him understand the innate tragedy of life in these United States.

MAX: The ticking clock is we have to get this pilot pitch fleshed out before our agents order in the SWAT teams—

DAVE:—or give the job to somebody else.

MAX: Then we have to write the damn thing.

DAVE: And polish it.

MAX: And wait for notes from the agents while they set up the meeting.

DAVE: And bitch about the notes.

MAX: And take the meeting.

DAVE: Which will be with some kid young enough to be our son—

MAX: Named Josh, Jason, Jacob, or Jared . . .

DAVE: Which will go great—

MAX:—and we'll walk out of there ready to buy new houses—

DAVE:—and then we won't get the job.

MAX: Right. So what's the ticking clock? Wait—I've got it!

Well, that little conversation sure focused our minds. Max is like that, always keeping my eye on the ball, always bringing me back to reality, always helping me understand the importance of the here and now instead of the pie in the sky, although I do love pie. Whenever I'm stuck on a plot point, whenever I get a note from the studio that says: great script, now can we transpose the action from a sixteenth-century French nunnery to a feminist colony on Mars and I want to kill myself, he's always there with a handy suggestion about the Martian climate and topography, showing me how all that stuff I learned about medieval pig farming can easily be turned into a background of Red Planet strip mining operated by a company he insists I call d'Anconia Copper.

So I often feel like a heel for the way I've treated him, the way I've mocked him and his beliefs (mostly behind his back, to be sure, since he's twice my size and could easily beat the crap out of me, but for some unfathomable reason never has)—but not enough of a heel for me to give those beliefs any credence, mind you, much less accept them. I prefer remaining my wry, fashionably revolutionary persona, the Pride of Horatio Street, as I like to think of myself, and I'm not about to sell myself out for anything less than—

MAX: . . . so what do you think?

DAVE: I think it's great. So now we're out of Gitmo, the jewels are on their way back to the Tower of London—the part about "just borrowing" them for Nixon's inauguration was brilliant—

MAX:—that was Carter's inauguration—

DAVE:—same thing. Anyway it was fabulous and I totally stole it.

MAX: You didn't steal it. We're partners, remember?

DAVE: Whatever. So as we head toward the big plot point—

MAX:—tell the civilians what that is.

DAVE: That's the twisteroonie that comes about three-quarters of the way in. You know, where you find out the good guy is really the bad guy, he is really a she, or we're not on planet Earth at all, but a parallel universe. The thing that really puts our heroes in a pickle.

MAX: You mean the part where they've been working together all this time, and even though they look exactly alike but hate each other's guts, one of them suddenly finds out that his partner has double-crossed him?

DAVE: I guess so.

MAX: The part where Chuck finds out that Syd hasn't just been a lovable, irascible wastrel, but has actively been working for the other side?

DAVE: More or less, yes.

MAX: The part where he goes back to the brownstone on Horatio Street—it's always Horatio Street with you, isn't it?—and finds all of his stuff trashed, his money, weapons, and passports missing, and his secret decoder ring gone?

DAVE: Pretty low, huh?

Suddenly Max breaks into a big smile.

MAX: Gotcha.

DAVE (confused): Gotcha?

MAX: You really don't see it, do you?

DAVE: Huh?

MAX: I just won the argument. Because you just blew Syd's cover and admitted who he is, at the plot point.

DAVE: Oh-oh . . .

MAX: Now the audience sees him for the shitheel he's been all along, instead of the harmless slob. Now they can go back over the events in the show and put them in context: every time Syd did something hinky, something that he later explained away with a quip or a shrug, they now can see was malevolent and not just a difference of opinion.

DAVE: Damn.

MAX: So Chuck is the hero.

DAVE: When you put it like that, yes.

MAX: Which leaves us with one major problem.

DAVE: What's that?

MAX: We can't have the audience hate Syd. If we want to go to Week Two, this has to be a feint.

DAVE: Right! He's just pretending to be bad! The pirates have his mom and dad and his pet hamster hostage back in Bali, so he's just been *pretending* . . .

MAX: Go on.

DAVE: . . . pretending to cooperate and double-cross his buddy. But in

the end, we have to know that he's not a hopeless case, that he'll do
the right thing.

MAX: And what's that going to be?

DAVE: I have no idea.

To be continued . . .

INTERMISSION

In Which "Che" and I Discuss the Sleep of Reason

I have a nightmare that someday the scales will fall from people's eyes and they will see us as we really are.

Relax, my son. The Patients have by now almost completely lost their faculty of reason. We have done our work well. The progress of Progressivism is always upward, ever forward. So it is written, so shall it be done. Remember the Brezhnev Doctrine.

Dad—the Soviet Union collapsed. Half the empire spun off, went democratic, went down the drain, or fell to the Muslims. How is that progress?

O ye of little faith.

You know I hate it when you quote Scripture. What, are you going soft in your old age?

The Devil can quote Scripture to his own ends. How many times have I told you that?

Yeah, but how do you know?

He told me Himself.

I was afraid of that. But I'm still having these nightmares.

What sort of nightmares, my son? Remember, the sleep of reason produces monsters—

Which is exactly my problem. For example, I have a nightmare that the Patients reading this book will read C. S. Lewis's The Screwtape Letters *and realize that it is not fiction.*

Not a chance. No one in this culture, in this society reads anymore. They are too busy watching television and playing video games. True, the Enemy has made some successful *Narnia* movies, but they were not a patch on *The Lord of the Rings*, box-office-wise. Although, come to think of it, the *LOTR* books were also written by a friend of the Enemy . . .

Which got him exactly bupkes in royalties. The estate, whatever . . . But still, I have nightmares—

Tell me, my most beloved son.

I have a nightmare that our Patients will read Plunkitt of Tammany Hall *and get firsthand instruction in how we steal elections, hire our relatives for make-work "public service" jobs, and generally slurp like pigs at Circe's trough.*

I'm sorry—who's this Plunkitt guy? I don't see him down here.

Never underestimate the power of prayer. But c'mon, Dad—you remember the great GW . . .

Ah, yes. That was a fine time in New York . . . around the turn of the last century. He was one of the sachems of Tammany Hall, the Aaron Burr–founded Wigwam that first melded the thugs of New York City's gangland with our beloved Democratic Party to create the ruthless, power-obsessed criminal organization of which we are all so proud. But I am confident that 99.9 percent of our readers will not have the slightest interest in reading the Democrats' aphoristic playbook at this late date. Rest easy, my son.

Nonetheless, I have a nightmare that our Patients will read Machiavelli's The Prince *and realize that we beat them to the punch.*

Meaning what? We're always ahead of them. It's the only advantage the Big Fella deigns to give us.

Meaning that their touching notions of "honest government" are just fantasies. But we can't let them know that.

You have got to be kidding me! When I was a kid, we used to read that book in high school. Today, they wouldn't dare teach it at the graduate level, since nobody would understand it. Don't worry about a thing; ol' Niccolò's going to stay where we left him—six feet under. What else is worrying you?

I have a nightmare that they will read Ayn Rand's The Fountainhead *and recognize us in the figure of Ellsworth Toohey—the "friend" who is in fact their mortal enemy.*

Another interminable book that nobody's ever read. A novel about an architect? Please. And as for who is John Galt . . . who cares? No chance of a Rand comeback in our lifetimes. Why do you keep worrying about archaic technologies like books when we are in the brave new world of universal ignorance?

But still. They might stumble on it on their handhelds. That's happening more and more these days. What if they read Dickens's Bleak House *and see us in the character of Mrs. Jellyby, the "telescopic philanthropist," who lets her own family go to hell while she frets over the fate of an African tribe.*

Can I possibly be any clearer? Why would they read when there are so many more entertaining diversions out there? Nobody even saw the Gillian Anderson BBC miniseries version of that ode to the enduring, corrosive powers of lawyers and lawsuits. And what's wrong with Mrs. Jellyby, anyway? She sounds like a typical progressive, devoting her time and money and energy to people she's never going to meet instead of the people who actually depend on her. I call her a secular saint, whatever that is.

I have a nightmare that one day, perhaps during another Great Awakening, the Supreme Court will overturn Murray v. Curlett, *which outlawed school prayer.*

Yawn. You've already discussed this Murray broad. The sainted Madalyn was our wedgie in the panties of the Christian body politic, the elevation of the Singular to the Universal. Remember—we only have to find one exception to destroy their precious little *Weltanschauung*; they have to win actually a unanimous verdict. Gaia Bless America!

But still, Pop . . . what if she was . . . wrong?

Don't even go there. The removal of religion from the public square was the fundamental building block of our revolution—or, rather, the removal of the cornerstone from the Enemy's great edifice. Look how far we have come to making atheism the new Established Church of the United States, one that will have no real gods before it! Can't you just enjoy the moment?

I have a nightmare that one day the Supreme Court will overturn Roe v. Wade, *thus returning abortion to the states—although, alas, we will never get those forty or fifty million dead souls to pay into the Social Security system.*

You make the one good point the evil anti-choice side has in its unrelenting assault on the original Emanation from the Penumbra of the

Riddle wrapped inside the Enigma of the Constitution. It's true, we didn't quite think through the consequences of largely unrestricted abortion. We were too busy knocking up our girlfriends with impunity and then convincing them it was a heroic act to kill an unborn baby by scissoring open its head and sucking its brains out. As a matter of fact, when your mother, What's Her Name, and I first found out that you were on the way, we sat down and had a serious discussion . . .

What?

Relax—you're here, aren't you? Still, I would have been mighty proud had she chosen to exercise her Gaia-given, constitutional right to—

But, still, isn't there a contradiction here? When you establish a mammoth welfare state—

—You say that like it's a bad thing—

—*Let me finish. When you erect a giant welfare state predicated on an ever-expanding population to fund the nonworking elderly, don't you, you know, need more . . . people?*

There are too many people on this planet already. Just like we said back in the 1960s: how can you possibly bring a child into this hateful, hurtful, sinful world?

But who's going to pay for it all?

What are you, stupid? Undocumented aliens, of course. Next nightmare.

Well, now that we've brought it up, I have a nightmare that I will still be alive when the Mother of All Ponzi Schemes, Social Security, finally beggars the nation, and the heroic, eco-friendly childless couples starve to death as they realize they forgot to manufacture their old-age meal tickets.

Already discussed. Anyway, there's always euthanasia—for the other guy, I mean.

I have a nightmare that, one day soon, The New York Times will collapse into irrelevance, along with Time, Newsweek, and The New Yorker, and no one will be there to set the TV networks' agendas, forcing a population in desperate need of our wisdom to think for itself.

I wouldn't worry about that. Sure, the print media is not what it used to be, and millions of people have discovered that they can live perfectly happily without a weekly newsmagazine, or even the *Times*'s op-ed page; as a friend of mind once said: "Today, I have become a man. I canceled my subscription to *The New Yorker*." But the people, united, will never be defeated, and that goes for the progressive *nomenklatura* too. After all, we've got to figure out a way to pay for those houses in the Hamptons and Bel-Air.

I have a nightmare that the Other Side will pick up a copy of Saul Alinsky's Rules for Radicals *and actually read it, boring and poorly written as it is.*

Now you're starting to go too far. That book is top secret.

I have a nightmare that they'll organize and rally to take back their country from the frauds, poseurs, hollow men, gangsters, communists, atheists, perverts, Daley Machine hacks, ballerinas, and Jake Lingles who have parlayed a desire for Change, a touching but absurd reliance on Hope, and a huge dollop of racial guilt into something this country has never seen before.

Hold on a second there . . .

I have a nightmare that they will come to understand the truth of Goya's axiom that The Sleep of Reason Produces Monsters.

Monsters from the Id! Monsters from the Id! One of my favorite movies. Didn't Anne Francis look dishy in that little skirt . . .

I have a nightmare that even the Father of Lies can't fool all of the people all of the time and that . . . oh my Gaia . . .

Stop, son. It's time to wake up. Come on, David—calm down!

And that, you know, the truth . . . will . . . out, scattering us like so many scuttling Gregor Samsas when the Man flips the light switch—

Get a grip!

I have a nightmare that—Ow! You didn't have to hit me!

Yes, I did. Now get back to work.

★ PART TWO
THE SOLUTION

or The Fight for
Freedom Is
Never Over

Life and how you live it is the story of means and ends.
The end is what you want, and the means is how you get it.
To say that corrupt means corrupt the ends is to believe
in the immaculate conception of ends and principles.

—Saul Alinsky

RULE NO. 1:

Know Your Enemy, His Intentions, His Weapons, and His Weaknesses, and Use Them Against Us

By now I hope you understand the nature of the fight you're in. I have tried my best to lay before you, in all its bracing malevolence, the history of our program regarding your destruction. Forget the tired old saw about the Devil's greatest achievement being to convince humanity that he does not exist; we little devils are, as they say, out and proud. Because at this point, just as in any great B movie, where the villain has the hero up against the wall and then gets a moment or two of glorious self-justification, I'd like a little recognition from you losers as to just how delightfully diabolical our handiwork has been.

For what sport is there in beguiling you into your own self-destruction? Far more challenging and enjoyable to confront you with the truth and to prove to ourselves once and for all that you lack the will or the skill to prevent it. We can't have you looking for an "exit strategy" at this point, else where would the fun be? When one side is in it to win it, while the other is in it to lose gracefully, it's not a battle that paying customers will line up to see. They want blood and red meat, and by Gaia, that's what we're here to give them!

Which brings us to Corollary No. 1: *Know your enemy.*

I mean—what the hell happened to you? Up to this point in your history, you've risen to every challenge—indeed, have met any challenge, borne any burden, and paid any price. Oh, you were something else in the old days. The British threw Washington's forces out of Manhattan— New York City, you must realize by now, has never been on your side—

and chased him around for years, but he crossed the Delaware and never gave up, fighting on until he managed to checkmate Cornwallis at Yorktown and won the day. For Washington and the rebels, there was no such thing as an exit strategy: it was either total victory or a short dance at the end of His Majesty's rope.

During the Civil War, things looked pretty bleak as a succession of loser generals got the North into hot water and put Lincoln's presidency on the line, until the Great Emancipator found a hard-drinking, cigar-chompin' buzz saw of a man named Ulysses S. Grant, who then promptly opened up a can of whup-ass on the South and gave them a licking they remember to this day. Grant wasn't looking for the exits, he was looking for Sherman and Sheridan and when he found them he unleashed himself and them on the enemy: up the Mississippi, to split the Confederacy at Vicksburg (New Orleans surrendered without a fight), smashing through Georgia, and gradually pinning down Lee's forces so that by the end of the war the Army of Northern Virginia was basically confined to quarters at Appomattox.

The U.S. tried desperately to stay out of World War I until the Zimmermann Telegram revealed an offer by the Kaiser to restore Texas, New Mexico, and Arizona to Mexico in exchange for the Mexicans entering the war on the side of the Germans. Well, that did it—no *Reconquista* allowed! And when the Americans did enter World War I, General Black Jack Pershing flatly refused to have his troops parceled out among the allies, and kept a unified command that halted the German advance on Paris at Château-Thierry and Belleau Wood, and destroyed the German salient at St.-Mihiel. During World War II, the U.S. bombed the German cities into rubble, fought the Japanese from island to island in the Pacific in brutal, take-no-prisoners battles, firebombed Tokyo, and dropped the Big One on Hiroshima and Nagasaki.

In other words, you used to know how to fight. You used to know how to recognize a mortal enemy, used to know how to deal with that enemy—by destroying him. Unconditional Surrender was Grant's motto, and Eisenhower's too. Since then . . . not so much. Now you're in another kind of war, not bloody but bloody serious, a war for your soul and the survival of your country, and you're looking for the exits.

In the fight of your life, up against an implacable foe that has loathed you and sought your destruction not for years or even centuries, but for millennia, you can't even name your enemy. No, I'm not talking about Islam, or even radical Islam if you insist on a distinction; I'm talking about us. This is, in case you haven't noticed, a fight to the death. For you, elections are a means to an end, usually some sort of corrective to what you see as our excesses. Action and reaction. For us, elections are the ends in themselves, and we won't be happy until we get to the last election. After which, there will be no more elections. The Apostle Saul laid all this out for you to see in *Rules for Radicals*, but of course your side never bothered to read the American equivalent of Mao's *Little Red Book*.

If you had, however, you'd understand the truth of Corollary No. 2: *Have no illusions about our nature*: Pride Incarnate, brimming at once with anger, resentment, and an overweening moral superiority based on nothing more than our own inflated self-esteem.

Assess accurately and clearly the nature of the challenge you face, and the kinds of people you are battling. Because you have all had learning and poetry and imagery and literature and music and high culture beaten out of you over the last half-century, you pathetic weaklings have been left to fight this fight on the only battlefield we have deigned to leave you—our turf! Which means the political arena, and thus the legal arena, where you are hopelessly out-manned, out-womanned, and out-gunned. Symbolically speaking, of course.

In the legal arena—the "guilty until proven innocent" arena—everything is a game, which you must play by our rules. As highly stylized as a Shakespeare sonnet, the courtroom is not a forum for truth but for nonmortal combat in which victory goes to the clever, not to the strong (which is, naturally, why we love it—no physical danger!). And yet Milton limned for you the essential nature of the conflict in a poem you no longer read, because—thanks to our infiltration of the educational system—you no longer can. And Shakespeare (who?) taught the world more about the nature of evil in a single speech by Iago in *Othello* than all the lawyers' summations since Cain murdered Abel. In this new phase of the struggle that goes back to the war between God and Satan, it's imperative to realize that this is our go-for-broke moment. A miraculous combination of events—or perhaps not so miraculous—has delivered Amerikkka into our hands, now to feel the wrath of our terrible swift sword, so if you think we will now perform the traditional "pivot" toward the center in hopes of winning "bipartisan" support for our agenda, think again. We've got you on the run now, and there you will stay, until we finally hunt you down like the dogs you are.

Who knew that when Rousseau was leaving all his bastard children on the steps of the churches of Paris, he was also conceiving and effecting a social revolution that is still going on? Or when the good burghers of Königsberg were setting their clocks by Immanuel Kant's daily constitutional, that his notions of the *Ding an sich* (the "thing in itself") would eventually wind up occupying the president of Columbia University's chair during the student uprising of 1968, with the said *Ding*bat wearing sunglasses and smoking a cigar? Ideas matter, especially big, crazy ideas, and if the history of the past half-century has taught us anything, it's that no idea is too crazy for us to give voice to, or for you to fall for. There is no institution we will not attack, no social norm we will not question. What seems solid and eternal to you, to us is written in sand. When you win a victory, you lay down your weapons and return to your jobs, your families, and your lives. When we win one, we redouble our efforts, especially since our jobs tend to be either government boondoggles or academic sinecures, our families come second to the Struggle, and the Struggle *is* our life. To you, every triumph is definitive; to us, every loss is negotiable. You are Cincinnatus, home from the wars. We are Hannibal, spoiling for a fight.

Why are we like this, simultaneously so angry and yet so miserable, and consumed with our primal but irrational desire to inflict our emotions on you, so that you might share our misery and feel our pain? Whenever we institute elements of our beloved, and eternal, goal of "social change," we quickly move from simple tolerance to acceptance to, ultimately, a fierce and rancid insistence on forcing you publicly to embrace everything about our cause, no matter how distasteful you might find it. It is not enough, it is never enough, for us to win a single victory. No, we must not only win the war, we must crush our opposition—you—and force it to accept everything. Like Grant, the only terms we understand are unconditional surrender. Except that we call it tolerance.

So in order to fight this battle, you're going to have to fight it on our terms. You're going to have to think ‚like us, get down in the mud with us, seize our weapons, and turn them against us. Martial arts masters will tell you that the way to defeat an opponent is to use his strength against him, and even a weakling movie buff like me can figure that out from watching *Independence Day* (the most conservative movie ever made, although that will surely come as a shock to its writer and its director), when Jeff Goldblum draws the little diagram and explains that the aliens are using our satellites against us. Of course, he's proven spectacularly right when those silly hippie chicks somehow get up to the roof of Library Tower in Los Angeles with their New Age "Welcome, Undocumented Conquerors from Outer Space" signs and immediately get blasted to kingdom come.

We are nothing if not always on message.

Which brings us to Corollary No. 3: *Forget political correctness and speak your mind, no matter what the consequences.*

You might file this one under: "Pair, Grow a." As we've seen, PC is an all-purpose tool for your subjugation, expressly intended to prevent clear speech and thus clear thought. Those two things alone can defeat us, which is why we cannot permit them in our Orwellian version of a "free country."

The first battle that must be won, therefore, is the overthrow of the PC culture that we have built so assiduously over the past five decades. And that means taking a chapter of our own playbook—the comedy of the 1950s and 1960s that pushed the envelope (Lenny Bruce et al.), a direct challenge to the prevailing authorities—and wielding it against us.

Oh my sweet beloved Gaia, I can hear you muttering—Lenny Bruce? That pornographer? That foul-mouthed, unfunny . . . *New Yorker?* (Actually, he was from Long Island, but I can read your subtext.) Dave, are you kidding?

No. One of the reasons you've been on the losing side in the culture wars since the 1960s is . . . well, how can I put this? **YOU'RE NOT FUNNY.**

Why is this important? Humor changes from generation to generation, like tastes in music, like tastes in dramatic structure (try watching a movie from the 1950s and see how slowly it moves—the four-year-olds in the audience are crying from boredom, they're so far ahead of the plot). And what's funny to one group is not necessarily—in fact, usually is not—funny to another. Big deal. There's no such thing as an absolute in humor or other cultural issues, and if you don't believe me just ask Red Skelton. The point is to be on top of things. The point is to move the ball. The point is *to change the culture*.

And that's what Bruce and others like him did. They changed the culture. Whether you lot liked it or not, and you didn't, they changed the acceptable standards of discourse, and they retrained the nation's attention away from one set of preoccupations to another. It wasn't always pretty and it wasn't even always particularly funny, but it worked. And all of a sudden the standards that your side had assumed were immutable were gone.

So learn to speak your mind, even if—especially if—you are threatened with arrest, fines, imprisonment, whatever. So was Lenny Bruce. As the old Tammany hacks knew, them what holds the nightstick enforces the laws via the cracking of heads. Unless you break the magic spell of political correctness, you cannot defeat us, because each time you censor yourselves is one fewer time we have to try and do it for you.

Which is why I am thinking of *The Public Enemy*. The Cagney character—the snarling, vicious layabout and psychopath named Tom Powers—that's us. As tough a legend in our own minds as Powers is, until the night he tries to test his manhood one last time and emerges into a driving rainstorm, ventilated. "I ain't so tough," he mutters, and then collapses into the gutter. Strip away the myth and you are left with only the man—who, in our case, really ain't so tough. From the lake of fire to the gutters of Chicago is not such a long journey after all. That is our circle of life, not dust to dust but arrogance to discomfiture, endlessly looped like a bad porn movie starring Lucifer, Beelzebub, Moloch, Belial, and me.

Know this about us. *Use* that knowledge against us. Or else, as Ivan Drago says to Rocky Balboa: "You will lose."

Use our weapons against us.

Since there's no idea too ridiculous for us to entertain, take out to dinner, and even home to meet the parents, I'm surprised that up to now you haven't been putting your best minds to work on this problem. Just as, during and after World War II, the U.S. recruited some of the smartest and most daring young people in the country to join the fledgling CIA and other intelligence agencies, in order to have some defense against the attacks that had already started with the theft of the Manhattan Project's secrets by your country's "ally," the Soviet Union, so should you be training a cadre of faux lefties, to zip up the ladder from Andover to Harvard to *The New Republic* to the networks. Heck, if Josephine Baker and Julia Childs could do it, you clowns can do it.

Here's what I'm talking about:

- Pretend to be like us, so do what we do: lie. Adopt all of our manners and mores, right down to our mannerisms. Preface every statement with a handy "I read in the *Times* today that . . ." or, "As I was saying to Bill Moyers a few years ago out in Quogue . . ." and watch heads swivel and eyes light up with a Strange New Respect. Before you know it, you'll have your own talk show on MSNBC.

- Or don't. Even rigid Stalinists like ourselves, every once in a while, have to fake diversity in something other than our Frankfurt Schooled "race, gender, and class" categorical imperatives. Which means that, any given moment, there's room for up to three straight, white practicing Christians at any given gathering—except, of course, the editorial pages of *The New York Times*, which are strictly segregated—so why not be one of them! Think of the fun you can have as you're whisked around our cocktail parties like some exotic animal, and put on exhibition to show just how darn broad-minded we are, that we can tolerate someone like you in our presence. Why, the next thing you know, we'll actually start inviting black people over for social occasions instead of photo opportunities.

In other words, develop your own network of spies, infiltrators, and fifth columnists. You've ceded vast swaths of the information infrastructure to us, which in one sense turned out not to be a bad thing for you, since it eventually gave you Fox News and us MSNBC, but let me tell you from personal experience it really helps to have people on the inside, taking the pulse of the movement, probing its defenses, pushing the envelope about what you can or cannot say in polite company. Fox News has unleashed a vast army of babes, apparently all raised on the same hydroponics farm that produces *les Girls* of the world-famous Crazy Horse nightclub in Paris, except smart enough to have earned law degrees. And we're putty in their hands!

This is what keeps us up at night; in the good old days of the U.S.S.R., it was one of the dirtiest words in a good Young Pioneer's vocabulary: revanchism. Which means, more or less, revenge.

Although we have done spectacularly well with the youth—young people are naturally on our side because, as the old saying goes, if you're not a liberal at twenty you have no heart and if you're not a conservative at forty you have no . . . never mind—we can never really trust them. The job of young people is to revolt against their parents, and when the parents go from smiling patriarchal fascists like Robert Young in *Father Knows Best* and Fred MacMurray in *My Three Sons*, to guys like my dad, the sainted "Che" Kahane, big, hairy bears who didn't quite make it to Woodstock, but lied about being there just to get chicks, well, some young people are going to naturally start questioning authority.

I mean, think about it for a moment. Put yourself in our Birkenstocks. We're the Man now—fat, sassy, and socialist. Which means we're also ripe for a takedown.

This may, in fact, be one of the Enemy's little jokes, to keep both of us locked in the *dar al-Harb* until the final day of reckoning, but since we don't believe in any of that religious stuff, I choose to think that we can keep on co-opting the hearts and minds of young people *ad infinitum* or until you finally wise up and show us otherwise:

Bring in the kids. Your ideals and their idealism are made for each other.

Many of them are already wising up to us—after all, they're the ones who are going to be left holding this big stinking bag of you-know-what we're leaving for them. Follow our game plan from the 1960s—mock us at every turn, in every venue at your disposal, particularly those with youthful constituents. Refute the labels of prig and hypocrite we've pinned on you and slap them on us. Then offer the next generation a *real* alternative. Give them something to fight for.

I have a horrible suspicion that you may be surprised—again!—at how quickly the establishment turns when its children are set on bringing it down . . .

Another of our favorite weapons is to break your system from within, the old Cloward-Piven one-two punch. So why aren't you trying that on us? Instead of rolling over, apologizing, and retreating constantly, why aren't you merrily acceding to our every idiotic idea, thus hastening the day when our version of Socialism in One Country collapses just as it did in the Soviet Union? Admittedly this is a riskier strategy, but think of the fun you could have by voting for every tax increase, expanding welfare, promising every American—including illegal Americans who haven't even stolen across the borders yet—a guaranteed annual wage, one that would allow them to live in "affordable" housing anywhere in the U.S. of A. at taxpayer expense. Why, there's no end to it! If Jonathan Swift could offer his "Modest Proposal" to eat Irish babies, and thus reduce the number of the starving people, why don't you do the same sort of thing? Come to think of it, a few new "Modest Proposals" on the right Internet sites might do some viral wonders.

And don't just stop with taxes. Universal health care? Sure! A chicken in every pot and two cars in every garage? Make it some lentil soup and one green car and a couple of bicycles and you've got yourself a deal. Free energy? Why not—the sun's free, isn't it? Energy ought to be a human right, just like in Europe, where six-week vacations and spa time at state expense would be enshrined in their Bill of Rights, if they had a Bill of Rights. After all, FDR famously floated his ideas of a "New Bill of Rights" and his "Four Freedoms," which included "freedom from want" and "freedom from fear," so why not keep going, right down the line?

Yeah, I know that that lunatic Russkie babe Ayn Rand tackled some of this material in *Atlas Shrugged*, her perfectly ludicrous novel of an America run by petty little frightened men who speak in NPR voices and have mastered the art of sophist discourse to the point where they almost believe it themselves. It's a wonderful world she paints over the course of the novel's first one million pages or so, a place where one lone evil capitalist—the super-slim, super-smart, super-determined, super-slinky, super-sexy Dagny Taggart—holds out against the legitimate demands of the various People's Republics until her whole ill-gotten railroad empire is finally forced under and America is severed in the middle and forced to regress to a simple, more agrarian time, when we lived as one with Nature.

Luckily, you don't have the guts to go all the way and call our bluff. There probably isn't a John Galt among you, whoever the hell he is—I couldn't finish the damn thing. Anyway, you may not have to. You have a terrific case study unfolding before your very eyes in the imploding "social democracies" of Europe. A smoking time bomb of all our crackpot ideas in action, they're going to go up a bit ahead of your good old U.S. of A. The chaos is unfolding now—call attention to it, at dinner parties, in the office, in cabs, at the grocery store, at your barbershop and hairdresser: *Oh my God, can you believe what's happening in Europe? Sure hope it doesn't happen here! We've got to get some sane people in Washington!* It's not so hard to start a few stampedes if you push the right buttons often enough.

I realize that many of you pathetic Clowards—excuse me, I mean cowards—and weaklings are positively Piven—oops! I mean riven—with doubts about yourselves and the rightness of your cause. You're squeamish about adopting our tactics, that they are somehow beneath you, that our ruthless amoralism may not be to your fastidious liking. Well, tough. There is plenty of time down the line for you to get all turn-the-other-cheek Christian on me, but right now you are in a fight, and from Saint Louis at the Crusades to MacArthur on the beach, great leaders have learned to set aside the dictates of scripture in order to get the job done.

In fact, you're sitting there reading this and thinking, right this minute, *"Hey what the hell this Dave guy makes a pretty good case for just giv-*

ing up and giving in and after all in the long run we'll all be dead so what does it matter anyway?" Or words to that effect.

Go ahead, keep thinking like that.

Which brings me to David Mamet and *The Untouchables* and the most important question I can possibly pose to you, courtesy of Jimmy Malone.

RULE NO. 2:
Become What You Behold

David Mamet's screenplay for *The Untouchables* is one of the most oft-quoted scripts in Hollywood history, and for good reason. After all, it contains the clearest and most vivid explication of the now notorious "Chicago Way," which comes as Sean Connery (Jimmy Malone, the honest cop) and Kevin Costner (Eliot Ness, the uptight fed) sit in a church pew. Costner desperately needs the veteran Malone's advice on how to get the man he's after, the notorious gangster Al Capone, who seems to hold all of Chicago in his malevolent, fearsome sway. In what follows, think of yourself, the average, timid, clueless conservative, as Costner and me—the crazy-brave truth-teller—as Connery:

"You said you want to get Capone. Do you really wanna get him?" asks Connery. "You see, what I'm saying is: *what are you prepared to do?*"

"Anything within the law," Costner answers, to which Connery replies, "If you open the can on these worms you must be prepared to go all the way. Because they're not gonna give up the fight until one of you is dead."

Costner whines that he doesn't know how to do it. And then Connery delivers the most famous lines in the picture: "They pull a knife, you pull a gun. He sends one of yours to the hospital, you send one of his to the morgue. *That's* the Chicago Way. And that's how you get Capone."

Time to man up, ladies. Time to realize that Mao was right all along, and that power really does flow from the barrel of a gun. Do you think the Thirteen Colonies won their independence from Britain by sitting down and negotiating their grievances over cucumber sandwiches? (That's what we'd like you to think.) As we've been busily disarming you, both physically in the form of our blatantly unconstitutional gun laws, and intellectually, through the medium of political correctness, we've been busy burnishing our arsenals, sharpening our spears, and looking forward to the day when you're too weak to oppose us, and we, as the card-carrying cowards we are, no longer need fear that you'll do anything as rash as, you know, fight back.

But there's another line in the movie even more applicable to our purposes here, which I want you all to commit to memory right now. It belongs to Ness and comes near the end of the film, when Ness realizes that in order to get Capone, he's had to compromise every moral position he once held, and to become as ruthless and amoral as his adversary:

"I have forsworn myself. I have broken every law I have sworn to uphold, I have become what I beheld and I am content that I have done right!"

And that, boys and girls, is how you get Capone. Therefore, and for however long it takes:

Become What You Behold. Because unless you lose your fastidiousness, and are prepared to get down in the trenches with us, your opponents, you're going to lose. Because if your enemy really is the Liberal/Progressive/Socialist/Communist/Marxist/Fascist axis of "evil" that has so long bedeviled you, it's long past time that you put aside your nice-nancy-boy ways and come out swinging. Because whereas you see politics as a necessary evil, we see it as a combination of our life's work and a blood sport, the thing that makes our day jobs worthwhile—even if, as in most cases with us, our day jobs are also the things that provide us with the wherewithal to screw you. After all, who's paying our public sector salaries? Suckers!

And yet, time and again what we hear from your side is that you wouldn't want to adopt our tactics, that you wouldn't want to lower yourself to our standards and principles (your first mistake, since we don't have any, other than holding you to yours), that you would rather be right than win if it means fighting as dirty as we do. To which I say: that's why you're losers.

HOW TO TALK LIKE A LIBERAL (AND YOU MUST)

As I've noted, if you guys are going to be able to fight us effectively, you have to know not only the territory, like Professor Harold Hill in *The Music Man*, but the lingo as well. And I'm not just talking about words like "swell" and "gee whiz" and "so's your old man." I'm talking about being able to pass for one of us until we've got our guard down and then—whammo!

To that end, I've assembled a few handy phrases, which you're going to have to learn to deliver with a straight face, like Mr. Orange in *Reservoir Dogs*, practicing his cover story in front of a men's room mirror, with the requisite raised eyebrow and our patented Lefty Sneer™ dropped in at key junctures. You're deep in enemy territory now, so pay attention:

1) You can't possibly mean that. This is our way of saying you're full if it, but it goes beyond simple disagreement. It means that whatever it was that you just said, it has put you beyond the pale of polite discussion; it also very likely means you're a racist, a bigot, a homophobe, and/or a practicing Roman Catholic. All of which are, among our crowd, grounds for instant expulsion from polite society. *You can't possibly mean that* means that whatever you just said has wounded us grievously, has challenged some fundamental core belief of our *Weltanschauung,* and struck at the very heart of the fantasy world we mostly live in. It may be something as complex as a point-by-point refutation of *An Inconvenient Truth*, the truth about which we most definitely do not want to hear, or a minor statement of personal or political belief, such as, "I'm not really comfortable with the idea of gay marriage," or "I think we ought to cut taxes to encourage private investment," or, "You know, Michael Jackson really sucked."

In short, just about anything you can say that goes against our herd-like instinct to always be on the politically correct side of every issue will elicit this rejoinder. Which is why, when you hear one of us utter one of our usual *ex cathedra*–like pronunciamentos, just respond with *You can't possibly mean that* and watch the fur fly! (Your words in "quotation marks," our words in *italics*.)

You know, those Tea Party types look mighty dangerous to me. Why, there could be another Tim McVeigh or Lee Harvey Oswald lurking among them. Whereas the G-12 protesters and the Cinco de Mayo crowd are the very models of engaged political theater.

"You can't possibly mean that!"

As far as we're concerned, the Christian Right and the Midwestern militias are by far the greatest threat to the republic, much worse than the Muslims.

"You can't possibly mean that!"

If only the Catholic Church would allow its priests to marry, we wouldn't have all these pedophiles running around, preying on altar boys.

"You can't possibly mean that!"

Or better yet, wield this handy phrase preemptively, as we especially like to do. When we're prattling on about one bit of Received Wisdom or another, cut in with your own verbal karate chop to the jugular, whether it addresses the immediate point we're making or not. The point is to stop the argument in its tracks, to assert *your higher reality*: You *can't possibly mean* that you support what's going on in Washington! You *can't possibly mean* that you support forcing people into unions! You *can't possibly mean* that you want to flush our children down the drain for the sake of the corrupt educational establishment! You *can't possibly mean* that you think the Great Society was a good thing! You *can't possibly mean* that you want to go to the post office to see your doctor!

You get the picture.

2) Everyone knows that. Another all-purpose put-down, signifying that you're a complete idiot. It's a riff on the old Soviet "as is well known . . ." boilerplate, which pretty much signaled that whatever statement came next was a complete and utter lie, although we preferred to use the term "higher truth."

Everyone knows that Al Gore really won the 2000 election; that John Kerry really was a war hero, even though he only spent sixteen weeks in Vietnam and yet won more medals-per-minute than Audie Murphy; that Teddy Kennedy was the Lion of the Senate instead of the Swimmer of Chappaquiddick; that Jimmy Carter was a misunderstood president; and that Alger Hiss and the other Soviet spies were really innocent (of course they're innocent, in our mind!). Gainsay any of these theses and we'll nail you to the door of that church in Wittenberg, just like Martin Luther King did.

Still, you ought to give it a try and watch what happens. WARNING: be prepared for some exploding heads.

"Everyone knows that the Democrats are the party of slavery, segregation, secularism, and sedition."

You can't possibly mean that!

"Everyone knows that *Avatar* sucked."

You can't possibly mean that!

"Everyone knows that global warming is a complete crock, that a bunch of crooked scientists faked the data in order to siphon even more tax money out of our pockets, and that the polar bears are friskier than ever."

You can't possibly mean that!

"Everyone knows that the *real* war is in the electoral trenches, where the Left has been rigging the game since the get-go."

You can't possibly mean that!

But, of course, you do.

3) You're not really . . . This one's meant to indicate that the person you're speaking with is little better than a cave-dweller, a superstitious moron whose walnut-sized brain is probably stuffed with religious "dogma," and who is profoundly uninterested in all the Major Important Truths discovered in the late nineteenth and early twentieth centuries by Marx, Engels, Lenin, the Frankfurt School, Marcuse, and Oprah. Categories include practicing Catholic, Orthodox Jew, Republican, conservative, resident of flyover country, gun-owner, heterosexual, member of a two-parent family, and a driver of a 1984 Chrysler LeBaron.

Time to turn the tables. Come on, this one's easy—you can do it:

"You're not *really* still a Democrat, are you? Everyone knows that all right-thinking people were switching to Independent, and not moving in lockstep with the neo-Stalinists."

"You're not *really* still an atheist, are you? Everyone knows there's no upside."

"You're not *really* still going to stop at one kid, are you? Small families are so antisocial. Besides, everyone knows that we need lots and lots of kids to support the Social Security system."

"You're not *really* still buying that a 'free' market blew up the economy, are you? Everyone knows that what the Democrats did for decades with Fannie and Freddie made the *Hindenburg* look like a soap bubble. Let's analyze this" (another invaluable phrase, guaranteed to send us shrieking for the exits if you're ready to call it a night).

"You're not *really* going to drive that piece of hybrid crap, are you? Because everyone knows that they run up everybody's electricity bill, cause more polluting coal-fired electrical plants to come on line to meet demand—unless you want to build a few nukes—and endanger your own and your kid's life!"

To which, of course, we will answer: *You can't possibly mean that!*

Which brings us to Corollary No. 1: ***Forget being liked***. You don't have time for a popularity contest, especially insofar as we're concerned. Take the battle to us at every opportunity. After all, we never stop—we attack you in the supermarket, in restaurants and dinner parties—so why should you? Remember, the Left feels emboldened because—based on absolutely no sense of traditional "morality" at all—we feel we are *right*. Whereas, you *know* you are right, but have always been too polite to mention it, preferring to indulge our whims rather than run the risk of being called intolerant.

Never cede anything to us, philosophically speaking. Force us to argue facts, not emotions. We hate that.

The greatest failure of the George W. Bush administration was its incomprehensible failure to fight back against the calumnies of the Left. I mean . . . Cindy Sheehan! Can you imagine? But our media lackeys took this poor suffering woman and turned her into the human face of our animus, until we had chopped the hated $%$#BUSH&^%! down to size with her. And then, of course, we dumped her, left her to pursue her lonely, loony crusade against the Right after she was no longer any use to us. We are nothing if not cruel, especially in our quest for the Greatest Good for the Greatest Number.

People often ask me why we hated George W. Bush so much. And you know, when you stop to think about it, it's a really hard question to answer.

First, of course, he had to go and beat him an Algore in the election of 2000. Look, Albert Arnold Gore, Jr., did everything he could to blow an election he should easily have won, including paint himself up like an orange Indian and sigh like Scarlett O'Hara during the debates, claim to have invented the Internet (as is well known, the Soviets did that), and play Dialing for Dollars with a bunch of Buddhist monks, or whatever, from the White House. He totally blew it, and deserved to lose. But we did our damnedest, us and our pals in the media, on election boards, in the public employee service unions and ACORN's army of fraudsters, to put him over the top and if it wasn't for the dopes in Palm Beach County and the gun nuts in the rest of "Che's" home state, he woulda coulda shoulda won.

But he lost, by a measly few hundred votes, which meant that, under the fascist system outlined in the Constitution, the Sunshine State's votes flipped to &^%#BUSH@#$!, and not even the brazen attempt by the Florida Supreme Court to seize control of the electoral process from the state legislature could, in the end, prevent those seven conservatives and two liberals, or whatever, on the U.S. Supreme Court from putting paid to our little attempted coup.

And we went nuts. (Don't bother to say it.)

I think this was the moment—no, not when the seas stopped rising, that came later, during the election of 2008—that finally confirmed our longtime conviction that the Constitution was not our friend, and that in order for us to fully implement our program for fundamental change, we'd have to just go over it, around it, or through it.

But after that, Bush jungled up with the late Lion of the Senate, Edward Moore Kennedy—the only bootlegger's kid ever expelled from Harvard—on the No Child Left Behind boondoggle, passed a prescription drug benefit for seniors, even though they didn't need it and could afford their own drugs, while we youngsters eventually will need it and our country won't be able to afford it. He was for open borders and pretty much unlimited immigration from Mexico. He held out his hand to the ancient Conscience of the Senate, Robert "KKK" Byrd, even gently steadying him when the old man was teeter-tottering during a photo op. Aside from that appalling "Heck of a job, Brownie" cock-up during Katrina—when he cruelly and fascistically expected the governor of Louisiana and the mayor of New Orleans to, you know, do their jobs, as the Category Five hurricane bore down upon the levees, instead of throwing up their hands helplessly and (in the case of ex-governor Blanco), bursting into tears—he pretty much acted like the basic RINO that he was. Just like his dad.

You see, we didn't hate G. H. W. Bush. Naturally, we weren't happy when he was riding high in the polls after the first Gulf War, and of course we were nearly inconsolable when our beloved Soviet Union fell on his watch. But Bush's lackadaisical response to that dreadful event— leaning back in his chair and barely reacting to the news that the goal of American foreign policy for forty years had just been achieved—told us more than mere words that he was, at heart, a State Department/ stability kind of guy, and that he was almost as sorry as we were to see the Soviets crack up. Once we realized that about him, it was but the work of a moment to finish him off with a young Bill Clinton and get the process of selling out the country to the Chinese in exchange for campaign cash seriously under way.

The reason we came to despise &%@#BUSH!&! so was that, after 9/11, he didn't remain the dumb, inarticulate, Connecticut-born, Texas-bred liberal Republican we had him pegged for. We could have forgiven him his tax cuts, especially since the play-nice Republicans allowed our minority to force through a sunset measure, thus ensuring the return of America's wealth to its rightful owners, the federal government. And we might even have forgiven him his Supreme Court nominees, including the inoffensive chief justice, John Roberts, although we certainly would have preferred the hapless Harriet Miers over what we got, Sam Alito; and remember it was you wingnuts who sank her candidacy, not us.

But the one thing we could not, and forever cannot, forgive him for was for treating the attacks on New York and Washington as acts of war instead of what they so obviously were, simple criminal matters. While it's true that it's not every day that a group of mostly Saudi Arabian hi-jackers commandeers four airplanes and then flies them into very large buildings with the intent of killing as many Americans as possible, including the leaders of our so-called "Department of Defense" (we really should change its name back to the War Department), it could be. I mean, I can easily envision a scenario where, say, right-wing Christian extremists hijack one of those new Dreamliners—the Boeing 787 that can seat more than three hundred passengers—filled with Michigan Militia crazies all wearing "Palin for President" buttons and carrying large framed photographs of Jefferson Davis and Ronald Reagan, saying the Rosary as the plane crashes into the headquarters of NARAL Pro-Choice America.

It was quite obvious to us that the "tragedy" of 9/11 was what happens when you let religious extremism get a grip on the body politic, which is why we immediately went into hysterical overdrive concerning Bush's neo-theocracy. After all, moral equivalence is one of our favorite trump cards, and after the requisite period of "mourning," where our congressional leaders were forced by decency to stand on the Capitol steps singing "God Bless America" (the irony is too delicious), we soon enough were merrily encouraging our stooges in the media to climb back into the parrot cages and start squawking about how the "Christian Right" was every bit as bad.

Thankfully, by the end of 43's regime, the hapless president was little more than a punching bag; even years later, he continues to absorb punishment, blamed for all the ills that currently bedevil America. So it's well past time you learned Mamet's "Chicago Way": *they put one of yours in the hospital, you put one of theirs in the morgue.*

Yep. Truth to tell, and I am nothing if not truthful, Bush did only one thing wrong in the aftermath of September 11. Up to that point, he was reading *The Pet Goat* to those school kids in Florida, which considering his education at Yale and Harvard was just about his speed, and futzing with government around the edges, and not having a very clear idea about anything else. The famously tongue-tied president, "selected, not elected," as we like to say (even though, I remember now, the vote in the Supreme Court was 7–2 in finding "equal protection" clause violations in the Florida recount, and 5–4 in finding that the Florida Supreme Court had overstepped its authority in overruling the state legislature's election laws), bid fair to be a one-term, "I'm not Bill Clinton," typically Bushian wonder, unable even to muster his father's sinister CIA connections, or patrician inabilities with a common cash register. And what was that one thing? He took Mamet's advice.

He fought back.

Therefore:

Corollary No. 2: **Treat us with the same contempt with which we treat you.** Or, to put it in language you might actually understand: **Treat us with the same respect we give you, which is none.** Same difference.

After all, you don't see us being nice to you, do you? (Unless it's when we desperately need something, or when the "lone" foreign crazy manages to rattle us for a minute or two, or when we're looking down the barrel of an electoral gun.) You don't see us ever reaching across the aisle, extending the olive branch. Laurel wreaths are for winners, but olive branches can go pound sand. If a tie, to use the old sports cliché, is like kissing your sister, losing is like . . . well, don't make me go there. Remember that poor schmuck Sully in Arnold Schwarzenegger's 1985 movie *Commando*? You know, the part where Arnold quips: "Remember, Sully, when I promised to kill you last"?

Like Arnold: *we lied.*

Think of politics as the cage in *Mad Max: Beyond Thunderdome*: two men enter, one man leaves. The old cozy peculiarities of the Demopublican racket that the Great Plunkitt once knew and celebrated are long gone, the snuggly relationship between the parties that resulted either in the seesaw swing between "progressives" (Democratic thugs) and "Goo-goos" (idealistic Republican nudnik reformers) in New York City, in which both parties would share more or less equally, in Albany, in the booty pillaged from the suckers and rubes upstate, or the "Combine" that evolved in Chicago, in which both parties would share more or less equally in the swag looted from the suckers and rubes downstate.

It was fun while it lasted, but once the baby boomers and their congenital high moral dudgeon came into their majority—yes, at the dreaded age of thirty, over which no one was to be trusted—the old beneficial truce between God and Satan was abrogated. Half that generation cast off its organized-religious moorings as quickly as possible, and "experimented" with alternate lifestyles, sexualities, belief systems, and political movements. When the time came to make a living, they gravitated back to what they already knew, academe, or landed positions in law firms and in government. Today, we call them "activists" and "advocates." The other half graduated from college, found jobs, got married, raised children, and went to work every day whether they felt like it or not. We call them "suckers," or "you" for short.

"But Dave what can a bunch of poor schnooks like us do without no access to the big-time media and all huh?"

1) Every time a scandal on our side breaks out, pound it into the thick skulls of the American public. Pin it to our chest like a Muslim holy warrior attacking a movie director. Look what we did with Mark Foley, a Florida congressman nobody had ever heard of before: we made a few text messages to male pages a scandal equivalent to the Girl on the Red Velvet Swing, you know who I mean, Evelyn Nesbit, one of the celebrated Florodora Girls and that horndog Stanford White's sixteen-year-old mistress, whose dalliance with White eventually earned him three bullets in the head atop the old Madison Square Garden—on Madison Square, can you believe it?—which he himself had designed. The assassin: her nutbag hubby, Harry K. Thaw. Now *that* was a sex scandal.

By comparison, the odd furtive congressional gay nonencounters and Holy Roller preachers rolling in the hay with various hookers hardly seem worth getting all hot and bothered about. And yet we gleefully hang them around your necks like the Ancient Mariner's albatross, while our collection of perverts, child-molesters, and intern-abusers goes its merry way, secure in the knowledge that the only fate that awaits it is that of Elder Statesmen of the Democratic Party. Nice work if you can get it!

Hypocrisy, you say? *Au contraire*—you can't be a hypocrite if you don't have any absolute morals to begin with! When everything is situational, then nothing really matters; as Scarlett O'Hara said, "Tomorrow is another day."

2) Pin the tail on the Donkey. Yes, I know that's rude, but go ahead, try it: it's actually a lot of fun. We've pretty much retired the trophy on the "racist" meme, in part because it's our side that has been among, and continues to be, the most reflexively racist group of people this country has ever seen. No need to revisit our glorious history at this juncture, but suffice it to say that, operating on the principle that we always pre-

emptively accuse you of what we're either planning or what we know, deep in our black hearts, to be true about ourselves, we agree with the old Southern general Nathan Bedford Forrest, who famously advised a commander to "git thar fustest with the mostest." It must be true: I read it in *The New York Times* in 1917 . . . online. Forrest, by the way, was also one of the first leaders of the Ku Klux Klan, which means he would be right at home in today's Democratic Party, just as he was back then. And just when we think we've finally put one scurrilous charge to rest, *move the goalposts* and accuse us of something else! Endless fun and an all-purpose debating technique as well.

So call us out. But whatever you do, please don't . . .

3) Label us. We hate labels. We especially hate them when they are applied to us. Labels are sticky and tough to get off—they're what we do to you, with our media shills always willing to apply an extra coat of stickum, probably left over from those old glue pots they used to use to paste their stories together back in the good old days when Teletype machines ruled the earth and you could trust what you read in the newspaper, instead of the seditious crap you see on the Internet today. And please pretty please, never never never never—

4) Mock us. Because, if you could see us as I do . . .

INT. BEVERLY HILLS—NIGHT

A modest, private 24,000-square-foot home on one of the less fashionable streets above Sunset. Red-jacketed, suspiciously Mexican-looking valets take temporary possession of an array of late-model, expensive, but certifiably green, cars. Our hero and main character, DAVID KAHANE, an incredibly handsome and talented young man who looks like a cross between Cary Grant and Albert Einstein, pulls up in a new Toyota Prius. The valet is impressed as he takes the keys—

INT. MINI-MANSION, BEVERLY HILLS—NIGHT

A swan-necked hostess, wearing a form-hugging Little Black Dress, greets Dave with a kiss and a glass of champagne. Her name is ROSA LUXEMBURG—

ROSA

David, darling—it's grand, grand of you to come.
(conspiratorially)
I'd better lock this joint before the acrobats and midgets start
flocking in.

DAVE

Stop running old lines from *Gold Diggers of 1933.*

ROSA

But my darling, that's the only movie I know. Come in, join us.
We're all here, Vlad, Brad, and Dangerous to Know. Ha ha ha!

DAVE

(chucking her under the chin in a friendly but sexy way)
You always were a kidder, kiddo.

INT. MINI-MANSION, BEVERLY HILLS —
CONTINUOUS
DAVE smiles as he enters the dining room, which is about the
size of Soldier Field in Chicago. There must be fifty tables of six
in the modest room, with a view of the Hollywood Hills, Century City, and the Olympic-sized pool out the French doors.
Over the WALLAWALLA, Dave greets the other Hollywood
celebrities in attendance.

At last DAVE comes to his table.

CUT TO: INT. DINING ROOM—LATER
The aftermath of the meal . . .

DAVE'S TABLE—
A BUXOM STARLET, who's obviously had a little too much to
drink, speaks up.

BUXOM STARLET

So . . . what do we think? About how well everything is going, I mean?

Silence greets her query. She giggles, embarrassed—

BUXOM STARLET

Did I say something wrong?

DAVE looks her over, likes what he sees, decides to go for it—

DAVE

I agree with what's-her-name. What more could we ask for? We've gotten just about everything we've wanted, and if you don't believe me, just ask my sainted father, "Che" Kahane.

QUERULOUS GUEST #1 (RIVAL AGENT)

But there's so much more!

QUERULOUS GUEST #2 (FORMER STUDIO CHIEF)

The work is never over, the dream shall never die, the fight goes on, whatever, yadda yadda . . .

QUERULOUS GUEST #3 (MAJOR PRODUCER)

Frankly, the thing that worries me is the Christian Right . . .

DAVE glances over at his agent, who's seated across the way. The AGENT avoids his glance, pretends not to know him. DAVE turns to a little guy on his left, a stranger. Shabbily dressed, with bad teeth, the guy is obviously a fellow writer.

DAVE

What do you think?

FELLOW WRITER

What do I think? I'll tell you what I think. I think you're all a bunch of prats. Wankers who don't know how good you've got it.

This being a movie, his remarks come at a moment of COMPLETE SILENCE in the room, so everybody hears every word. A seething undercurrent of fear and rage ripples through the crowd. Murmurs of "Kill him!" can be vaguely discerned.

Undaunted, the FELLOW WRITER continues—

FELLOW WRITER (cont'd)

I mean, here you sit, expostulating, bloviating, ejaculating, and generally fannying about . . .

Dave notes that the man has an English accent, and mentally memos himself to imitate it, especially if he wants that coveted job as the executive assistant to that B-level studio executive he's been trying to get to buy one of his scripts.

FELLOW WRITER (cont'd)

. . . and the point is, none of you has the slightest idea what you're talking about, nor the least desire to actually act on what you espouse, nor the foggiest inclination to actually leave this room and drive south and east of here and come face-to-face with the people you profess to care about so much. You know, the people south of Pico and east of . . . well, at this point, pretty much east of Fairfax. So how dare you call yourself liberals, when your definition of Los Angeles is far more restrictive than even Chief Parker's ever was?

At the mention of "Chief Parker," an even uglier silence descends over the party. For a long, agonized moment, nobody says a word. Then Dave speaks up:

DAVE
That's fascinating. Can you repeat that?

HULLABALOO, HUZZEREI, and HYSTERIA erupt. Handsome men and beautiful women toss drinks, throw plates, rush for the exits, even jump into the swimming pool. Emboldened, the FELLOW WRITER rises, Evian water in his crystal goblet:

FELLOW WRITER
Here's to us, the "creative community." The most monolithic group of freethinkers ever to put their thoughts to treatments, scripts, or contracts. We preach individuality but we practice "revolutionary" conformity. We celebrate the individual even as we break him on the wheel of "social justice." Long may we live and prosper!

For a moment, nobody speaks. At last Rosa Luxemburg pipes up:

ROSA
Thank you so much for your candor, Mr. . . . Mr. . . . Whatever your name is. A real throwback to the good old days, when we fought the Man in all of his Satanic guises. When we were always on the lookout for racism, sexism, ageism, homophobia, hydrophobia, triskaidekaphobia, and all the other ills this mortal flesh is heir to. Luckily, as the poet said, them days is gone . . .

The FELLOW WRITER blanches, embarrassed, tries to regroup.

FELLOW WRITER
Thank you, Frau Luxemburg.

He picks up his glass, raises it—

FELLOW WRITER (cont'd)
A toast—to speaking your mind in a free country!

A PAUSE while all the guests look to Rosa for guidance. A beat . . . and then she PICKS UP HER GLASS—

ROSA

Vsya vlast sovyetam!

A couple of burly SECURITY GUARDS rush into the room. The guests cheer as the FELLOW WRITER is hauled away . . .

DAVE realizes that everyone is looking at him. He has to do something, fast.

DAVE

(suddenly inspired)
Peace, bread, and freedom!

SFX: Gunshots in b.g.

ROSA

(smiling sweetly, to Dave)
Now, then . . . where were we?

DAVE

Um . . . 1933?

Hey, it's a tough town, but as I said to that starlet, what's her name, after a mad night of passion in my palatial Echo Park pad, somebody's got to get the ball rolling. Being a conservative in Hollywood is a little like being a Christian in ancient Rome, but look on the bright side— they can't kill you all!

Which brings us to Corollary No. 3: *Give no quarter.*

Fight like we do: to the end. Because by now it should be apparent: we will never leave you alone. And here's why: you are our meal tickets.

Those we might term the Party of Take are sitting pretty. With the genius that has characterized our side since they battled their fellow boomers for the choicest seats in kindergarten, my father's generation now sits comfortably in their academic or governmental sinecures, their "workload" light, their pensions secured, which gives them plenty of time to think up more mischief at your expense. Meanwhile the Party of Give—the boomers approaching retirement in the private sector now— are staring into the abyss of a pretty bleak future. Their homes are worth half what they thought they were, they've been beggared by the high cost of prep schools and private colleges, when they could afford them at all, and now they find themselves being ruthlessly downsized by colleagues young enough to be their kids, without enough money in the bank and staring at Social Security as their flawed savior. Because they had to work and pay taxes and raise families larger than 1.0 kids, they never had enough time or energy to get involved in politics, not to the extent we of the Party of Take did, and so gradually, incrementally, they have been bled white as they watched the employment scales tip from private industry to government jobs, helpless victims of the great bloodsucking beast we like to call "public service."

For some of you it may be too late, but there's no reason the rest of you can't start fighting back, before we take everything you have and then some. Luckily for us, and those racist, gun-toting "teabaggers" notwithstanding, you remain politically fairly pathetic. After Sarah Palin rocked us back on our heels during the election of 2008, we regrouped quickly and soon began to carve her up, reducing the woman—who, were she a progressive, would have been a heroine and a role model— into a caricature of a dodo bird, too stupid to name a single newspaper or magazine when confronted by Katie Couric's stiletto.

You could tell we were floored by Sarah from the viciousness of our reaction. After Palin's electrifying convention speech, Andrea Mitchell of NBC looked like someone had just shot her dog, flapping her gums in impotent rage and amazement as the cheers echoed throughout the Xcel Energy Center in St. Paul. Suddenly, Senator Stockholm Syndrome's moribund, pathetic candidacy had been transformed and invigorated; a new fascist star, a deadly combination of Evita and Annie Oakley, had been born. And would have to be stopped.

If you really want to get back in the game, never let that happen again. The first step is to know when you've hurt us. A little tip: the louder we shriek, the more names we call you, the deeper you've wounded us. Think of us as Dracula, at the end of both the book and Coppola's movie; just thrust the blade home and your work is finally done.

So start punching back. You ever heard the word "demonize"? Well, get used to saying it. Adopt it. Make it your best friend; after all, given our pedigree, it fits us so much better than it fits you. Go after us. Call us out for what we are: bloodsucking ticks attached to the armpits of academe, Hollywood, Wall Street, the media. When we carve up one of your fat cats with a knife, you should take out one of ours with a gun—symbolically, of course!

There's so much of us to hate and hammer: our preening, useless intellectuals, always good for an anti-American op-ed whenever our house organ, *The New York Times,* needs one. At the drop of a Rolodex—virtual, of course, since we now keep our Rolodexes on our iPhones—we can come with a rotating hit squad of well-placed academics ready to pounce and opine upon just about anything having to do with you. (We're a little short in the Captains of Industry, Members of the Clergy, and the Four-Star Generals departments, so please let me know if you can find any for us.) Remember, our people are trained practically from birth as an instant-response team, the weaklings and the physical cowards who sought the safety of a sinecure in lieu of the mortal combat of life but who still get the thrill of shooting inarticulate fish in a barrel.

Always strike first. The dying news organizations like to pride themselves on their editorial independence, and fiercely resist pressure from, you know, the reading and viewing public who pay their salaries. But never again let NBC do unto another of your candidates as it did unto Sarah. Flood the switchboards and e-mail in-boxes with calls and letters of support. Hammer the editors with demands for more coverage of this wonderful new personality. Make it clear that you will take a very dim view not only of the newspaper/network but of their corporate parent, which treats you with such habitual and joyous disrespect. In other words, do what we do: organize, boycott, intimidate. Of course the producers and editors will sneer at you stupid civilians, but remember this: there are a lot more of you than there are of them.

Even better, act preemptively. With our friends in the media long since having declared their membership in the Democrat-Media Complex, you and I both know exactly how they're going to react to any given circumstance or personality. We are nothing if not laughably predictable in our malevolent behavior toward you, so why not head us off at the pass, pardner? Hammer us into submission before we can set the template and lay out the narrative.

Letters to the editor? (We just ignore them.)

E-mails? (That's what the spam folder is for.)

Phone calls? (One word: robots.)

So what do you do?

All three and then some. You're fighting a war of attrition here. Who do you think is going to crack first?

Withhold your most sought-after people from these snake pits and instead faithfully watch and listen to their appearances on your alternative media. Mount news-making ratings events to which the "mainstream media" is not invited. Underscore the fact that these dinosaurs are no longer the anointers of the accepted and the arrived. When they come begging—and they will—if they haven't pulled in their fangs, do it again. They'll get the message . . . eventually.

And now I'm going to tell you to do something really nasty: go after them personally.

Do unto them as they've done unto you. Look into their backgrounds for irregularities, for thin credentials, for any and all chinks in the cloaks of infallibility they proudly wear. Undermine their credibility and call them out for their biases and false premises at every turn. And smile while you're sticking in the shiv. Yes, I know you fastidious sewing-circle gals hate the very thought of getting your skirt hems muddied by stepping in a puddle or two. But what choice do you have, really? It's us or you and while we obviously prefer us, you had better start looking out for you if you want there to be a you much longer. So here's what you do:

There are few groups of pontificating clowns more vulnerable than the bigdome journalists who pass for wise men these days. (How Walter Lippmann would laugh at these *pishers*!) I could name names, but the point really isn't the names—they will come and go, the hacks, the one-trick ponies, the conflict-of-interest crew, the sozzled old broads who phone it in, in the best tradition of the old Hollywood gossip grand dames, the former drama critics, the influence-peddlers, the "access journalists"—but the archetypes. Let's limn them:

- The legacy crew. Like any fiefdom, journalism has become a hereditary feudal hierarchy, with sons and daughters following their fathers and mothers into the limelight and greasepaint of *Meet the Press* and its imitators. They come in waves, boosted on their sires' reputations, heading directly from the Ivy League colleges (the worst possible place at which to recruit a reporter, but a splendid place to find and groom a "journalist") to the New York and Washington bureaus of their respective newspapers, newsmagazines, and networks, wet behind the ears, without the seasoning that accrues from covering zoning boards in Pierre and street crime in Oakland, but absolutely cocksure about their skills and political judgments. When, in truth, they are little more than Xeroxes of parrots, squawking into the same squawkbox their late old man enjoyed, but with only half his talent, if that. It's as if Edward R. Murrow somehow begat John Gotti, Jr., or Joe Kennedy begat Patrick Kennedy.

  Oh, wait—he *did* beget Patrick Kennedy, more or less. Case closed!

- The Sammy Glicks. That would be the real-life counterparts to the irrepressible Schmelka Glickstein, Budd Schulberg's eponymous antihero of *What Makes Sammy Run?* But these days you don't have to be Jewish to be a Sammy Glick! A member of any ethnic group or sex can join in the fun, as long as he's prepared to sell out his friends, always seek the main chance, suck up, fuck down, and generally look out for good old No. 1 until he finally makes it to the top of the greasy pole. Or not, as the case may be. Still, the top of that pole looks mighty fine, because the "top" is not what you've always thought it was—"managing editor" of some storied but failing name brand in American journalism. Oh, no—that's not it at all. The top of the greasy pole is—

- Washington, D.C., and Hollywood, California. The only two towns that matter anymore (New York, eat your heart out). If Washington is Hollywood for ugly people, Hollywood is Washington for people who can't quite make it in Washington, and so will settle for the money and the sex and the lifestyle, all the while still carrying out the work of fundamental change. Scratch any top-tier journalist and I guarantee you that you will find a miserable sod who wakes up every morning either rehearsing his Oscar acceptance speech for Best Original Screenplay or coveting an office in the West Wing, or at least the Old Executive Office Building.

All of which means "journalists" can't afford to be quite as snooty as they used to be. With the carcass of AOL Time Warner still stinking up Rockefeller Center for miles around and for decades to come, a great object lesson lies before them: what happens when small-minded but well-educated fools ignore their audiences.

Never forget: it's all about the narrative. That was the fatal mistake Palin's handlers made after her spectacular launch: they never realized the speed or the intensity of the mainstream media's counterattack. They still thought the media was supposed to be "neutral," even though they had been warned four years earlier by Evan Thomas of *Newsweek* that the media's support was worth . . . well, let's let him tell it in his own words, uttered on *Inside Washington*, a local television show, during the 2004 election cycle:

> There's one other base here: the media. Let's talk a little media bias here. The media, I think, wants Kerry to win. And I think they're going to portray Kerry and Edwards—I'm talking about the establishment media, not Fox, but—they're going to portray Kerry and Edwards as being young and dynamic and optimistic and all, there's going to be this glow about them that some . . . is

going to be worth, collectively, the two of them, that's going to be worth maybe 15 points.

In the end, it didn't quite turn out that way, and while it's clear that the media's support of—and blocking for—the International Man of Mystery, Barack Obama, contributed mightily to his victory—and they're proud of it!—it may well be that 2008 was a last hurrah for the MSM that will make Frank Skeffington's *ave atque vale* in *The Last Hurrah* look like a modest Irish wake. There is no beast like a wounded beast, especially one with enough self-realization to know that the wound is fatal, and so I'd advise your candidates to be ready for anything as the beast dies.

But, of course, they won't be. They'll continue to believe that politics is still politics-as-usual, that we're all in basic agreement about society's general goals, that we're all talking in good faith about working within the system—even as we "fundamentally change" it!—and . . . any moment now . . . we, the "friends" they ushered into power, will pivot and move to the middle and do the same old things every politician has done since time immemorial and—

Forget it. We're not your grandpa's Democrats.

All this fighting back against the media is going to take some organizing. After all, we have at least a half-century's head start on you, with our ACORNs and our labor unions and our government employee unions. And now we have the massive power of the state behind us, as well as that of many professional organizations, including the American Bar Association, the American Medical Association, and the American Association of Retired Persons. And what do you have? The National Rifle Association. (Well, okay, that's a little scary.)

But most of all you have to start thinking like us. Stop assuming the best about your enemy and instead assume the worst. Assume that our motives, no matter what we say they are, are inimical. Assume that the outcome we desire, no matter what we say it is, will be disastrous. Assume that "by any means necessary" means exactly that.

You may not like who you see in the mirror the next day, but at least you'll still be alive and kicking (us), and not crushed under our boot heel, which we normally apply to evil corporations, but in your case we can make an exception. And you'll have begun to take your country back—for the children!

So take it from Jimmy Malone, and ask yourselves: What are you prepared to do? Are you prepared to become what you once beheld? At long last, are you ready to fight?

Because if you're not, you're dead.

RULE NO. 3:
The Culture Is the Message—
So Seize It

This is crucial. Accept the fact that the "culture"—by which, of course, I mean "us"—is never going to reflect your version of reality until you change it from within. Our infiltration and takeover of the "narrative" has been going on since the 1960s and reversing it is no small task. If you're looking for acceptance or, worse, love from the mainstream media, your old college professor, or Hollywood, forget about it. This is a war you've long ago lost—but which you can still win if you choose to fight it. But the first step in fighting lies in picking up an (eek!) weapon and choosing to use it, so until you do that, buddy, you are standing there as bare-assed as Mel Gibson and his band of Scottish merry men in *Braveheart*. And look how far they got.

Well, okay, so they got farther than Longshanks and the English would have thought, given their lack of underwear and their reliance on rusty old swords and blue face paint. And in the end Mel got what he wanted—namely, being disemboweled in front of a cheering audience while Sophie Marceau wept—so it all ended happily ever after, after all, and Mel lived on to direct Jesus at Golgotha. But you lot are neither crazy Celtic warriors, nor six-packed Spartans spoiling for a fight with Brazilian drag queens—oops! I mean "exalted rulers of the Persian Empire"—so you're going to need a little something more in the way of armaments in order to win your battles.

The culture is where the action is, and it's high time you folks started battling for the high ground—you know, the redoubt from which your archers can launch their arrows, the place from which your castle defenders can pour down vats of boiling oil on our heads, just as we do to you every week from the pages of *The New York Times*, *The Washington Post*, all three broadcast networks, *Time, Newsweek,* and two of the three cable news channels.

And yet, as we've seen, it's a battlefield you've almost completely abandoned, and instead left to us. Where armies of the night once clashed, today only the lonely crows flap about in search of fresh eyeballs to peck; why, there hasn't been a good Armageddon in these precincts since, well, the last Armageddon, and that was back in the days when Egyptians, Assyrians, and Babylonians roamed the earth. So it's long past high time you picked up your stubby little sword, checked to see that you're packing what every self-respecting Scotsman packs under his kilt, and got on with the party.

So what do you do? Let's take your objectives one at a time:

Corollary No. 1: **Get back in the media game**. And how do you do that? Simple: Start by taking your media back.

Let's face it: at this point the U.S. is pretty much a banana republic, riven by two factions that are not quite in numerical equilibrium. Which is a fancy way of saying that there are more of you than there are of us, always have been, but by using our pet media as a kind of kinescope, the illusion of an illusion, we have been able to fool you throughout the last century into believing that we have both right and might on our side. On the one side are you, the revanchists, clinging desperately to your faith and your guns and your charming belief in your cherished "Constitution," while on the other is us: revolutionary, amoral, and wanting nothing more than the complete destruction and remaking of your country—a mote in our eye since its inception!—in the egalitarian-collectivist mode. Which, after all, only fulfills the prescriptions inherent in your Declaration and constitutional Preamble. From the Shining City on a Hill to Satan's Throne of Royal State of which Milton sang—that's the descent we have outlined for you.

Forget about *The New York Times* and the legacy dinosaurs still lumbering along Sixth Avenue in New York City, at least until you follow my advice and take them over. Good Gaia—*Time* used to be the flagship publication of that noted right-wing nut Henry Luce, and somehow we managed to change it, mostly through our Harvard degrees and our Rhodes Scholarships (which I gather from Old *Time* Hands they used to dispense along with the free booze in the corridors of the Time & Life Building across Sixth Avenue from the real Rockefeller Center on Thursday and Friday nights as the magazine went to press). Some of them may stumble around for a while, but in the end, unless they change their business models and give up their lavish, Harvard-expectation lifestyles, the twelve-room apartments on Central Park West, the houses in the Hamptons, the European vacations, they are looking at the Last Rites very soon. The action has moved elsewhere.

A few years ago, the conventional wisdom was that newspapers would be around forever—where else could you find such a compelling and timely package of information conveniently printed on the finest fishwrap, that gathered all of the important events of the day and delivered them right to your doorstep? Then the Internet came along with its near-instantaneous delivery of news and content that people might actually want to read and the media moguls scoffed and said yes, but, where is the editorial judgment, the wise chin pulling, the scintillating prose, and the shameless shilling for the Democratic Party and the local sports teams that made the daily newspaper such a joy and a pleasure? Then the Internet began to spontaneously generate its own magazines, its own news aggregators, its own pundits, many of whom developed enormous followings that far outstripped the circulation figures of their dead-tree rivals, and the editors scratched their heads and said maybe we better get a piece of this racket, and so what did they do? They put their marquee writers behind a pay wall and drove readers away in, well, droves. The next thing they knew, they were selling off their fancy new corporate headquarters, laying off employees by the hundreds, and making disadvantageous loan-shark deals with rapacious foreign billionaires to keep themselves afloat as they stared bankruptcy in the face.

So the way is clear for you to take over. The war for the soul of America is no longer being fought in the editorial boardrooms of *The New York Times* and *The Washington Post*, but in the freewheeling precincts of the new media, where ideas are not fugitive and cloistered virtues—"unexercised and unbreathed," as Milton said—but are constantly being tested on the field of battle. Take your fight not to the letters columns but to your own Web sites; like the pamphleteers of pre-Revolutionary America, let your voice be heard, on the Internet, to anybody who'll listen. Relentlessly fire down upon us from the bluffs above the arroyo, seize and hold the high ground and herd us into a small corner of nowhere, the way Sitting Bull did to Custer, and finish us off. It's really much easier than you think: just ask Andrew Breitbart, whose collection of "Big" Web sites has in just a couple of years become a formidable force in Hollywood, politics, and journalism.

For decades, our useful idiots in the media have been gnawing away at the foundations of your society like a beaver working a particularly choice tree. The tree seems invulnerable, eternal, and then all of a sudden it's on the ground, where it can be best measured, and then it's just another log, on its way to being kindling, firewood, or the newsprint of *The New York Times*. The circle of life, indeed. The *Times* they are a-changin' and it might as well be you who picks up the pieces of the Sulzberger Empire. After all, they're ripe for defeat. As Arthur "Pinch" Sulzberger famously said at a commencement:

> It wasn't supposed to be this way. You weren't supposed to be graduating into an America fighting a misbegotten war in a foreign land. You weren't supposed to be graduating into a world where we are still fighting for fundamental human rights, whether it's the rights of immigrants to start a new life, or the rights of gays to marry, or the rights of women to choose. You weren't supposed to be graduating into a world where oil still drove policy and environmentalists have to fight relentlessly for every gain. You weren't. But you are. And for that, I'm sorry.

Frankly, we don't like to hear defeatist talk like that, but there's not much we can do about it. You've just found our Achilles' heel: the media is our mouthpiece and yet *everybody loathes the media*. Which, when you stop to think about it, I guess means that they really hate us too. And after all we've done for them!

And yet, because you haven't fully realized how fundamentally the world has changed around you, you still insist on placing your trust in, and cede societal validation to, the old dead husks of institutions like

NBC News, *The Washington Post,* and some schismatic divisions of the Anglican Communion. After years of our infiltration, they're now like the bodies of the poor inseminated victims in *Aliens,* dying shells of human beings harboring the alien vipers in their breasts, choking out a last plea—*Kill me!*—before the nasty little critters burst through their chests and go scurrying into hiding, there to grow and molt and increase in size and strength until: chomp!

Without the media's running interference for us, acting as the curtain in *The Wizard of Oz,* you would have, as I've explained, seen us for what we really are far sooner: courtiers, shills, hacks, overinflated, like the *Hindenburg,* with a sense of self-importance and yet, deep down, as consumed with a crushing sense of failure and irrelevance as Rosencrantz and Guildenstern in Tom Stoppard's play. We are Richard Rich in *A Man for All Seasons,* ready to sell out our mentor, Sir Thomas More, and indeed all of Christendom, for . . . Wales. And just as deserving of as much contempt.

Our pet media has created an alternate universe, one in which none of you lives, but which they've made you believe in through sheer dint of repetition. In the guise of bringing you information via words, they've taken the words right out of your mouth, and not only rendered you speechless, but powerless. But as one newspaper after another topples into the grave, the former "big three" networks continue to hemorrhage viewers (most of whom are simply dying off), there is a huge vacuum waiting to be filled. You bitter clingers, like battered wives still married to abusive spouses, have persisted in the foolish belief that this is all transitory, that one day you'll wake up and your local daily rag won't be a seething cauldron of leftist hatred, blatantly misreported stories—especially evident when you have firsthand knowledge of the events in the report—and shadily and selectively edited "news judgment" that leaves out anything of interest or importance to you in favor of a conformist *Weltanschauung* that presupposes a single, Stalinist contextual view of how the news of the world is to be apprehended.

In general, conservatives have come late to the alternative media party, but that the audience exists there can be no doubt. Rush Limbaugh seized the high ground of talk radio decades ago, and now Fox News routinely outdraws its rivals CNN, MSNBC, and CNBC combined. The fact that liberal publications and TV networks, despite their overwhelming numerical superiority, react to Fox News like vampires to the cross ought to tell you something, since their greatest scorn (like that for Sarah Palin) is reserved for that which they fear most.

So reinfiltrate the media, already! *All* of it, Old and New. Create alternative institutions that reflect a way of looking at and dealing with the world that mirrors what you call reality. It's no accident, back in the good old days of *la Revolución*, that the Sandinistas or whichever raggle-taggle band of taco- or non-taco-eating Marxist guerrillas holding Soviet AK-47s in one hand and Mao's *Little Red Book* in the other (even though we support all Latin American revolutionary movements, like most *gringos*, everything from Tijuana to Tierra del Fuego pretty much seems the same to us) always made it their first order of business to seize the local *prensa* or radio station. Because they knew that reality is best dictated by the media, as opposed to the peasants' lying eyes, and so the sooner they could play "Won't Get Fooled Again" over the imported Rundfunk, the quicker the tequila could start flowing again, and the money start rolling in (and out).

Go thou and do likewise. Oh, you don't have to do anything as messy and as, frankly, terrifying as threatening us with all those guns we know you have locked away against the day when some wingnut calls for an armed march on Washington, or at least Austin. But those of you who have been smart enough to see the future—talk radio and the electronic media—know by now that the way to break the power of *The New York Times* is not to finally get one of their columnists to find Jesus, but to simply ignore them.

Yes! Ignore them. I myself haven't read the *Times* for years now, and it hasn't done me a bit of harm. Why, I could write a mock op-ed piece right this minute and I'd defy you to tell me it wasn't composed by one of their highly paid scribes, who collectively waste what was once the most valuable journalistic real estate in the world by scratching each other's backs, quoting each other's columns, phoning each other's sources, and buying each other lunch. I too can abuse the first-person pronoun with the best of them, publicly confess my congenital timidity and cowardice, whine about the dearth of good men in this world, reach for cheap pop cultural references, sing show tunes, and otherwise turn in copy that would disgrace a high school newspaper. And so, probably, could you.

So forget about conquering the *Times*. It's a lost cause and you don't need to assume their debt payments. Instead, for a pittance, you can set yourself up on the Internet, writing about things you know about. Who cares if you're not a great writer? (See paragraph above.) If you know your subject you know your subject, and surely we have all experienced the truth of the dictum that whenever you read about something you actually know about in a newspaper, you realize that it is a great steaming load of horse apples. But then when you turn to the other sections—gospel!

Well, only you can break that cycle, and you don't even have to be a "professional journalist" to do it. You can set pixels to blank cyberspace and, presto, you are a whistleblower, a guru, an expert witness. No longer will it be possible for one product, such as a newspaper, a magazine, or a television network, to pretend to truth. Glenn Reynolds, the Instapundit himself, calls the blogosphere writers an *Army of Davids*, slaying the Sixth Avenue Goliaths from the comfort of their dens, and in their pajamas to boot.

Which brings me to Corollary No. 2: ***Stop thinking that "Hollywood" is a dirty word.*** And this, ladies and germs, is where your pals in the "Christian Right" are going to have to suck it up for a while. You see, here in Hollywood there is nothing we fear more than the "Christian Right." Why, even the seventeen politically conservative Christians out here fear the "Christian Right" because we all—yes, every man jack of us at Jerry's Famous Deli and Nate 'n Al's and Dominick's across from Cedars and the Casa Vega in Sherman Oaks on Ventura in the Valley and Pinto Bistro and, hell, even Teix in my neighborhood of Echo Park and, well, you get the idea—worry that they might mess with our deathless art instead of reserving that privilege to our super-smart studio execs, agents, production assistants, drivers, and caterers.

I don't mean you should throw your Nazi brethren overboard, or under the bus, or wherever the current cliché is headed nowadays. I mean that you simply are going to have to ask them to put aside their cultural squeamishness and bear with you for a while until, way down the line, after the victory is won, they may find more takers here for their own kind of flicks. I mean, it's not like they are going to make common cause with us or anything . . .

My private opinion: they're noisier than they are dangerous. Sure, they squawk every time we celebrate some alternative lifestyle but—and I'm speaking as one who's spent plenty of time in the heartland, in my imagination anyway—they're plenty frisky themselves when the lights are down low, the moonshine's flowing, and Pappy's on a business trip to the big city and won't be back until a week from Tuesday. Their bark is worse than their overbite. Anyway, they don't go to movies, except for *The Passion of the Christ*. So the hell with them.

The reconquest of my beloved Tinseltown should not be that hard. After all, in its heyday there were no more patriotic Americans than the sons of the *shtetl* who invented the town in the first place, and if you don't believe me you need to read Neal Gabler's book *An Empire of Their Own*. Aside from the odd commie propaganda film, such as *Mission to Moscow* and *North Star*, Hollywood churned out patriotic film after patriotic film, recognizing an enemy when it saw it in those Heinies and them dirty little Japs. So what if those pictures are jingoistically embarrassing and, in the case of the Japanese, amazingly politically incorrect today? We won the damn war, didn't we?

Here's what you need to know: Hollywood runs on fear and greed and as soon as the money lies on the opposite side of the Left–Right equation, fear and greed will switch teams. For a long time its unassailable position as the driver of the popular culture left it immune to the vagaries of the marketplace: as long as big "tent pole" movies made money, it could afford to indulge its leftist political leanings with films designed not to succeed at the box office but to succeed at Beverly Hills dinner parties. Hence the spate of Iraq War duds like *Rendition* and *Redaction* and *Return to Bethlehem* (okay, I made that last one up, sort of), all made with malice aforethought and with the full knowledge that they wouldn't recoup a penny (not that any Hollywood film ever recoups—just ask any writer with monkey points!).

But, when you stop to think about it, in the larger culture—the "real" culture, as opposed to the imaginary culture that is served up in the cinema, seen on television, and delivered to your progressively autocratic breakfast table each morning by the likes of Frank Rich, Paul

Krugman, and Thomas "I, Me, Mine, and Did I Mention Myself" Friedman of *The New York Times*—we've created a Bizarro-universe in which we've forced you to live, through the simple expedient of your having taken yourselves *out of the game.*

There are plenty of conservatives—what you guys call "real Americans"—in Hollywood. It's just that you don't know them because, like the early Christians, or gay men in the 1950s, they have been forced underground, and communicate with each other through signs and wonders, like drawing the sign of the fish in the sand, wearing green on Thursdays, or acknowledging in public that *Taken* turned out to be a hit at the box office. In fact, I happen to know where they congregate, where they share ideas, where they draw sustenance from each other, the very revelation of which locations would have all the studios and agencies calling down air strikes on certain bars and restaurants on both sides of the Santa Monica Mountains, thus killing an amazing number of famous actors, producers, writers, and directors.

Still—and I'm letting you in on a deep, dark secret here, one that we confess only to our shrinks and that cute girl or unhappily married cougar sitting next to us at the bar at Tom Bergin's on Fairfax—we're outnumbered and we're starting to get scared. Oh, sure, there's plenty of us holed up here in West Hollywood, West Los Angeles, and west of the Hudson, where I live. But our takeover of your country has been, to name a famous movie, a "Grand Illusion," something we carried out in the darkness of the movie theater where, while you were fumbling with Mary Jane's bra strap, we were stealing your patrimony and leaving you a very messy mess of pottage instead.

So vote with your dollars. You've already skipped enough of the bash-Bush, slander-the-troops stinkers that we churned out in order to prove to our friends down the block in Brentwood how brave we are. But you need to do more—you need to continue to get out there and, more than ever before, actively support those books, movies, TV shows, and publications that reflect your values. Make a point of it. Open your checkbooks if you have to—how the heck do you think we've kept magazines nobody reads, like *The Nation* and *The New York Review of Books,* alive all these years? We just get one of our friendly capitalism-hating social progressive zillionaires to cough up some dough and we're good for another ten years or so.

One other thing: *remember who your friends are*. That's a problem we stalwart men and chicks of the Left often have, although we joke about it a lot ("circular firing squads" and Will Rogers's hoary old chestnut of not belonging to any organized political party, on account of he was a Democrat). You shouldn't fall prey to such internecine warfare: after all, you don't want to take over the world, you just want to finish your shift at the plant and go home to live in peace. So use all these new-media platforms your kids are down there in the basement inventing at this very minute, and plug your buddies. Make us know their names—we ain't gonna like it, but the louder we scream, the greater effect you'll be having. Especially if we start yelling about the "unfairness" of it all.

Amerikkka, you fools, has always been conservative, in the worst sense of the word—"conservative" of the ancient values of Western Civilization, of the legacy of Milton and Locke and Hume and Bishop Berkeley and even Hobbes. That's the truth. So start acting like you believe it, and stop having your kids studying animal husbandry or whatever it is they study at their loser community colleges and start studying screenwriting. Trust me, screenwriting's a lot easier, you make far more money from it, and you get to change the world out there, alone, in the dark.

Hence Corollary No. 3: *Reclaim academe*.

This is a longer-range proposition; we have had, after all, nearly half a century to completely hollow out the major colleges and universities, especially your so-called "Ivy League" institutions, largely in the name of our most sacred of sacred cows, the Great God Diversity. The Ivy League sent a disproportionate number of its sons (no daughters allowed in those benighted old days) off to fight in the Civil War, World War I, and the Big One. But after the collapse of the Germany of the National *Socialist* German *Workers* Party—and what part of that name sounds like the Reagan Revolution to you?—and Imperial Japan, our elite colleges, especially in New England and on the West Coast, became infested with the scions of Moral Relativism, so that a few short decades after the defeat of socialist fascism in Europe, the children who fled the socialist fascists were suddenly overrepresented among the socialist-communists of Harvard, Yale, and Brown students. *Viva la Revolución!*

That's good old Amerikkka for you, always willing to extend the olive branch to an enemy, to bend over backward, even at the risk of becoming a prison girlfriend, to the super-bright kids (like me!) who want to do "your" country harm. We are nothing if not ungrateful when it suits our purposes.

But the weakening economic climate has severely damaged many institutions' endowments and the end of the "Echo Boom" means that fewer middle- and upper-income kids will be competing for college places in the near future. Colleges will therefore be in the position of being more responsive to their customers. So . . .

Stop sending your kids to Harvard, Yale, the University of California, or any other elite university, whether public or private, unless and until they clean up their acts—fundamentally.

If there's a bigger, more brazen racket in the country than the showcase colleges and universities, I don't know what it is. Sure, they may still be okay for real subjects, like languages and math and science— although that "climate change" racket, which we almost got away with, had you going there for a minute!—but when it comes to stuff that's either imaginary (the "social sciences"), useless (English departments), or just plain nuts (pretty much everything else), they are a complete waste of your kid's beer and sex time and your money, which would be around fifty grand a year heading northward in an uninterrupted straight line, especially now that the federal government is going to administer college loans.

"Hey, Dave, just you wait a minute buster. Sending my kid to the Ivy League and beggaring my family not just in this generation but for future generations to come has been my lifelong dream. Who are you to tell me any different?"

Bear with me. The reason you don't want to waste upward of $50,000 per annum getting little Johnny, Shaniqua, or Abdul one of those fancy degrees in deconstructionism is that, unless you are absolutely certain that your little genius is a liberal, there will be no job waiting for him or her upon graduation. You see, those "disciplines" are our rackets. They're where we stick our progeny who really don't have any talent for anything else; having been raised on a diet of propaganda and counterintuitive nonsense since they began their education (as I did) in the Little Red School House in Greenwich Village, they can swallow the nonsense of Derrida and Foucault without batting an eye. Whereas your kid . . . well, as the white folks down south and in certain Boston neighborhoods used to say about black folks coming into their segregated towns and villages, "They wouldn't be happy here."

Having attended elite schools—Little Red, St. Ann's, Columbia—since practically the day I was born, I can tell you firsthand that you'd be better off sending your kid to the School of Hard Knocks, or training him to be a hobo on a freight train. After all, why spend a nickel to enroll and then drop out, like those losers Bill Gates and Andrew Lloyd Webber, when you can cut out the middleman entirely? And if by chance it's a real subject they're studying, well, the last time I looked two plus two equals four both at Dog Tooth State Teachers College in Rancid, Wyoming, and at Penn. Plus, the students actually get report cards at Dog Tooth State.

So don't do as my dad, the sainted "Che" Kahane did (not that he paid for it), and send your little genius to an Ivy League school—they're not going to get any grades, anyway, other than pass/fail, although they will get laid a lot, by members of both sexes. Send those little buggers to Dog Tooth State. And before that you've got home schooling and innovative charter schools (unless we can kill them first—right near the top of our list). Hell, start your own colleges! I think you have a few experts tucked away here and there who might not mind sharing some dollops of "traditional" wisdom before they totter off to the great country club in the sky.

The only reason, and I do mean the only reason, to want to torture your kids with stints at Hotchkiss, Choate, Andover, Exeter, and Punahou, thence to forward them to Princeton, Stanford, Kenyon, Yale, and Cornell, is to make sure they meet the right people on their way up. Every elite school will tolerate a certain number of townies and Not Our Crowd Dears, especially if they are black or Hispanic—although the obligatory celebration of diversity will end immediately upon graduation, and then Wall Street and Melrose Avenue will return to what they always have been: nearly all-white professional enclaves for those who work in finance or in the picture business, which we call the Industry.

However, on the off-chance your kid is one of that demographically dwindling number of nonconnected, up-by-its-bootstraps "little people," well, all he or she has to do is make a friend or two for life among the "others" and voilà! Instant elevation from the servants' entrance and the maid's bedroom to the front door and the guesthouse out back near the pool and the cabana. And if that's worth the roughly one zillion dollars over eight years such an education/social mixer is going to cost you, after taxes (and remember: a lot of us don't pay income taxes since, like the Kennedys, we inherited our money), then go ahead and knock yourself out. Just remember this: your kid will enthusiastically be playing for our team by the time we get through with him. And all to get revenge on you for his crappy upbringing.

Elite opinion is, frankly, going to be a tougher nut for you to crack. It's the stuff that gets bandied about at the better dinner parties on Fifth Avenue up near the Metropolitan Museum, and in the hills above Sunset Boulevard—you know, the part we called "Trousdale Estates." The likes of you is never going to get invited to those parties. You're too low-rent, too uncool, too *hoi polloi*. You're the kind of people we write movies about, not the kind of people we want to send our kids to school with. What do you think this is, a meritocracy?

So remember this: the families—okay, the single gay guys—throwing those parties in the "bird streets" off upper Doheny and in the big prewar, rent-controlled apartments along Central Park West, mostly began as glove salesmen, kinescope operators, pushcart vendors, fruit and vegetable salesmen, hod-carriers, water-tunnel-diggers, and the guys who built the Seventh Avenue IRT. They came from nothing—okay, they came from Minsk, Pinsk, the Pale, Killarney, Kildare and Kilkenny, Palermo, Agrigento, and Caltanisetta. So there's hope for you too. As long as you never admit where you came from, except in the vaguest, most *Barton Fink* sort of way.

Just don't get your hopes too high.

RULE NO. 4:
Get on Offense and Stay on Offense— and Take No Prisoners

So there you are, lying flat on your back on the canvas and wondering whether the referee got the number of that truck. For decades, we've pummeled you and pounded you, if not quite into submission then pretty close to it. We've robbed you of your tongue, of your fighting spirit; we've hamstrung you with lawyers and political correctness. We've made you doubt the worth of everything you once held dear— now there was a practical application of "Critical Theory" if there ever was one!—including your culture, your history, and, well, you. We've practically criminalized everything about you, including your thoughts, and it's just a matter of time before we get those too. Why, we've got top government-funded scientists in their labs working on a brain wave reader right now!

The key to our success is our relentlessness: we are like the Terminator before he went all girly-man in California, except whinier. Unlike the Terminator, who laughed as bullets bounced off him, plucked out his own eyeball and walked through searing flame until he was little more than a scary metal skeleton, got half his body ripped away by a machine press, and kept coming at Linda Hamilton, however, we don't like to get punched. So start punching.

And I don't mean pattycake. Reagan was able to deflect us with wit and good humor and pretty much got his way. True, he didn't really deliver on any of his campaign promises except cutting taxes and destroying the dear old Union of Soviet Socialist Republics—the Panama

Canal still belongs to Panama, and the departments of Energy and Education are happily still with us, continuing their irresistible, malevolent bureaucratic growth and giving birth to hordes of new Democratic voters every day—but we sure hated his guts while he was around, although we wept copious crocodile tears after his demise.

But humor isn't going to cut it anymore; this is no laughing matter. Back when the Great Communicator ran against Mr. Mush from the Wimp—that was Jimmy Carter, in the *Boston Globe*'s inadvertently famous phrase—it was still possible in this country to believe that both sides were acting in good faith, that both candidates shared a love for their country, that each political party was dedicated to the betterment of the nation, and that, in the main, we all shared the same goals and aspirations, as well as a common history.

Hah! Them days is gone.

The election of 1976 came too soon for us; after all, we had only just completed our conquest of the Democratic Party in 1972, and Nixon's resignation, though it was devoutly to be wished and celebrated, caught us flat-footed, as did Ford's suicide pardon of the old Trickster. But, as is our wont, we found a candidate nobody had ever heard of five minutes earlier, a standard-issue guilty white Southerner, the kind that either end up on our tickets or editing *The New York Times*, and we ran him against the Pardoner, whom we mocked mercilessly via our favorite television comedy show, *Saturday Night Live,* and the rest of the tale is well told.

It's true that in 1980 Reagan whaled the tar out of Jimmah, and then clobbered Mondale and for a time there it looked as though we were well on our way to becoming a permanent minority party—you know, the way the Republicans are supposed to be when all's right in hell and Satan is on His throne. Your big mistake—and believe me, this is not simply gratuitous Bush bashing, fun as that is—came when it was time to consolidate the Reagan Revolution and really put a stake through our hearts, and the best you could come up with was a one-term G. H. W. Bush, who begat G.W.B. and before you could say "Saddam Hussein" three times, turn around, and spit, we had our very own Hussein in the White House and—unless you pay attention to what I'm telling you here—there'll be no stopping us now. Not only have the rules changed, we're no longer even playing the same ballgame, and you really haven't figured that out yet.

So *pace* Ronnie, the time for jokes is past: it's time to fight. Which brings us to Corollary No. 1: **No more Mr. Nice Guy**. It is better to be feared than liked.

Civil wars are tough, even when there's no actual shooting, but buddy you are in one now, so you might as well get used to the idea. And if for some reason you think you're not, just look around you, and listen to what people are saying. Tempers are frayed, four-letter words drop from the loveliest of mouths, the tip of the tongue taking a trip of three steps down the palate to tap, at three, on the teeth: Go. Fuck. Yourself. If you'll pardon my Nabokov.

Let me tell you straight up and up front: you're going to lose friends. A lot of friends. Hell, maybe all your friends, assuming you ever had any on our side. But that's okay, because they probably never liked you very much anyway. See, we can pretend to be friends and neighbors for years, gossip over the back fence, borrow cups of sugar from each other—you know, whatever it is you people out there in flyover country do—but you just so much as look askance at Elton John's lifestyle choices and buddy we will never speak to you again. To criticize one of us, however obliquely, is to criticize all of us.

Will you really miss us?

McCain's defeat should have made this clear. The "maverick" who relied on the civility of the Senate and never came to an aisle he didn't want to cross was woefully unprepared for the attacks launched on him by his erstwhile "friends" in the media; the man who had been for years the press corps's favorite Republican was suddenly suspect. "I don't know," a lot of my friends here in Los Angeles said to me over sushi at Fat Fish, "I used to like McCain, but something's happened to him." That something, of course, was running against our guy—not that he put up much of a fight or anything. In fact, the whole election was like watching one of those boxing movies from the late 1940s, like *The Set-Up*, except that this time the fighter does what the gangsters tell him to do, and that's take a dive. No heroic resistance here: having already alienated a large swatch of the conservative electorate, McCain was left alone on the field, and only the Warrior Princess at his side made his ultimate electoral showing as respectable as it was. Naturally, around our campfires, we don't quite tell it that way, since Sarah Palin is the one thing we Hollywood types fear almost as much as Saint Michael with a blazing sword showing up on our doorsteps just as we're about to do a line of coke and slip into the hot tub with a couple of Polish starlets.

So fight, fight, fight: fight us on the Malibu beaches and in the Hollywood Hills, fight us in the arena of conventional wisdom, fight us even in casual conversation. Never back down.

"But hey Dave," I can hear you saying, "how in the Sam Hill am I supposed to fight you guys when I don't know the difference between Westward Beach and La Costa Beach and the one time I tried to drive around in the Hollywood Hills I got so lost I wound up in San Francisco or maybe it was Burbank I forget which huh?"

Fight us in cyberspace. You've got quite an intelligence and distribution tool there.

I've already told you that cyberspace is where the wars of the future are going to be fought; hell, the Chinese, the Bulgarians, and the Israelis probe our electronic defenses every day, searching for weaknesses, vulnerabilities, and stray bits of classified intelligence left on former Director of Central Intelligence John Deutch's unclassified laptop, when he brought it up with him to Bethesda one fine day; his cashiering was, naturally, entirely unrelated to his breach of security.

You don't have to go to as dramatic a level as Deutch; all you have to do is inform yourself. In the interests of full disclosure, the government now buries almost everything in cyberspace: policy changes, personnel decisions, even the famous Friday night document dumps, during which all sorts of embarrassing information sneaks out while the crack press corps is heading to its country homes in the Hamptons or the horse country of rural Virginia.

So get on Whitehouse.gov and snoop around. You'll be amazed. Not since Leni Riefenstahl's *Triumph of the Will* has there been something so devoted to the Dear Leader as the official White House Web site. But hiding there in plain sight—especially if you are, as I am, a trained semiotician—is a blueprint of just about everything we have in store for you. Check out the appointments, the programs, the announcements. Look and see what the various "czars" are up to. You remember them, the group of unelected, unconfirmed BFFs who actually run the government, as opposed to the cabinet secretaries, who are just there for show. Once you've read all the propaganda—excuse me! I mean, all the pertinent information—you can branch out to other sites, some of them (sshhhh) oppositional, like the rebel outposts in *Star Wars,* or *Episode Four: A New Hope 'n Change,* or whatever George Lucas is calling the one good movie he ever made these days.

You should also read Drudge—the man who introduced the world to Bill Clinton, Monica Lewinsky, the cigar, and the blue dress—and Glenn Reynolds's Instapundit.com, and of course my very own beloved *National Review Online,* where my mom-away-from-moms, Kathryn Lopez, introduced me to the world in February 2007. Sick of being force-fed mainstream media spin via the usual suspects in *The New York Times* and *Washington Post*? Then just turn the horse around and go right to its mouth, and check out the wealth of primary sources freely available at places like Thesmokingun.com, which specializes in arrest documents and other fun legal stuff. Poke around. As always on the Net, a healthy dollop of skepticism is vitally needed, since it's easy to fake *anything*, including your own high school graduation pictures. But, armed with your trusty BS detector, you should feel confident about taking the battle where no man had gone before until Al Gore came along.

The beauty of the Internet is that it's all serendipity—you might go looking for something and find something else, very much different indeed. And fall in love with it. So get off your duffs, you couch potatoes, put down that remote, shut off your plasma flat screen TV, waddle over to the computer, or just pick up your iPhone, and get online. Sure, you might have to read a little, but that's the whole idea—leave the bread and circuses to the chumps and suckers who wonder why their taxes are going up and why suddenly everybody on their block speaks Spanish and runs whenever the cop car drives by, and why everything you might want to do suddenly needs a very expensive permit.

Educate yourself. Get the facts. The truth shall set you free. And then spread the word. Set up e-mail lists and use them.

The thing is, we're no longer interested in the old go-along, get-along political culture, the rigged poker game in which the two parties only pretended to compete as long as they could fleece the marks (you) and divvy up the swag later. As the Great Plunkitt might have said, we're seein' our opportunities and we're takin' 'em, so you'd better wise up, Janet Weiss.

I realize most of you don't want to spend half your lives surfing the Net and living in an alternative universe like I do—as a liberal, I live almost completely in an alternative universe, except when I leave the house to go get the Jag washed by illegal immigrants—but the least you can do for yourselves and your country is to get out there and get into the fight.

You want a romantic notion to help fire your newfound patriotic activism? Then think of yourselves as Rick Blaine, the expatriate saloon keeper in *Casablanca*, who sticks his neck out for nobody, which is how he wound up isolated, loveless, and alone in one of the crummiest cities in North Africa. Then along comes his old flame, Ilsa Lund, unfortunately tethered by marriage to a heroic Czech freedom-fighter, and all of a sudden he gets that old feeling and one thing leads to another until there they are on the tarmac at the end, and what does hubby say but, "Welcome back to the fight. This time I know our side will win."

You're Rick Blaine. We're neither Ilsa, nor Victor Laszlo, nor even Captain Renault, the Frenchman of lascivious taste and easy virtue with whom Rick strikes up such a beautiful friendship at the end. No, we're Major Strasser, the swaggering avatar of the National Socialist German Workers Party, which you have to admit seems right up our alley. Plus Conrad Veidt, who played Major Strasser as the snarling but lovable beast that he was, also portrayed the sleepwalking "killer" Cesare in *The Cabinet of Dr. Caligari,* and as far as we're concerned any movie about shrinks, hypnotists, or somnambulists is our kind of picture. Case closed.

I know this one isn't going to be easy. You're too well bred, or at least too polite, to want to get right in our faces with this fight. To you, raised in your lower-middle-class, faux-genteel households, directly confronting someone, calling them out, is rude. You would no more think of telling Uncle Dan he's drunk and repetitive as he launches into his world-famous story about the time he thought he met Damon Runyon on the streets of Manhattan, Kansas, and it turned out to be Bob Barker of *The Price Is Right* instead, than you would punch him in the face. But we—

We come from big squabbling families—or small, poisonous ones, take your pick—where survival of the fittest and meanest is the operative ethos. No matter what our ostensible "religion," the only code we abide by is the Law of the Jungle. We scream and yell at each other, treat each other with contempt, lay guilt trips on one another, keep score when it comes to money owed and presents given and slights endured or unanswered. No Ingmar Bergman silent rooms and ticking clocks for us, no sir. The only ticking clocks in our lives are the clocks that tell us to wake up, get out of bed, drag a comb across our head, and go out and screw our fellow man. If that fellow man happens to be Mom or Dad, so much the worse for them. After all, we didn't ask to be born and, frankly, we're still pretty peeved about our nativity, if you want to know the truth. It's one of the many things we visit our shrinks to complain about.

This, by the way, is the answer to the mystery of why the coasts tend to be liberal and the interior of the country—flyover land—tends to be conservative. The coasts are where the immigrants landed and to which they continue to flock. The big coastal cities, which include the country's largest population centers, are also where the money is and by money I mean "government money"—you know, the kind of stuff that comes either out of your pocket or via the printing presses working overtime down at the Mint. Money, like water, flows freely, although unlike water it most often flows uphill, toward Them What Has as they pretend to be solicitous about Them What Don't. It's a simple equation: big cities + federal money = nearly unlimited graft and corruption. And that's a principle we've operated on for generations.

Meanwhile, the interior sections that take some effort to get to and thrive in, with the obvious exceptions of big railroad hubs like Chicago, where our political machines and gangsters could comfortably set up shop, tend to be populated by what we laughingly call "real Americans," the ones who continue to allow us to use their best qualities against them: trusting natures, big hearts, open wallets, innate "decency," tolerance, a willingness to live and let live on the assumption that we all share the same values, the same hopes, dreams, and aspirations.

When, of course, we did and do not and have no intention of ever so doing.

Yeah, we could always point to our 1.0 beautiful children (assuming we had any at all) and say it was all for the kids and who wouldn't want a better country for them than the one we were born into, and you fell for it, as we knew you would. You never stopped us in midsentence and said something like:

Hey, mister, wait just a darned minute, the country I was born into was pretty gol'-durned good; we stove off the Depression, whipped Hitler and them kamikazes, came home from the war, raised our families, educated our children, moved to the suburbs, got rid of legal segregation and then watched our cities burn anyway a few years later, watched our schools fall apart, watched our politicians assassinated, watched our taxes soar, watched our institutions crumble, watched a president or two get impeached, watched our economy collapse while the Wall Street fat cats skated, watched our norms about love, marriage, sex, and faith be first challenged in the name of "dissent" and "diversity" and then clawed to death, watched our immigration laws change the entire character of the country under the rubric of "antiracism," saw moral equivalence destroy morality, watched our country falter in one, two, three wars, watched our military fall prey to the intellectual fascism of "political correctness," learned to be afraid of saying what was on our minds and in our hearts, which used to be our right as Americans, whether you agreed with us or not, until now here we cower in flyover country, watching illegal aliens gather on our street corners while you tell us we're supposed to be grateful because we never had a Mexican restaurant in Bismarck before and now that we come to think of it, goddammit, we liked our country plenty just the way it was before you fellas showed up with your olive oil voices and your Irish charm, and we shoulda put you down and out and in the ground when we had the chance, but no, and look at us, we were too damn nice and now we're screwed.

Luckily, you never say that. Because the minute you so much as *think* a single one of those hateful, racist, bigoted thoughts we will be on you like a swastika tattoo on Charles Manson's forehead. How dare you demonize us? How dare you characterize the events of the past half-century or so as anything other than the obvious moral triumphs they have been? How dare you put your country as it once was up against our country as it will be once we get finished with it? How dare you riff on Jack Woltz's famous line to Tom Hagen in *The Godfather*? How dare you *defend your way of life*?

Well, maybe it's about good and goddamn time you did. When we're in your face like this, I mean back-to-back and belly-to-belly, you should come right back in ours. Let the spirit roar and the spittle fly.

Lose that "Minnesota nice" weirdness, that Midwestern naïveté, and try to put yourself back in the shoes of your forefathers, the clodhopper Europeans who got off the boat from Bumfück, Norway, or Dinkelscheisshausen, Deutschland, and instead of doing what we did—staying in Manhattan and immediately falling in with one of the ethnic street gangs whose thug ethos has made the island such a swell place for all these years—yanked themselves up by their bootstraps (after we had fleeced them) and trekked westward to the flyover states, which was basically the last we ever heard of you.

So here's my advice: call us out, each and every time. Refuse to accept our premises. Refuse to go along with our reflexive indictments of everything you stand for. Refuse to tacitly accept guilt as we make our routine accusations that we "know" what you *really* mean when you talk about things like "the Tenth Amendment," "Marxism," "You lie!," and "date night." (To us, as I think I've made perfectly clear, they all mean "racism.") Writing in *The Weekly Standard,* the brilliant essayist Noemie Emery has termed our little trick of projecting upon you what we feel in our black hearts "secondhand hate," and that is what it most certainly is.

And yet, like the suckers you are, you fall for it every time. You stand there and let us whale away on you, imputing every sort of ignobility to you, your culture, your belief system, your faith tradition, and your families unto the generations. By our lights, since we despise you so roundly and so thoroughly, any weapon to hand is useful, and so we club you to death with your own good manners, telling you all the while that to fight back would be wrong, would be advocating at least symbolic violence and hate mongering, would be trying to force your opinion on us.

And so you take it, when what you should do is punch us right in the face.

Okay, maybe not literally, although Gaia knows we deserve it. After all, you, like everybody else in this soon-to-be-great land of ours after we finish our modern updating of *Mission to Moscow*, have grown up with Hollywood films, and if there's one thing you can count on it's the arrival, in the third act, of what we Industry types call the "cheer moment." That's the part in the movie when the long-suffering hero, after having suffered indignity after insult, finally snaps and strikes back at his

tormentors. Down they go in a heap of blood, spitting teeth and grop-
ing around the floor for their eyeballs as our guy, his bloodlust finally
roused, romps, stomps, and otherwise kicks some serious ass as he wipes
the floor with the bad guys—and with nary a tort lawyer in sight. From
High Noon to *Born Losers* to *Straw Dogs*, the cinema has made the worm-
turns revenge drama a staple of popular entertainment. We leave the
theaters with our own bloodlust satiated, confident that at least in some
writer's fevered imagination, righteous payback gets delivered in spades.

Now, in real life, at the first punch someone would shriek and call a
lawyer and before you knew it our main character would be doing six to
twelve in a medium-security prison. Which actually is okay with us,
since we'd then get to write the sequel, in which an unjustly imprisoned
man busts out of prison (*The Shawshank Redemption*), or somehow returns from the dead to hunt down his tormentors (*Point Blank*) and kill
them. And then you'd cheer all over again and, after the movie, ask
yourselves: was there ever a time when people actually did that?

Yes. It was called the American Revolution. Did they punch back?
You bet your sweet patootie they did.

So should you. Punch. And punch. And keep punching until we cry
like little girls and run away. When we attack you, defend yourselves, by
any means necessary. When you've tried this in the past, and hauled off
and given us a good old-fashioned trip to the woodshed, you've had to
listen to the requisite caterwauling about "fringe" behavior, and the
chin pulling in the media wondering whether this is the start of another
Oklahoma City–type situation. And of course if we can play the race
card, you can bet we will. But we do back off. Today, we're doing our
level best to criminalize your means of self-defense. Not that I'm advocating violence—like all good liberals, I hate violence. As General Webb
says to Heyward of the French in Michael Mann's dreadfully regressive
The Last of the Mohicans (which celebrates a benighted time when men
were men and women loved them): "They have not the nature for war.
Their Latinate voluptuousness combines with their Gallic laziness and
the result is: they would rather make love with their faces than fight."

You simply need to find a way to relevel the playing field after we've
spent half a century tilting it in our favor. Right now, as in the French
and Native American War, we're waging asymmetric warfare against

you, which come to think of it is another reason we can barely contain our admiration for the terrorists who, after all, are simply doing the job we real Americans won't do, i.e., actually kill you. We know you're not lawyer-savvy, that you don't come from families and social circles brimming with lawyers, that you don't routinely personally employ (as I do) at least three attorneys for different purposes, that calling *Car Talk*'s resident law firm of Dewey, Cheetham and Howe is not the first thing you think about when someone is trying to break into your home, the way we do from the safety of our panic rooms, which come equipped with a two-week supply of Evian water, a month's worth of raw walnuts, and satellite radio that pipes in NPR 24/7.

If I were you, I would change the system. Put the lawyers back in their place, to serve the law and the people, instead of to function as attack dogs against the very system that gives them shelter. I would make filing frivolous lawsuits a seriously expensive matter for the aggressor. I would make it almost impossible to win punitive damages—don't you just love that phrase, *"punitive"* damages? Music to our ears—and allow only the most reasonable actual damages.

If I were you, I would get rid of the legalistic mind-set that tells innocent people they must retreat in the face of a threat, that they must resort to force only as a last, desperate act of self-defense, that it is better for them to sacrifice themselves to a larger legal principle than to prevent their wives and children from being raped and murdered.

If I were you, I would rise up as one and shout that the rights and plights of defendants in capital cases would henceforth be of secondary concern to society's need for restitution and, when necessary, revenge. That you will no longer allow us to impute racism of any kind in the handling of such matters. That the days of the antebellum South are as dead as Jeff Davis and that you will no longer tolerate us trying to tar you with that brush.

If I were you, I would reject the notion that the perfect must always and everywhere be the enemy of the good enough. That, since there is no hereafter in which to sort things out, we must shackle ourselves in the here and now, obsess over every case, never close what can be reopened, and never but never accept that the fact that humanity is not itself perfectible if only you kill enough people.

If I were you, I would try to reassert the old ways of thinking about the human condition, that some people got tough breaks, that life wasn't fair, that sometimes through no fault of your own or conspiracy by the Christian Right, you got the short end of the stick, but that in the sweet by-and-by every mountain shall be humbled and every valley exalted. That philosophy was good enough for the Founding Fathers, so why isn't it good enough for us?

That's what I would do, if I were you. But, of course, you won't.

Because your answer to Jimmy Malone's question—"What are you prepared to do?"—is this: Nothing.

Which brings us to Corollary No. 2: *Get rid of the RINOs.*

You clowns cannot hope to win if you consistently return to office Republicans in Name Only, candidates who make all the right noises on the campaign trail (i.e., conservative), then turn around, pivot to the "center" (i.e., left), reach across the aisle—hell, tap-dance across the aisle—and then function as quislings for the next two or four or six years. If charity begins at home then so does housecleaning.

Therefore, the first thing you've got to do is get rid of the enemies within. As you know, our motto has been for decades: no enemies to the left. It's not that we don't hate each other's guts, which we surely do. It's just that we realize that the principal Enemy is and always will be you until that happy day when you are all gone, and we can get back to the circular firing squad and disorganized political parties of Will Rogers's dream.

Every time you accept another RINO because "he can win," or because "he's better than the other guy," or because "we can trust him to mostly do the right thing," I want you to think of three little words: Franz von Papen. The "wily" (as he's always described) Papen, the tool of the right-wing Junkers and industrialists who had their senile puppet president in Hindenburg during the Weimar Republic, thought that by bringing the head of the National Socialist German Workers Party into the government they could "control" him. Whoops! Barely into his term as Chancellor, Hitler moved swiftly upon the death of Hindenburg to consolidate power and turn Germany into a police state in which the members of the armed forces swore a loyalty oath not to their country, but to him personally. And the wily Papen? Totally out of luck. Never trust anybody, and that goes double for politicians.

As far as you losers are concerned, every RINO is, in effect, on our side, because he or she has already surrendered the high ground of moral principle for the squishy soft middle ground of "compromise." But as that lunatic Rush Limbaugh keeps shouting at you at tiresome length, there can be no accommodation on principle: the minute you agree to meet in the middle, then you've already abandoned your redoubt and are now engaging us right where we want you—on the killing fields of compromise. Those fields are already littered with the whitening bones and bleached skulls of your earlier Hectors, whose corpses we tied to our chariots and drove round and round the walls of your shining city on the hill.

So what have you got to lose by abandoning the old aisle-reach and nominating some real warriors—young men and women who have already been tested on the field of combat, both actual and intellectual. Just as the CIA ought to be recruiting agents from the South Side of Chicago—guys who know how to sense danger—instead of the leafy precincts of the Ivies, so you ought to be out there, right now, looking for Spartans. The last thing your side needs at the moment is more middle-American Rotary Club types, like the ones who've led you into this electoral ditch and thus delivered you, willy-nilly, into our hands.

Although we're doing our best, the one institution of American life we thus far have not been able to corrupt totally is the military. Sure, we've made some strides—you really have to hand it to us, the way political correctness plastered the Fort Hood killer with more al-Qaeda decals than your average Nascar driver and still nobody did anything about him until it was too late—but by and large the military is yours. And why is that?

The easy answer, and the one we desperately want to believe, is that the armed services are filled with life's losers, rednecks, and hillbillies who couldn't get into Harvard and thus had to settle for learning how to properly do what they'd do for free—kill people. The truth, which we've completely forbidden our pet media ever to let slip, is that the American officer corps is far better educated than the average University of Chicago grad, far more able to take command of difficult circumstances, and trained to apply his book learning and his practical experience on the spot, when it's a matter of life and death. For the University of Chicago grad, the only life-or-death situation he's ever likely to encounter is whether to take public transportation back to Hyde Park from the Rush Street bars at two in the morning, instead of springing for a cab.

And don't forget the enlisted ranks, either. Our contempt for these guys and gals basically knows no bounds, except when we need one of them to back us up in a fight we accidentally picked in one of those dive bars we like to frequent to show how "edgy" and "tough" we are, and the next thing we know some bruiser is threatening to feed us a knuckle sandwich. These enlisted johnnies have gone through some serious physical training, know how to handle weapons, and—assuming they're lucky enough to come home with most of their limbs still attached— actually get real jobs in the private sector, something that most of the folks on my side never quite managed to figure out how to do.

Look at the conservative clubs on campuses and start grooming those kids for office too. Believe me, anybody brave enough to confess to conservatism on campus has the stones to take on anything Washington, D.C., can dish up.

In general, focus on those groups that we most despise and you'll find yourselves some pretty good contenders. Think about all the once successful businesspeople we're pumping out into the street each and every day! Not to mention small business owners. Running a state—or a country—can't be half as complicated as fighting their way through the mountains of impenetrable paperwork and regulations we tortured them with all those years until we finally pulled the plug. Your state capitals and our beloved District of Columbia might not look half bad to those filthy capitalists right about now.

So there's your talent pool and it's high time you exploited it. After half a century of ponytailed hippies, some of whom stayed on the pot farms of Mendocino and others who cleaned up their act and went to work for *The New York Times,* preaching license, secularism, and sedition, I betcha the country is more than ready for a little of the old, you know, God and Country stuff.

And perhaps this was the hated *&^$BUSH#$@!'s plan all along when he started his mendacious wars against countries that never even attacked us, like Iraq: to give the younger generation a taste of real combat and real command, so that when they came back they could apply those lessons in the real world, and hammer the crap out of us.

Uh-oh.

Rule No. 5:
Let the Dismantling Begin

As is well known, as my dad's favorite newspaper, *Pravda*—or was it *Izvestia*, I can't remember, it's all Cyrillic to me—used to say, one of the dirtiest words in a fellow traveler's vocabulary is "revanchist." You could look it up—the meaning, I mean, not the fact that it is one of our dirtiest words, right alongside "America," "religion," and "the Constitution"—but why bother? "Revanchist" means a backslider, a counter-revolutionary, the guy who wants to overthrow the overthrowers. Someone out for payback. In other words, you, if you're doing it right.

And this is where we always have you Knights of Columbus clods at a disadvantage. Given the nature of the game, it is always we who are the heroic ones, the fighters, the revolutionaries, the progressives, the people *demanding* change for the Betterment of All Mankind, or at least ourselves. Whereas you are the bad guys, the Basil Rathbone character in *Robin Hood*, the sneering scions of privilege who are standing in the schoolhouse door, crying "Stop!" to the great forward march of Progress. No wonder everybody hates you, including you.

You see, there's nothing romantic or glamorous about being a conservative. Aside from occasionally polishing the bust of Edmund Burke, there's no great cause to serve, no glory to be won, no chicks to impress. There's absolutely nothing about it that fires the hearts, minds, and gonads of young people, no *la Causa* to *viva!* No Finland Station train, no Long March. Where's your slogan to compete with, say, *The people, united, will never be defeated?* "Morning in America"?

What you need, my pathetic friends, is a cause, and that's what I'm here to give you in this section. Ask yourselves this simple question: what is it about revolutions that gets young Westerners all wee-wee'd up? It's not the food, or the sleeping conditions, or the occasional tear-gassing. It's not the Lincoln Brigade stories round the campfire, or the sweet young thing willing to share your sleeping bag, or the feel of cold steel up against your rib cage. Hell, it's not even the ultimate victory; after all, the Who taught my dad's generation that the new boss would be pretty much identical to the old boss, so the whole thing really didn't end up amounting to a hill of beans in this crazy world.

It's *destruction*.

We've been selling that since the Vandals or whoever sacked Rome, since the Turks took Constantinople, since the Brits burned Washington during the War of 18Whatever, since the Nazis tossed all those books on the great bonfires of the European vanities, since the Russians rolled through Berlin and just about blew away every man, woman, child, dog, cat, horse, building, and beer hall they could get their hands on. Fact is, we love to blow stuff up, especially when it's your stuff, and the longer and harder you worked at it, the more it means, the more cultural freight it carries, the sky-higher we want to send it. And that's basically all there is to it.

So get busy wrecking stuff—only this time, it's our stuff you'll be wrecking. Turnabout is fair play: for the first time in eons, you guys will be the Visigoths and we'll be the effete Romans, still searching for the perfect rhyme in a language nobody speaks anymore while the raping and the looting were going on behind them. Part of the fun, of course, is you get to hear us squeal, and that ought to be sweet music to your ears after all these years of having to take it from us.

Indeed, make destruction your campaign slogan: *Roll it back!* Get those clean-cut young military officers out there on the hustings with a vow not simply to restore the status quo ante, but to revel in the destruction. Describe lovingly how each brick is going to be taken down, each monstrous agency of the federal government—a government that, by now, pretty much everybody hates, even us—is going to be cut down to size or eliminated altogether. How lazy, shiftless bureaucrats who make twice what you do are going to be de-unionized, forced to actually work in the dismantling of their own agencies, of their own jobs, and then summarily and publicly fired. How budgets will be first slashed and then eliminated entirely, how excess government property will be closed down and auctioned off, how taxes will be drastically reduced on the productive class and increased on the freeloading class—you know, the 47 percent of all taxpayers who today pay not one dime in federal income taxes. You want to be a part of this country, you gotta pay something. As Blake, the Alec Baldwin character, says to the bunch of schmuck loser real estate hustlers in the film version of Mamet's masterpiece, *Glengarry Glen Ross*: "It's fuck or walk."

Here's the best part, the way you're going to sell this. You're not just tearing stuff down and blowing shit up for the fun of it, the way we do, and the way history's first rebel, Satan, tried to do in heaven. Oh, no. *You're tearing down the walls of the socialist prison we have been building around you.* You're not destroyers, you're liberators! Just like we were back in 1968!

In retrospect, 1968 was a pivotal year for a lot of reasons, but it's the violence I keep coming back to, because it fascinates me. When those heroic boomers went at the pigs with hammers and sickles or tongs or whatever, it was a whole generation attempting parricide, just for the hell of it. We—I use the term loosely, since I'm channeling my dad here—went up against the pigs, against Mom and Dad, against the university presidents and provosts, against the Man, against the whole damned system. It was liberating in so many ways to realize that our hero, Mao, was right when he said that all power, even flower power, flows from the barrel of a gun. Which is one of the reasons a lot of us look upon our Islamic enemies with a healthy awe and respect, since a guy who will saw your head off with a large kukri knife obviously is playing in a league of his own.

So this is what I mean about it's better to be feared than liked. Once "Che," "Uncle Joe," and the rest of their cohort realized that you feared us and there would be *no consequences for their actions*—aside from that little unpleasantness at Kent State—well, that was pretty much the ballgame. Something they had thought was a monolithic construct, a vast conspiracy, turned out to be a Potemkin Village, and before you knew it, they were running around naked inside the hallowed halls of the culture, defacing the art and crapping on the floor. After all, it was the National Guard that rescued half those soggy, freezing, drug-addled kids at Woodstock, and the thanks they got was getting spittle in their faces. We are nothing if not entitled.

That sense of entitlement certainly permeates my generation of progressives, because, after all, we learned it at the feet of the masters, in my case "Che" and What's Her Name, my mom. We were never threatened with the lash at home, because this feared/loved thing is only meant to apply to you. No sir: we were coddled like young Persian princelings, indulged in our every whim, constantly told how wonderful we were. The boomers were rebelling against their hard-assed dads, the ones who had just come home from the wars—or did not come home from the wars, as the case may have been. These were guys who had grown up in the Depression, who had graduated from high school and actually learned something, who had been drafted or volunteered, who had fought and killed. They weren't in any mood to take any guff from junior. And the boomers loathed them and plotted their revenge.

I guess what I'm trying to say here is that we play hardball. We may be unprepossessing, unattractive wimps, but in our minds we're tough guys and that's the way we want you to think of us too.

Amazingly, you do.

So turn the tables on us. As I pointed out in the preceding section, we don't like it when you punch back. And given that it's your side that has all the guns, marksmen, crazed militias, hot biker chicks, and the entire armed might of Nascar, you could roll right over us if you wanted to. You could crush us like the vermin we—let's be honest—know that we actually are. You could stub out your cigarettes on our eyeballs, steal our collection of Pete Seeger records, and run off with our women, assuming you don't mind mustaches, although we'd probably draw the line and actually put up a little fight if you tried to move into our neighborhoods; at the very least we'd call the cops or a private security force, whose presence we announce with those signs in our front yards, the ones that say: ARMED RESPONSE. Which basically means we've hired minorities to do the job—our own self-protection—that we just won't do.

Now I know that some of you wingnuts are going to read this and immediately start spreading the word that I'm advocating armed insurrection or some sort of wacky notion. If today's crop of progressives had been around for the battles of Lexington and Concord, well, the Revolution would have had to start without us, because frankly we just don't have the taste for such things; the beatings we took in Chicago and the deaths we suffered at Kent State sort of reduced our bloodlust, physiologically speaking.

But they never lessened our animosity. We remain down for the struggle, in for the long haul, committed to your unconditional surrender and our ultimate victory. Which is why we've labored so mightily to convince you that resistance is futile, that our ideas have already proven themselves and that no further discussion is necessary. As they say about "global warming"—the science is settled!

So don't call us either Mr. Nice Guy or Late for Dinner: we come with Tammany brass knuckles in one hand and the little tin box in the other, equally ready to beat you up or shake you down. We just hope we don't faint at the sight of blood.

Which brings us to Corollary No. 1: *Challenge every one of our premises and our "accomplishments."* Expose their true nature and consequences for real people, and pin them on us, hard. *Freeze them, personalize them, polarize them,* as we love to repeat *ad nauseam.*

I used the phrase "Potemkin Village" above, but in truth it's much more applicable when describing us and what we have wrought. I mean . . . what exactly have we done that's so all-fired great? When push comes to shove, about all we can come up with is the civil rights movement, but you had at least as much to do with that as we did and, besides, it was the racist Democrats—how it pains me to type those words!—who fought it till the last fire hose ran dry and the last German shepherd died. Other than that, we've pretty much crapped out. So now—when we're at our cockiest and most overconfident—is the time for you to break us.

It's easier than it might look. Since our only real defense against any of your philosophical challenges is to call you a Nazi and walk away in a huff, get in our face at every conceivable opportunity. Do not let us make one single statement unchallenged; do not let us frame and dictate the terms of any debate. Wouldn't it be one of the great cheer moments in modern American history if once—*just once!*—you saw a military officer or a captain of industry testify before Congress, subjected to the preening, self-indulgent stupidity of some leftist man-of-the-people millionaire, when all of a sudden the man or woman stops, turns on his tormentors, and says something like this:

You know, I have been sitting here for more than an hour, being lectured by a bunch of clowns who can't tie their own shoes without a pollster, a bunch of boobs I wouldn't hire in my mailroom, if I still had a mailroom, a bunch of lying, malevolent skunks who have used their offices as "public servants" to further enrich themselves and their friends, all at the expense of the Little Guy they profess to care about. By rights, you all ought to be hanging from the lampposts along Constitution Avenue as penalty for the sins you've committed against our great country. You deserve to wind up like Mussolini and Clara, upside down in the village square, where the kids can throw rocks at you. You deserve to be frog-marched out of here, placed under arrest, your finances opened to public inspection, your private papers exposed for all the world to read. In a show trial, broadcast live on national television and streamed live to every computer, iPhone, BlackBerry, PDA, iPad, and other devices not yet invented, you should be made to confess your malfeasance, offer restitution, beg forgiveness, and then be shot for the crimes you have committed against our country, its people, and its Constitution—a Constitution you swore to uphold and defend, but which apparently meant to you loot and pillage. That's what ought to happen to you, Senator, and in a just nation, under God, that's exactly what's going to happen.

[Sounds of doors being forced open, a great crowd rushing the hearing room. Senators and their aides scream as an enraged populace, unmolested by any police, seizes the solons and drags them from the chambers . . .]

That's not likely to happen anytime soon, although I have to admit it's a great scene and I'm definitely going to put it in my next movie. But what you can do is refuse to play along anymore, refuse to be bullied by a bunch of high school presidents who couldn't get and hold a real job if Enron was still hiring and Paul Krugman was the head of the Human Resources Department. Don't let another statement of the "everybody knows that . . ." variety go unchallenged, including from our pet goats in the media; remember that we, at all times, must conceal our true intentions behind a fog of Newspeak. Dispel the smoke, brimstone, and naphtha and see us for what we really are. Recall that wonderful scene in *Faust*, Part One, outside the Auerbachs Keller in Leipzig, in which Mephisto (the real hero, as we know) frees a group of students from a spell with the words: "Loose the bonds of illusions from your eyes!/And remember how the Devil joked."

But the best way is to go after the very soul of our philosophy, the way Mephisto did to poor Faust: that life is a zero-sum game. How we managed to impose that alien, European, and altogether nutty *Weltanschauung* on good red-blooded American boys and girls is still beyond me (Dad is a genius!), but the fact remains that we did. When you stop to think about it, the notion that the economic engine of capitalism is a finite pie is even crazier than thinking that the world is carried on the back of a giant turtle, but there you go. We sold this package of shared misery—shared by you, not by us—by gift-wrapping it in a bunch of tired old Christian bromides about loving thy neighbor and charity beginning at home and other such hoo-hah, given that we were now enforcing "charity" at the point of a gun, which in another time and place was called "highway robbery."

So go after this. Texas Guinan, the Manhattan nightclub hostess with the mostest during Prohibition, always used to tell her girls: "Never lose the purple mantle of illusion," but this zero-sum, beggarthy-neighbor bushwa is our purple mantle, and when you tear it away from us we become little more than an especially old and ugly Salome, writhing naked on the floor and kissing the severed head of John the Baptist. And you should do what Herod does at the end of Wilde's play and Richard Strauss's opera: he orders his men to crush her beneath their shields.

Because what's perfectly clear by now is that our socialist-redistributionist policies are as bare-assed as Salome after she lost the seventh veil, and buyer's remorse is beginning to set in. What you must do is conceive and launch a well-coordinated, intellectually coherent campaign against our brand of Frankfurt School nihilism, Cloward-Piven deconstruction, and the entire postwar edifice of neo-socialism that we have erected on the backs of the hardworking people of this country. Which means:

- Shouting it from the rooftops. Buttonhole everybody. If need be—and the need is great—make yourself a complete bore on the subject.
- Say No to Nihilism! Party of No? Party of Hell, No! Two negatives make a positive, so put that spin on it and Say No to Negativity, and all the Party of Death (that would be us) stands for: cultural disintegration, abortion, governmental intrusion, euthanasias, death panels, the nanny state. P. J. O'Rourke once quipped that living in the Soviet Union was like living with your parents forever—and for many Russians that was literally true—but you ain't seen nothing yet. If we complete our mission to destroy your "way of life," it will be like living with Noah Cross from *Chinatown* and Ma Barker.
- And by all means, recruit candidates explicitly committed to rolling it back, not ameliorating it around the edges, in your usual doofus way. To that end:

Corollary No. 2: ***Think the unthinkable***. Go ahead, it's fun!

Get rid of Social Security? Why not? It's always been a giant pyramid racket, borrowing from the unborn Paul to pay the sixty-five-year-old Peter today—and to keep paying him for the next twenty or thirty years. The problem is, there is no unborn Paul, since some young woman proudly taking control of her body just aborted him. And without the Pauls of the future, we have to print extra money to cover the unfounded liabilities inherent in a pyramid scheme such as this one, which was sold to the public (duplicitously, as usual) as both a "safety net" and a retirement plan, as both a "tax" and "not a tax" as it withstood the legal challenges that rightly ought to have strangled it in its cradle. For decades, Social Security was considered the "third rail" of American politics, touch it and you die, but pretty soon we're all going to be like Mr. Blue in the original *Taking of Pelham One Two Three* and deciding it's easier to touch that rail and get it over with rather than face the consequences of having given birth to the Thing That Devoured Cleveland—and every other American city.

Same goes for state and local pensions—as one town and city after another collapses into bankruptcy, all those promises to keep will come home, like the Reverend Jeremiah Wright's chickens, to roost, even though we've got miles to go before we can sleep. The public employee unions, such as SEIU, need to go, along with the featherbedded, gold-plated contracts they've been negotiating—in a breathtaking conflict of interest—with politicians over the heads of their real bosses, the taxpay-ers. Think of them as the new leisure class—the fat cats and robber barons of the twenty-first century, except for the railroads and steel mills and oil wells and automobile factories and international banking systems they haven't built. Their rackets are hundreds, thousands of mini–Social Security time bombs, each one waiting to go off with max-imum detonation when we can least afford it. Sure, by our lights a soci-ety in which 60 percent of the people—"public servants"—retire and then live off the taxpayer for the rest of their lives, while the 40 percent still dumb enough to be working in the real-world private sector—"schmucks"—have to keep working until they drop, is a thing devoutly to be wished. This is Revenge of the Proletariat, and it serves those darn exploiters right; they're just getting what's been coming to them since Marx was scribbling away in London and banging the chambermaids. Public employee unions have only been legal since the Kennedy admin-istration, so that ought to be an easy fix, if you don't mind a little blood in the streets, because they *will* fight for their right to take you down with them. But with all the money that will be flowing back into the private sector, your companies may even be able to hire them to do, you know, a little honest and productive work.

Repeal the health care bill and at least half of the useless laws enacted since the Johnson-Nixon administration (domestically, they were pretty much the same thing). Get rid of all that feel-good legislation whose un-intended consequences are currently, inexorably changing the fabric of the nation and crushing its economy. Have your candidates run on a platform that all bodies of government—municipal, local, state, federal (we Americans just can't get enough government)—must repeal at least one law, and preferably more, for each new one they pass. If we could exhume the Founders and, before we put them all on trial for crimes against humanity, could ask them how many laws they would have con-sidered enough, and then showed them the Federal Register alone, they'd all hop back into their graves and commence spinning.

The lawyers will hate this, of course, because they have the best racket going: they study law in order to run for office, where they can make more laws that will employ more lawyers until, *reductio ad absurdum*, the entire country, minus a few drones, consists of lawyers suing other lawyers over laws written and passed by still more lawyers, implemented by a Chief Executive who's also a lawyer, and adjudicated by a Supreme Court consisting of nothing but lawyers—all of whom went either to Yale or Harvard. Paradise!

This is no joke, and it's about time you realized it and your candidates started getting vocal about it. The American people have an almost infinite capacity for tolerant forbearance, but sooner or later even their largesse is finally exhausted. The old Tammany sachems in New York had it right: they knew that if you didn't steal everything, there'd always be something left to steal, and the rubes would never be any the wiser. But in our arrant hubris, we've forgotten that simple lesson. Take advantage of it.

And now penetrate our last defense mechanism: your own willing suspension of disbelief. Surely, we cannot have *intended* all this wanton destruction, this overturning of centuries of shared values and goals?

Au contraire, mes amis! While you may wonder why we would so enthusiastically continue to support crippling legislation that will accomplish nothing that anybody actually asked for and will destroy the country's economy, the answer is very simple. It's not an answer you're prepared to believe, since it goes against every decent impulse you have.

It's not a bug, it's a feature!

In other words, what's happening now is the *result we wanted all along*. That's how you "fundamentally change" America, by collapsing its institutions under the weight of their own implicit good intentions, just as Cloward & Piven advocated. And each step of the way, you can continue to peddle the same old snake oil: that it's in the best interests of the country; that only churls, Nazis, and conservatives could possibly oppose it. And then, one day, it will all be over and a new phoenix will arise from the ashes, inhabiting a new world in which, alas, there's no place for you.

Which brings us, *in extremis*, to Corollary No. 3: ***Having thought it, act on it.***

Do not accept the validity of our version of the Brezhnev Doctrine. Which, after all, is as dead as Brezhnev, when you stop to think about it; ask the Russians how well that worked out after the fall of the Berlin Wall.

The country is ripe for a huge rollback. Abolish many or most of the regulatory agencies, sunset the laws that have outlived their usefulness or accomplished their objective, put a moratorium on new legislation until the old debris is cleared away. Actually act on campaign promises to eliminate wasteful federal agencies, such as the departments of Energy and Education as well as the cumbersome and Orwellian Homeland Security Department. The goal: to try and restore the proper balance between productive citizen and "civil servant," with the former the master of the latter once more.

So stop talking and start acting. At every level, no matter how small, put your best people forward, starting with the PTA and the local political town committees; even community organizers have to start somewhere. If some of you have to make politics your lives for this generation and into the next, tough—what do you think we do? Like Ulysses, you have been summoned on a great and royal mission, and while you'd like to feign madness and try to plow the sand, we both know that this madness is simply a ruse. The stakes are too high and besides, instead of staying home, this time Penelope will be right beside you, fighting for home and hearth and the future.

Conservatives of the world unite! You have nothing to lose but your chains.

RULE NO. 6:
At All Times, Think Constitutionally

Not even a liberal like me would dispute the notion that the U.S. has wandered very far away from its founding principles, which has been part of our push all along. When you have a founding document as simple, as lambent, as lucid as the Constitution, which lays out the nature and structure of the federal government—which was intended to be a compact among the sovereign states, remember?—in a way that not even a lawyer could possibly misinterpret, you have a problem. And, practically from its adoption, we have striven mightily to fix it.

The key, of course, is to get the lawyers on the case. As we've seen, one of our objectives was to turn the U.S. into a nation of the lawyers, by the lawyers, and for the lawyers, and in that you'll have to admit we have succeeded spectacularly. A kind of mystic aura has grown up around the law, as with wine or classical music, except that if you get it wrong you can go to jail. In fact, though, the law is nothing more than shared morality and social goals given written expression. Everything else, as they say, is commentary.

And that's where we come in! For centuries, the figure of the lawyer has been pilloried in popular entertainment, including the opera, as a clueless, pettifogging, half-blind nitwit who's a stickler for details while the handsome baritone spirits the saucy serving wench into the bedroom. Lawyers were necessary evils, obsessed with dotting *i*'s and crossing *t*'s while the rest of the world got on with life, love, and the pursuit of whatever.

Today, they're just evil. Like some degenerate futuristic tribe—Morlocks with glasses—they can parse but they cannot understand plain language anymore. They are the perfect tools of our deconstructionism: a horde of intellectual sappers we have bred and unleashed upon you, programmed to convince you that nothing is what it seems, that for every meaning there is an opposite, far more than equal, anti-meaning, and that everything you used to think you knew about the United States—it was all a lie. They are our Janissaries, our Gurkhas, our Uhlans, and well compensated too. You cannot hope to beat them, not in the rigged system we currently have. All you can do is outbid the other guy for their services.

All of which means that, despite the lip service paid in the famous oath to "preserve, protect and defend the Constitution of the United States," nobody really believes that either. Not the Congress, not the Supreme Court, and certainly not recent presidents of the United States, whose names I won't mention here. We're way too sophisticated for that engraved-in-stone, Moses-down-from-the-mountain-with-the-tablets stuff. But the minute you accepted our cockamamie notion of a "living Constitution," with its reliance upon various emanations of penumbras of riddles wrapped inside of enigmatic sphinxes, your goose was cooked.

That's why it's high time—if it's not already too late—for Corollary No. 1: *Get back to first principles: the Declaration of Independence and the Constitution.* They're all that's standing between you and either anarchy or dictatorship, and the sooner you figure that out, the quicker you'll bring the eternal battle between your guy and our Big Fella back into some kind of weird, Buddhistic, Asian-fusion harmonic equilibrium.

So that's why I'm leading you on this brief but pungently simple look at the two most important documents in American history, the Declaration of Independence and the Constitution; while you were madly pulling the lever for "progressivism," we've been diligently trying to take them away from you, change their meaning, or even reverse it. Both documents can save your republic, if you can keep it, as that guy who went and flew a kite famously said. I'm not a lawyer, so I'm not as well versed in the arcana of the minutiae as some of the real shysters out there. Still, that isn't going to stop me from offering my two kopecks. This is supposed to be a citizens' republic, remember, not a country dominated by all my pals who attended Harvard Law and now view themselves as a kind of secular priest class, interpreting the Law for the amazement and limited edification of the rubes. And, as long as you believe that, you're in real trouble.

THE DECLARATION: TIME FOR ANOTHER AMERICAN REVOLUTION

I'm only briefly going to address the famous part, the section they used to make even us long-suffering atheist kids actually memorize in school, like it was a speech by Chairman Mao or something. You remember the tune:

> When, in the course of human events, it becomes necessary for one people to dissolve the political bonds which have connected them with another, and to assume among the powers of the earth, the separate and equal station to which the laws of nature and of nature's God entitle them, a decent respect to the opinions of mankind requires that they should declare the causes which impel them to the separation.
>
> We hold these truths to be self-evident, that all men are created equal, that they are endowed by their Creator with certain unalienable rights, that among these are life, liberty and the pursuit of happiness. That to secure these rights, governments are instituted among men, deriving their just powers from the consent of the governed. That whenever any form of government becomes destructive to these ends, it is the right of the people to alter or to abolish it . . .

Whoa! We don't like to hear that talk about abolishing government, because if this government of ours really was abolished we'd all have to get real jobs, and we're not about to do that. So that's why we fight—symbolically, of course. You read this stuff about "dissolving bonds" and even if you are as dumb as we think you are, you might start getting ideas about dissolving—oh, I don't know, the Democratic Party, just like the Russians did to the Communist Party after the distressing collapse of "socialism in one country." Anyway, this Jeffersonian document goes on to say:

> . . . and to institute new government, laying its foundation on such principles and organizing its powers in such form, as to them shall seem most likely to effect their safety and happiness. Prudence, indeed, will dictate that governments long established should not be changed for light and transient causes; and accordingly all experience hath shown that mankind are more disposed to suffer, while evils are sufferable, than to right themselves by abolishing the forms to which they are accustomed. But when a long train of abuses and usurpations, pursuing invariably the same object evinces a design to reduce them under absolute despotism, it is their right, it is their duty, to throw off such government, and to provide new guards for their future security.
>
> Such has been the patient sufferance of these colonies; and such is now the necessity which constrains them to alter their former systems of government. The history of the present King of Great Britain is a history of repeated injuries and usurpations, all having in direct object the establishment of an absolute tyranny over these states. To prove this, let facts be submitted to a candid world.

"Repeated injuries and usurpations" could just as easily describe our bracingly consistent MO for the past couple centuries, if you ask me, but putting that aside for a moment, the cure for what ails you lies in the next stretch, the stuff you never memorized, and probably have never even read. It's an eighteenth-century laundry list of all beefs that the colonists had against Good King George III, and it's amazing to look back on it now because a lot of them sound suspiciously like the same beefs you people have today. Think of what follows as the halftime speech being given by the coach of a scrappy underdog team as he fires up his troops to go out there and win one for the Gipper!

He has refused his assent to laws, the most wholesome and necessary for the public good.

We've flipped this one around on its head, but the effect on you is the same. Rather than refusing assent, we enthusiastically shoved volumes of new laws down your collective throats, so hard that you're gagging on them right now. We've packed as many of your state houses as we can with our drones and trolls and their taxpayer-supported staffs, whose numbers are as uncountable as the sands on the beach or the stars in the sky and yet growing. Every day we churn out new laws, new regulations, new executive orders, new edicts, new initiatives, all of which are designed to do one or both of the following: restrict your freedom and cost you money. And yet you sit there and take it.

He has forbidden his governors to pass laws of immediate and pressing importance, unless suspended in their operation till his assent should be obtained; and when so suspended, he has utterly neglected to attend to them.

Would that this were still true! The idea of a sovereign too busy playing golf, going on "date nights" with his wife at enormous taxpayer expense, choppering off to Camp David as often as possible, and careening around the country waving his hands and making increasingly ineffectual speeches while the state goes to hell in a handcart sounds like paradise even to us.

He has called together legislative bodies at places unusual, uncomfortable, and distant from the depository of their public records, for the sole purpose of fatiguing them into compliance with his measures.

Now this sounds like a good idea for your side, and my recommendation is that you see it King George's way (III, not Bush II). Imagine taking our legislative solons away from such gangland cribs as Washington, D.C., Trenton, Jefferson City, Sacramento, and Albany and mak-

ing them travel to some hick town in the middle of nowhere, sadly de-
priving them of their bars, cat houses, and bagman drops. Round up the
usual suspects and drag their tails off to Gary, Indiana, or another of
your dumpy little burgs, and make them stay there; a couple of days of
that and they'll be ready to repeal the entire Bill of Rights, or outlaw the
practice of psychiatry, or restore the Constitution, whichever comes
first.

> He has dissolved representative houses repeatedly, for oppos-
> ing with manly firmness his invasions on the rights of the people.

Again, you ought to take a leaf out of Crazy George's book and dis-
solve various legislative bodies, just for the hell of it. After all, you can't
do any worse than the venal and acquisitive Klepto-Klowns we already
have in there.

> He has obstructed the administration of justice, by refusing
> his assent to laws for establishing judiciary powers.

Now, this one is rich. Here you guys have been bitching about the
out-of-control judiciary and good King George was practically handing
what you wanted on the same silver platter that once bore the head of
Mary Queen of Scots and you complain about it?

> He has made judges dependent on his will alone, for the
> tenure of their offices, and the amount and payment of their
> salaries.

So what? That's how you do it, when you're doing it right.

> He has erected a multitude of new offices, and sent hither
> swarms of officers to harass our people, and eat out their sub-
> stance.

Okay, you probably have a beef here. If there's one thing we lefties
know how to do, it's to send out swarms of officers to harass your peo-

ple, eat out your substance, and then have the gall to ask for more. What's ours is ours and what's yours is not only negotiable (our old position) but outright forfeit (our new, more nuanced stance). In fact, swarming is one of the things we do best: when we see an opening, whether it's the New Frontier, or the Great Society, or the New Covenant (remember that one? neither do I) or Hope and Change, we give it all we got. So should you.

For taking away our charters, abolishing our most valuable laws, and altering fundamentally the forms of our governments:

For suspending our own legislatures, and declaring themselves invested with power to legislate for us in all cases whatsoever.

What all these antiquated kvetches basically boil down to is this: it sucks being on the short end of a political argument, especially when the other guy's got all the troops and the firepower. So start the counterrevolution already, why don't you?

He has abdicated government here, by declaring us out of his protection and waging war against us.

Don't get me started . . . We long ago declared your side out of our protection and have openly waged war against you, except you were too dumb to notice. Osama spent years of yelling at you and issuing *fatwas* and blowing things up in Africa before he got the notion to fly those planes into the World Trade Center—and then you finally figured out you were at war with an ideological movement, not just a bunch of street punks that the New York City Police Department could use the plunger on. Naturally, we immediately set about disabusing you of this conviction almost immediately.

He has plundered our seas, ravaged our coasts, burned our towns, and destroyed the lives of our people.

Yup.

He is at this time transporting large armies of foreign merce-
naries to complete the works of death, desolation and tyranny,
already begun with circumstances of cruelty and perfidy scarcely
paralleled in the most barbarous ages, and totally unworthy of
the head of a civilized nation.

I think you call that "amnesty," right?

He has constrained our fellow citizens taken captive on the
high seas to bear arms against their country, to become the exe-
cutioners of their friends and brethren, or to fall themselves by
their hands.

Except that now our own citizens voluntarily travel across the high
seas and take up arms against their country, everybody from Johnny
Jihad in California to the Somalis in Minneapolis who turn up on the
battlefields in the Middle East, al-Qaeda–trained and ready to punch out
their fellow Americans. And why shouldn't they? After all, they've emigrated to a country that tells them, thanks to us and our pet historians,
like the late Howard Zinn, that patriotism is a vice, not a virtue; that
America deserves every bad thing she gets, and still has a lot of payback
coming to her.

We, therefore, the representatives of the United States of America, in General Congress, assembled, appealing to the Supreme
Judge of the world for the rectitude of our intentions, do, in the
name, and by the authority of the good people of these colonies,
solemnly publish and declare, that these united colonies are, and of
right ought to be free and independent states; that they are absolved
from all allegiance to the British Crown, and that all political connection between them and the state of Great Britain, is and ought to
be totally dissolved; and that as free and independent states, they
have full power to levy war, conclude peace, contract alliances, establish commerce, and to do all other acts and things which independent states may of right do. And for the support of this
declaration, with a firm reliance on the protection of Divine Provi-

dence, we mutually pledge to each other our lives, our fortunes and our sacred honor.

Except for the God part, pretty stirring stuff. But you wouldn't have the guts to do it again, would you? Even though the circumstances you now find yourselves in eerily and nearly exactly parallel the plight of those First White Interlopers back in the eighteenth century. So, in order to prevent something like—oh, I don't know, a huge monolithic but brain-dead bureaucracy from taking over the country and making the lives of its free citizens miserable—they cobbled something together you like to call your Constitution.

THE CONSTITUTION: EVERYTHING YOU NEED TO KNOW YOU LEARNED IN 1791

For all the oceans of ink that have been spilled interpreting it, reinterpreting it, amending it, and, best of all, even overturning portions of it, the Constitution is a ridiculously simple and straightforward document. Even with twenty-seven mostly useless amendments added, it still runs barely eight thousand words, which is about half your average screenplay, such as *Terminator Salvation*, but funnier. What's more, the commentary three of the Founders provided in *The Federalist Papers*—Hamilton, Madison, and John Jay—as they attempted to sell this crazy idea of limited self-government is remarkable for the clarity of their writing and their dedication to their ideals. Gaia only knows what might have happened had Alexander Hamilton continued to proselytize on behalf of "freedom," but luckily the first Democratic Vice President, Aaron Burr, put a stop to that nonsense by shooting him dead in Weehawken, and that was the end of that.

Face it: we killed your republic before it was hardly even born. God bless a political party's right to choose!

Still, writing in sentences so simple that it takes a Yale-educated federal judge to willfully misunderstand them, the Framers laid out the basic principles of life in a state where the government leaves you alone. As far as Hamilton et al. were concerned, it wasn't the job of the federal government—or any government—to take care of you and your family, to ensure not just equality of opportunity but equality of results, and to divvy the nation up into aggrieved and competing ethnic groups. Instead, it was as easy as one, two, three:

Article One, and therefore by implication the most important one, concerns the Legislature: *All legislative Powers herein granted shall be vested in a Congress of the United States, which shall consist of a Senate and House of Representatives.* That's pretty much it. Sure, the document goes on to explain the qualifications (age twenty-five for the House, thirty for the Senate, residency and citizenship requirements), but the key thing here is that you wingnuts should govern yourselves through the simple mechanism of electing a whole new House of Representatives every two years, with the senators being selected by the state legislatures, their terms staggered so that every two years one-third of them can be replaced. Have you ever heard of anything so crazy?

The Constitution is quite clear on what the enumerated powers of Congress are. Notice that nowhere on this list is the Environmental Protection Agency, the Central Intelligence Agency, or the Department of Education—oversights that thankfully have since been corrected. Anyway, here's the list of stuff that Congress gets to do, right there in Section 8:

> The Congress shall have Power to lay and collect Taxes, Duties, Imposts and Excises, to pay the Debts and provide for the common Defence and general Welfare of the United States; but all Duties, Imposts and Excises shall be uniform throughout the United States;
>
> To borrow money on the credit of the United States;
>
> To regulate Commerce with foreign Nations, and among the several States, and with the Indian Tribes;
>
> To establish an uniform Rule of Naturalization, and uniform Laws on the subject of Bankruptcies throughout the United States;
>
> To coin Money, regulate the Value thereof, and of foreign Coin, and fix the Standard of Weights and Measures;
>
> To provide for the Punishment of counterfeiting the Securities and current Coin of the United States;
>
> To establish Post Offices and Post Roads;

To promote the Progress of Science and useful Arts, by secur-
ing for limited Times to Authors and Inventors the exclusive
Right to their respective Writings and Discoveries;

To constitute Tribunals inferior to the supreme Court;

To define and punish Piracies and Felonies committed on the
high Seas, and Offenses against the Law of Nations;

To declare War, grant Letters of Marque and Reprisal, and
make Rules concerning Captures on Land and Water;

To raise and support Armies, but no Appropriation of Money
to that Use shall be for a longer Term than two Years;

To provide and maintain a Navy;

To make Rules for the Government and Regulation of the
land and naval Forces;

To provide for calling forth the Militia to execute the Laws of
the Union, suppress Insurrections and repel Invasions;

To provide for organizing, arming, and disciplining the Militia, and for governing such Part of them as may be employed in
the Service of the United States, reserving to the States respectively, the Appointment of the Officers, and the Authority of
training the Militia according to the discipline prescribed by
Congress;

To exercise exclusive Legislation in all Cases whatsoever, over
such District (not exceeding ten Miles square) as may, by Cession
of particular States, and the acceptance of Congress, become the
Seat of the Government of the United States, and to exercise like
Authority over all Places purchased by the Consent of the Legislature of the State in which the Same shall be, for the Erection of
Forts, Magazines, Arsenals, dock-Yards, and other needful Buildings; And

To make all Laws which shall be necessary and proper for carrying into Execution the foregoing Powers, and all other Powers
vested by this Constitution in the Government of the United
States, or in any Department or Officer thereof.

That last line is where we, the Devil in the Details, came in . . .

Article Two is all about the executive branch. That's the President to
you: *The executive Power shall be vested in a President of the United States of*

America. He also gets to be the "Commander in Chief of the Army and Navy of the United States, and of the Militia of the several States, when called into the actual Service of the United States." Plus he gets to make treaties, with the advice and consent of the Senate. The end.

Article Three, the judicial branch, is even shorter. Here's basically all you need to know:

> The judicial Power of the United States, shall be vested in one supreme Court, and in such inferior Courts as the Congress may from time to time ordain and establish. The Judges, both of the supreme and inferior Courts, shall hold their Offices during good Behavior, and shall, at stated Times, receive for their Services a Compensation which shall not be diminished during their Continuance in Office.

Couldn't be simpler, really. And what are the Supreme Court's actual enumerated powers, you ask? Turns out—almost none! Tell that to Learned Hand—

> The judicial Power shall extend to all Cases, in Law and Equity, arising under this Constitution, the Laws of the United States, and Treaties made, or which shall be made, under their Authority; to all Cases affecting Ambassadors, other public Ministers and Consuls; to all Cases of admiralty and maritime Jurisdiction; to Controversies to which the United States shall be a Party; to Controversies between two or more States; between a State and Citizens of another State; between Citizens of different States; between Citizens of the same State claiming Lands under Grants of different States, and between a State, or the Citizens thereof, and foreign States, Citizens or Subjects.

This was modified slightly by the Eleventh Amendment with some babble about lawsuits "commenced or prosecuted against one of the United States by Citizens of another State, or by Citizens or Subjects of any Foreign State," but otherwise that's about it. Not a word about abortion, which continues to puzzle me since I was raised thinking that

A Woman's Right to Choose was as fundamental a cornerstone to this almost great republic as Plymouth Rock.

The rest of the Constitution is boilerplate stuff about the relationships of the states, how the feds guarantee each state "a Republican form of government," which I didn't like the sound of at all until one of my professors at Columbia explained to me the archaic meaning of the term, the amendment process, debts, oaths, supremacy, ratification, and then it was signed, sealed, and delivered and the wrap party began until somebody said, "Hey, wait a minute . . ."

And so the Bill of Rights was born. Those are the first ten amendments to you, and they have caused our side no end of grief since. In fact, it's safe to say that we are now pretty much at war with all of them, including the once sacred First Amendment, behind which we hid for decades. You know all about the Big Ten, so there's no need to go into detail here, except to observe their blunt language, which basically amounts to saying to the nascent Hercules-in-his-cradle: NO!

> 1st Amendment: *Congress **shall make no law** respecting an establishment of religion, or prohibiting the free exercise thereof; or abridging the freedom of speech, or of the press; or the right of the people peaceably to assemble, and to petition the Government for a redress of grievances.*
>
> 2nd Amendment: *A well regulated Militia, being necessary to the security of a free State, the right of the people to keep and bear Arms, **shall not be infringed**.*
>
> 3rd Amendment: stuff about soldiers in your living room. They were, like, totally against it.
>
> 4th Amendment: *The right of the people to be secure in their persons, houses, papers, and effects, against unreasonable searches and seizures, **shall not be violated,** and no Warrants shall issue, but upon probable cause, supported by Oath or affirmation, and particularly describing the place to be searched, and the persons or things to be seized.*
>
> 5th Amendment (we love this one): ***No person** shall be held to answer for a capital, or otherwise infamous crime, unless on a presentment or indictment of a Grand Jury, except in cases arising in the land or naval forces, or in the Militia, when in actual service in time of War or public danger; nor shall any person be subject for the same offense to be twice put*

in jeopardy of life or limb; nor shall be compelled in any criminal case to be a witness against himself, nor be deprived of life, liberty, or property, without due process of law; **nor shall private property be taken for public use, without just compensation.**

6th Amendment: stuff about speedy trials and the right to cross-examine witnesses. Whatever.

7th Amendment: trial by jury if the beef is worth more than twenty bucks. Got no problem with it. Everybody's got twenty bucks, if only in returnable bottles and cans.

8th Amendment: *Excessive bail shall* **not** *be required,* **nor** *excessive fines imposed,* **nor cruel and unusual punishments inflicted.** That last bit sure has been helpful to our side, since we've been able to roll it back from public hangings to mental distress.

9th Amendment: *The enumeration in the Constitution, of certain rights, shall* **not be construed to deny or disparage** *others retained by the people.*

And . . . wait for it:

10th Amendment: *The powers* **not** *delegated to the United States by the Constitution,* **nor** *prohibited by it to the States,* **are reserved to the States respectively, or to the people.**

There it is, hiding in plain sight all along. Every single one of our regulatory schemes, power grabs, aggrandizements, rules, regulations, orders, bureaucracies, departments, and civil service ranks are barnacles on the hull of the good ship *United States of America* that can be and should be challenged by the several states, as the Founders might say. Unless the Constitution no longer means what its plain language says it does—and we've had top people working to convince you otherwise for decades and decades—the real power in Amerikkka lies with the states, which can more or less tell the feds where to get off.

You've all been witness to the greatest unconstitutional power grab in the history of the world, grabbed by the very federal government the Constitution was meant to bind and control. And you let it happen, bit by bit, increment by increment, each diminution of your sovereignty acceded to (because, after all, it was the "right" thing to do), until today Leviathan is the unchallenged King of Beasts. Congratulations.

So what are you going to do about it? Which brings us to Corollary No. 2: *Time to clean up the amendments—and perhaps call a Constitutional Convention.*

The Constitution provides for its own updating, but after looking at some of the provisions and, especially, the amendments that, even with good intentions, shattered some of its foundational principles, maybe it's time for you *schmegeggs* to take a page from our playbook and get into that whole "living, breathing" thing. Only this time, make it live and breathe and suck the oxygen out of every single one of the deleterious amendments we've foisted on you in the name of "progress" over the past century or so.

Here's my short list: *the Progressive Era amendments Sixteen, Seventeen, and Eighteen.* One of which is already gone, which leaves only two to go.

Amendment Sixteen: the income tax (1913). The camel's nose under Hussein's—or whatever the President of the United States is currently named—tent. Once the principle was established that the federal government could reach into the pocket of each and every citizen and "lay and collect taxes on incomes, from whatever source derived, without apportionment among the several States," you were done, and so was your precious republic. Because that meant a vast expansion of the feds' police powers, in the form of the IRS; it mean a gross rearrangement of the relationship of the citizen to the federal government, and, most important, it *presumed that every citizen of the United States was guilty until proven innocent*—that he and she would have to declare, subject to government inspection, exactly how much income they had made, to the penny, during the filing year. Note that this did not include the rapacious fortunes of the Robber Barons, or the amassed moolah of the titans of the Gilded Age—no, this was a "progressive" amendment designed for one thing and one thing only: to prevent the emerging middle class, which made its living via "income" rather than "capital gains" or "inherited fortunes" or "gangster swag." From this black day in February 1913—with the great Gangs of New York running free while the former president of Princeton (another guilty white Southerner) rushed into the sweaty embrace of a bunch of German and Eastern European social philosophers—your fate was sealed. And until you repeal this *philosophical* abomination, and replace it with the Flat Tax or the Fair Tax or the Your Aunt Hilda Tax, you are doomed. It's Beggar Thy Neighbor, played by plutocrats, pitting the proles against the *schlimazels*, forever and ever amen.

Amendment Seventeen: direct election of senators (1913). The Founders wanted the Senate to be composed of senior statesmen, wise in the ways of the world, who were grounded in their states and did not necessarily see a President of the United States staring back at them in the shaving mirror every morning. They were supposed to be two equal voices, representing the several states; today, they're two equally plausible candidates for the next presidential election. In other words, they no longer serve their states, they serve themselves. And in case you doubt me, I have two words for you: John Kerry. What harm would it do for you lot to return the Senate to what it was supposed to be, a check on the hot passions of the House? Besides, think of the money you'd save.

Amendment Eighteen: Prohibition (1919). For which we bless the sainted Woody Wilson every day. The amendment that created Gangland, brought Tammany Hall to its fullest flower, and basically destroyed the United States of her Founding Fathers' vision. Like its sister amendment, the Nineteenth (1920), Prohibition was a backlash against a changing America, as the WASP establishment criminalized the simple pleasures of the Germans, the Irish, and the Italians who liked nothing better than to relax after a hard day's backbreaking labor digging the subways and water tunnels of New York with a beer, a shot of whiskey, or a glass of wine. Talk about fundamental change! WASP America thought it could keep down and control the wretched refuse of Europe's teeming shores, but it just kept on coming and eventually took over the place. No wonder the Eighteenth Amendment was repealed early in the first Roosevelt administration (1933). Still, the principle was established: that the federal government has a right to interfere in every aspect of your life.

The Nineteenth Amendment, women's suffrage, I'm not going near if I know what's good for me, which I do.

The point is, make Repeal your watchword, and brandish two of the forgotten amendments in the Bill of Rights—the Ninth and Tenth—as your sword. Although we've done our best to make you forget about them, make you think they are as outdated as the one about quartering soldiers, they're really among the most important ideas of the lot, and certainly equal to the famous First Amendment. Because what they basically say to the feds is this: this far, and no farther. You can add a few more amendments under the constitutional process (and even some of those were rushed through under, shall we say, hinky circumstances), but these are your enumerated powers, and everything else is reserved to the people and the states. A charter of negative liberties? You bet!

Completely unacceptable to the Left, of course, so we set to work on the Bill of Rights with a vengeance. We're like the annoying kids who won't take "no" for an answer, and instead constantly keep wheedling, testing the boundaries, hoping there's some give in that "no," some part of "no" that actually means "yes," and we deployed our crack legions of lawyers to push and probe while our crack legions of editorialists questioned and wondered and what-if'ed until after a century of this sort of hammering, some of these immortal principles began to crack.

We couldn't demolish the First Amendment, because we needed that one for a time, needed it to undermine the entire foundation that gave it birth. But we went right after the Second, especially during the gangland wars of the 1930s, when we used the tool of public revulsion over the St. Valentine's Day Massacre to get our stooges to pass the National Firearms Act of 1934 and our pet goats on the Supreme Court to see it our way in *U.S. vs. Miller* in 1939, which was the first time the court had ever examined the so-called "right to keep and bear arms." Shall not be infringed? Despite two recent Supreme Court rulings protecting individual ownership of firearms, watch us try!

From that point on, we basically stopped attacking the Bill of Rights per se, and instead turned our attention to an end run, which was simply ignoring the Constitution our lawmakers and executives were sworn to uphold and defend, and going our merry way with a vast expansion of the federal beat. World War II certainly helped, and though there might have been some small pushback in the 1950s, by the time the Johnson-Nixon administration was in power, there was no stopping Leviathan.

So if I were you, I'd start challenging the entire legal and regulatory structure post-1932 and I'd use the Ninth and Tenth Amendments to do it. Yes, it's an impossible task, but so was bringing down the United States of America, and look how close to succeeding at that we are! You've got lawyers on your side—stop using them defensively and sic them on us in full, teeth-bared attack mode. Every "unconstitutional" extension of federal power should be challenged in court and in the media—*every time*. And if we start barking, just say you're doing it for the children.

It's a measure of how far you've fallen when your best weapon against us is the basic law of the land, a law we've so corrupted and marginalized as to have rendered it almost moot at this point. Which, of course, *was* the point.

RULE NO. 7:
Adapt the Time-Honored Conservative Message for a New Kind of America and a New Kind of American

The demographic changes unleashed by the Immigration and Nationality Act of 1965, part of the late Senator Ted Kennedy's immutable legacy, are only now being felt. While in retrospect they seem inevitable, Senator Kennedy explicitly denied their likelihood:

> Contrary to the charges in some quarters, [the bill] will not inundate America with immigrants from any one country or area. . . . In the final analysis, the ethnic pattern of immigration under the proposed measure is not expected to change as sharply as the critics seem to think. . . . The bill will not flood our cities with immigrants. It will not relax the standards of admission. It will not cause American workers to lose their jobs.

Okay, so it didn't quite work out that way? So what?

Nativism—or as we call it out here in Hollywood, "jingoism"—is the sin most easily attached to the Right by the Left (although historically, we've been far more guilty of it, from the Klan on). And it's something we've been trying to pin on you since time immemorial. But by embracing the changing demographics—by treating non-European Americans as *Americans*, instead of various victim voting blocs whose votes must be bought and whose tender sensibilities must at all times be appeased through the enforcement mechanism of political correctness, abetted by the media's "narrative"—the Right has a huge opportunity to put paid to the Left's victimization meme once and for all. There-fore—

Corollary No. 1: *Put your money where your principles are and demonstrate that you welcome new-look America—as long as it stays America. Because either all men are created equal, or they aren't.*

By rights, you wingnuts should be a shining testament to the hypocrisy of our stated (although, in practice, nearly nonexistent) lib-eral virtues, the famous twins of fairness and tolerance. But, instead, you've let us project all of our many and manifold sins upon you for lo these last two centuries. If you'd ever learn how to articulate the princi-ples that created the United States in the first place—and that animate you now—in a language anyone, no matter their country of origin, can understand, you'd be dangerous. Nativism has been a scourge since the Irish started arriving in large numbers in the mid-nineteenth century, so it's long past time you Rotarians started displaying your faith in both the adaptive and the adoptive nature of this country. The country hasn't changed, but the ethnic makeup of the populace has, and will continue to do so. So either you believe in the "created equal" jazz, or you don't. Time to put your money where your mouths are.

And this is also how you're finally going to be able to lose that "racist" meme once and for all. As I've shown you, the real racists in this fight are us; the Father of Lies is to hypocrisy born and if you buy my theory that we consistently accuse you of what we're either thinking or actually doing, then you understand the truth of Rochefoucauld's dic-tum that "hypocrisy is the homage that vice pays to virtue." Frankly, if we were left to run things without any interference from you, we'd have the very Platonic form of a police state, in which rich liberals like me and my friends—philosopher-kings, the kind of people this country needs, and who ought to be protected—would live peaceful, contented lives, dabbling at professions like teaching and politics that don't really require much in the way of an education or even effort. We'd live in a world in which artists like me were publicly supported at taxpayer ex-pense—the example of Jean Sibelius in Finland comes to mind: worked hard, became famous, got a government stipend and then basically never composed another tune as long as he lived. Where a seat in state or na-tional government was tantamount to a lifetime sinecure (we're almost there now), and august solons could swan about, fretting over the plight of the Little Guy and then flying home for the weekend to oversee their vineyards in the Napa Valley.

And as for the Little Guy—well, that would be mostly people of color, hired as government employees for make-work projects or to sit in some air-conditioned office all day, watching television and pretending to work. The rest of them—we'd have to carefully calibrate the number so the tax base would be large enough—would either slave away all day at dead-end jobs, turn to crime, or . . . something. We don't care. Just as long as the cops can continue to protect us from our historic relationship with the proletariat, we're fine with it. After all, they don't live in our neighborhoods. They just vote like they do.

That's the great mystery and wonder of it all, of course—why they vote like they do—which is why you fools have a golden, hell, platinum opportunity to siphon off a huge voting bloc that you traditionally eschew: minorities, who soon enough will be majorities. Teddy's little immigration bill made that inevitable, and soon enough that day will be here. But remember this—most of you conservatives vote for the party that was founded on freeing the slaves! You used to own their votes, until we snatched them away from you during the Johnson-Nixon administration; as Nixon flipped the Solid South from Democratic to Republican, blacks abandoned their traditional home in the GOP on the theory that the enemy of my enemy was my friend, and never came back.

Still, that's no reason for you to surrender to our Brezhnev Doctrine. What we liberals have done to the black community since the 1960s should be a national scandal: though our vast panoply of soul-crushing (now *there's* a concept!) social programs, enforced by unelected bureaucracies, and a public school system that makes the Western Front in World War I look like just another day in the trenches, we have destroyed black families (and we're working on white families now), encouraged what used to be called antisocial behavior, celebrated the worst regarding matters of mores, and generally turned a culture upside down, so that it is now ruled by "gangstas." We swooped in, like drug dealers, hooking the people on hopelessness, and at the same time promising to cure the very diseases we had spread around. The beauty of our plan, something we learned from the crooked politicians of the Chicago Machine and Tammany Hall, was that the cure for misery was always more misery, to keep the people in a state of permanent desperation and illusion, a never-ending cycle, always spiraling downward. Sheer genius, really.

The black middle class has of course fled the old neighborhoods, just like all the other groups before it. And what have we replaced it with? Metal detectors.

So that's where you should be attacking us. Pin the tail on the donkey: you need a major talent recruitment drive, and one of the places it should start is at the historically black colleges like Howard, Morehouse, Bennett, etc. The great ones tend to be in the South, where the bulk of America's African-American population lived until World War II, and it is there, in the old Solid South, where the black conservative renewal is likely to begin. Nobody likes to be patronized, and we are nothing if not patronizing, so now's the time to act on decades of resentment.

You have an audience that's very receptive to your message. For half a century, blacks in America have had their passions inflamed—by us, and by "us" I mean the editorial pages of *The New York Times*—even as barriers have fallen. Race hustlers have made whole careers out of, in effect, preying on their own people, using them as props in their ongoing shakedown operations of just about anything in America that's still breathing and has a penny in its pockets. There's a tide of honest resentment out there just waiting to be tapped, and the only thing that's holding it back is the media's mind control over the issue: any black that steps off the plantation is hit and hit hard. Just ask Condoleezza Rice, Justice Clarence Thomas, and just about any other black conservative (or even moderate) who dares not applaud when the race card is played. In a just universe, black intellectuals such as Thomas Sowell and Shelby Steele would be on the *Times* editorial board.

So offer them more places at the table—offer them places at the head of the table. Remember how a Republican president, Teddy Roosevelt, electrified the black community when he invited Booker T. Washington to dine with him? And why? Not because the old Rough Rider was expiating collective guilt. On the contrary: TR was celebrating Washington's remarkable *individual* achievement—as a black man, yes, but as a *man* first and foremost. Washington's message of self-help and self-reliance has been out of favor practically since the founding of the National Association for the Advancement of Colored People, which was Du Bois's baby, but it's long past time that Washington be given his due. An aggressive recruitment effort, starting at the elite black colleges but also extending to the ranks of black military officers and enlisted men, can turn into a bumper crop of candidates before you know it. But, whatever you do, avoid the whiff of tokenism—that's our job. Naming a failed candidate like Michael Steele to be the head of the Republican National Committee was a blatant bit of post-Obama me-tooism that everybody could see through. Next time, think it through, and get it right. But, whatever you do—

Corollary No. 2: ***Mean it.***

Either you're all in this together or you're not; either this unprecedented experiment works or it doesn't; either America succeeds as humanity's last, best hope, or she's ours—another failed state, having fallen victim to "immutable" truths about humanity: that we really can't just all get along on our own and we need Big Brother to act as the enforcer. The country may be changing demographically but acceptance of the bedrock principles of the United States and its Founders must be universal and nonnegotiable. Conservatives need to return to the previous model, in place when great waves of immigration swept the country around the turn of the last century. Nobody gave a sucker an even break back then, and the newcomers were left pretty much to fend for themselves, to take care of their own and, most important, to get with the program. If America really is a state of mind, a collective dedication to the idea of individual rights, then what does it matter the country of origin?

So pay no attention to our victim model, which has been the only prism we've allowed you and the rest of the country through which to view race since we seized the Democratic Party in 1972. In fact, *explicitly reject* the victim model, and challenge others to do so. Americans love an underdog but nobody likes a loser, including minorities who have been on the short end of the stick for a long time. Stop tiptoeing, get down, and, while you're at it—

Corollary No. 3: ***Make new friends.***

There is no reason you racist reactionaries can't continue to make inroads among the Hispanics and the East Asians, including the Chinese, Vietnamese, Cambodians, and Filipinos, all of whom have strong streaks of self-reliance and intact families; and the subcontinental Indians, who have already begun to dominate entry-level capitalistic fields and whose numbers will only swell in the future, as they arrive here with a full command of English and well grounded in the traditions of British democracy. After all, who are the "Reagan Democrats" but the children of the white ethnics who took the Tammany shilling in the bad old days because it was shortest, swiftest, and most effective way up and out? You don't see many Irish on the Lower East Side of Manhattan anymore, nor Germans around Tompkins Square or in Yorkville. Things change, but *plus ça change* . . . they got replaced by more or less the same kinds of people.

So do what our Tammany forebears did, and co-opt them. Make them yours unto the generations—not by appealing to their basest survival instincts (nobody starves to death in America anymore, no matter what we and our media stooges try to tell you) but the better angels of their nature, which also happen to be singing in mighty choirs, not only to self-preservation, but to betterment and, ultimately, triumph. Triumph has been both the goal and the achievement of every ethnic group that has ever come to America. Because that's how you *Americans* roll when left to your own mysterious devices.

So go ahead and preach your corny gospel of Victory, not Victimhood. Take the hits from us when you boldly assert that there's nothing noble about being a Victim, that the fact that you were persecuted and sometimes murdered doesn't make you a saint—it only makes you a figure of pity. And pity is our job, right up there along with empathy, guilt, and fear. Proudly reject it. And if that's "blaming the victim," to use one of our favorite phrases, then so be it. We can always find more victims.

Anyway, you now have hordes of people entering the U.S. as legal immigrants who have nothing to do with the narrative. Since they're not white, none of them is crippled by "white guilt," unless we order our lickspittles in the media to turn them—like the Asians—into "honorary white people." When you stop to think about it, it's amazing how elastic our definition of "white" is, when it suits our ulterior motives. Which means you need to observe—

Corollary No. 4: *Expose the Left for who we really are*.

In the end, despite the relentless hammering from the anti-civilizational pseudo-intellectuals of the Frankfurt School and its American fellow travelers—as frustrating as we might find it—this country is strong enough to resist the importation of smug, and yet somehow victimized, Central European socialism as a response to its perceived (or imagined) problems. And once the larger population understands that our unctuous manner of speech, our assumed aura of "goodness," and our *faux* "concern" for anybody other than ourselves is just the same tired old act that fired the beast Marx as he howled in London; brought Mussolini and Hitler to power and sent Lenin to the Finland Station; seized China and North Korea and Cuba and half of Africa and condemned them to a life of squalor and misery and deceit and death—then I, for one, don't want to be on the business end of their wrath when it comes. Once it is frozen, personalized, and polarized, à la Alinsky, the black heart of Marxism will be as helpless as the Wizard of Oz—a deadly illusion that you will be well rid of, and will make me very happy I picked up that beachfront condo in Havana for a song. (I think it was a rousing, if slightly drunken chorus of "The East Is Red.")

And that, my stupid friends, is a day you should hasten. But, in order to do that, you're going to have to pay strict attention to our next rule:

RULE NO. 8:
Get Better Officers

Because, frankly, you've forgotten how to fight.

Let's face it, you haven't had a capable commander in chief since Reagan. I don't mean a real Commander in Chief, you know, like the one in the outmoded Constitution—who soon won't have any troops to order around, once we finish bankrupting the country for our "vital" social programs. I'm referring to the titular leader of your party, the guy in charge. And, brother, let me tell you: you should have followed Jesse's advice and "stayed out the Bushes."

I can hear you seething already. It's an article of faith among you mind-numbed Rushian Robots that Bush the Younger was one of the greatest presidents of all time, the man who fought back after 9/11. It's true that that pugnacity really fried us (although at the time we were secretly glad, because we were also secretly scared). But it's probably also true that even Al Gore, before he went crazy, would have done something similar—for which, of course, he'd still be a hero. Still, Shrub's approval ratings went through the roof after that little bullhorn moment of his, just as his old man's had after the quick victory against the paper tiger of Saddam Hussein's mighty "Elite Republican Guards" in the first Gulf War. But, naturally, being a Bush, GHWB didn't finish the job, which left the resolution of a million U.N. resolutions to the son for whom he had no particular hopes. Bingo! We had an issue: the "illegal" war in Iraq, fought at "Poppy" Bush's behest. In the moment of 43's greatest triumph, the seeds of his destruction had been well and truly sewn.

After the "we got him!" moment from the hapless Paul Bremer announcing Saddam's capture, it was all downhill. Donald Rumsfeld—once hailed by our chief mouthpiece, *The New York Times*, as a "rock star"—was quickly turned into the guy who invented the Maginot Line, and sent packing. Karl Rove, the "architect," "Bush's Brain," etc., was transformed into Lord Voldemort, the bastard idiot child of Lee Atwater and Pol Pot. Bush II watched his poll numbers sink under our relentless barrage and what did he do about it? Nothing! He didn't even order the arrest of those *Times* reporters—fences, really, like Mr. Peachum in *The Beggar's Opera*—who had been trafficking in stolen government secrets. And with that, we were off to the races. We are nothing if not opportunists, always looking out for the main chance.

Look, I have to admit there's nothing wrong with either the conservative or Republican base. Frankly, you guys terrify us, you and your damn fascist Tea Parties. Is there anything more frightening than seas of grandmothers waving American flags and singing "patriotic" songs? I don't think so. But the bozos driving your clown car need a complete upgrading in order to meet the new challenges of the twenty-first century, and one that the current crop of "leaders" is simply not up to. You morons need smart, ruthless, and savvy leadership, younger than your basic World War II veteran—hell, we've run a self-confessed draft dodger and a guy who quit on his comrades after a few months in Vietnam—not that there's anything wrong with that! If you're going to bring fruit salad and scrambled eggs to a knife fight, you might as well make sure your fighters are under fifty and are actually, you know, armed and ready to party.

You can't afford colorless Speakers of the House, or go-along, get-along collaborationists like most of your senators. You need officers who are going to inspire the troops, not dispirit them, commanders who've earned the love of their followers precisely by *not* crossing the aisle, instead preferring to stand on *principle*. These brave men and women are going to have to step out of the ranks and step up, and when they are attacked by our side—as they surely will be—you *must* defend them. Nobody wants to lead troops into battle and, halfway across the killing fields, find out he or she is all alone.

But how best to party like it's 1980? Glad you asked. Because this brings us to:

Corollary No. 1: *Turn in the direction of the skid.*

You know how, back east or in flyover country, when you're driving along some icy road and you hit the brakes and all of a sudden, instead of rolling to a controlled stop so you don't hit that nun leading twelve handicapped children over to the playground, your fabulous new Porsche starts heading off a cliff instead? So naturally you whip the steering wheel in the other direction, trying desperately to salvage something of the six-figure investment that you just made off your agent's word that Paramount is really, really interested in your new script, but what happens? You keep spinning out in the same damn direction! When what you should have done is to steer *into* the skid, regain control of the vehicle, stopping for the nuns and the little cripples, and then offering them all a ride to Knott's Berry Farm or wherever. In other words:

Do exactly the opposite of what your first instincts are.

After so many dreadful years in the post-FDR electoral wilderness, congressional Republicans more resemble battered wives than all-American men. They want to cover their heads and assume the fetal position in the hopes we'll stop pounding on them. But as the reaction to Sarah Palin—on both sides—demonstrated, the base is ready to follow its leaders into battle, *provided the leaders show that they really want to fight.* McCain's finest moment was his acceptance speech, in which he exhorted the audience to fight with him. Unfortunately, his lust for aisle crossing and the plaudits of his once-and-future buddies in the media got the better of him, so he kept his promise to lose—did he ever!—rather than challenge our definition of "dirty." By which we always mean asking questions about inconvenient truths that make our side uncomfortable and queasy. Stick to the issues! we shout, as our pet media poodles happily arf arf in the background. McCain was our perfect stealth candidate, a military man who didn't really want to fight.

If there's one lesson you need to learn from the debacle of 2008, it's this: never, ever, ever again nominate a man who tells you he'd rather lose honorably than punch our lights out.

Corollary No. 2: *Elections are not about programs, but principles.*

Hey, Dumbo—"programs" are our thing. Our candidates churn out books on "programs" all the time. They answer endless rounds of questions about "programs," helpfully posed by our plants in the media. In fact, we've made it seem that running for President or any other higher office is all about having the most ten-point plans, or five-year plans, or whatever. But what would you expect from a party that reveres FDR, but really hankers after the cultural revolutions and thousand-year plans that big-time statists of the past century so proudly hailed? We've got a "program" or a "plan" for everything, and you chumps have accepted the idiotic notion that one can plan further out than, say, five minutes (no wonder you've bought into the farce of "global warming"). Whereas those real military men you ought to be recruiting understand, like football coaches, the first rule of plans: that they go out the window the minute the first shot is fired. After which you rely upon the wisdom and guts of your commanders and the courage, training, and discipline of your troops to see you through to victory.

Principles are what counts. So stop trying to outdo us by rushing to the microphones with a silly plan to solve every social ill this side of halitosis whenever our pet frogs in the media croak about a new "crisis" in the daily news feed. In fact, forget about programs completely. Just say no! And if we call you out and demand to know—which we will, you can bet on that, it's part of the playbook—the details of your "plan," laugh and tell them to shove it and start talking about principles. To do otherwise is to accept our premises, which means you have already lost. Instead, stick to the big picture: liberty, self-reliance, faith, freedom. Those concepts are to us like a crucifix to a vampire, but heed not our squeals. Instead, keep brandishing your integrity and have the satisfaction of watching us collapse, writhing, on the floor into a puddle of putrescent malefaction, just like Christopher Lee in all those great Hammer movies.

To do otherwise displays weakness, and the last thing you want to do when dealing with us is to seem weak. So, keeping the principle in mind that we are bullies on the outside but cowards on the inside, let us now move to a discussion of how to fight.

One of your mistakes, as I noted earlier, is that for some weird reason you seem to think that being Mr. Nice Guy is the way to win friends, influence people, and once in a while succeed at the ballot box. We, of course, know better. As spiritual sons and daughters of the Society of Saint Tammany, we hold and keep a few principles firmly in mind:

- Promise the voters everything, deliver on almost nothing, but keep promising that the Promised Land is just around the next bend.
- Fan resentment as much as possible without actually starting a riot.
- If a riot starts, blame it on the other guy.
- Remember that some people are naturally credulous, some are naturally lazy, some are stupid, some are disadvantaged and content to remain that way, and some are born civil servants. Find these people and make them your constituents. If you take care of them, they will take care of you, pretty much in perpetuity. That's the deal.
- It is a surer thing to buy or steal an election than to win it.
- Never run an honest race if you can help it.
- Try to eliminate your opponent before the election. Challenge his filing papers, seek to have him removed from the ballot, get your friends in the media—especially if one of them is also your campaign manager—to call their lawyers and dig up any weapon to hand, including broken beer bottles, pool cues, and your opponent's sealed divorce records. Then tell people, more in sorrow than in anger, what a skunk he is.
- Always do it for the children, because even though your richer supporters don't have any kids, your poorer ones have millions of them.

In other words, a good general knows never to fight the battle on his enemy's turf, terrain, and terms unless he has no other choice. And yet your side constantly chooses to do so. You never grab the high ground when you can fight from the base of the hill or, better yet, the bottom of the ravine. You never marshal at least a three-to-one superiority of forces when you're on the attack—in fact, you hardly ever attack, de-

spite what we constantly refer to as the "right-wing smear machine"—
and you never take advantage of turf you know on which to conduct
your defensive measures. In short, your leaders stink.

So find and promote the folks who want and know how to fight.
Men and women who display the same kind of go-to-hell, don't-give-a-
damn lunacy as Barry Goldwater, who famously said, "Extremism in
the defense of liberty is no vice, and moderation in the pursuit of justice
is no virtue." Oh, how we shrieked at that! Goldwater was one of our
first experiments in word twisting and meaning imputation: we just
knew that he was one of those crazy John Birchers who saw Manchurian
Candidates under every bed. Why, he used the word "extremism"!
Whereas we, of course, are nothing if not moderate in all things except
our desire to eliminate you.

As history shows, you're very slow on the uptake. It's not for nothing that we call you—to your face!—the Stupid Party. You're like the
straight man in an old vaudeville show, the Washington Generals playing the Harlem Globetrotters, Gracie Allen to our George Burns. Let's
face it: your losing streak began with the very first Republican President, Lincoln, who fielded a stream of inept field commanders, one of
whom—that would be George McClellan—later ran against him in the
election of 1864 as the Democratic candidate. Sure, Lincoln fired him
and eventually replaced him with the man who would actually win the
war, Ulysses S. Grant, but McClellan took personal pique to a high
order of insolence: his party's Copperhead platform was frankly defeatist, as was his potential veep, a "peace" candidate named George
Pendleton. McClellan lost, Grant fought his way to Appomattox, and
Lincoln made the mistake of taking in a show at Ford's Theatre, but one
thing you can say for us Democrats: from the traitor Aaron Burr
through the "let's give up!" election of 1864, right up to our modern
day, we have distinguished ourselves by our treachery, our cowardice,
and our sheer inability to tell an enemy from a friend.

In other words, you lucked into Grant, one of the greatest fighting
men America has ever produced, as well as the greatest military man of
letters. And how did we repay his service during the War Between the
States? By slandering his memory—not as a general, because there are
some facts that even we can't argue with, but after his presidency, which

the country now remembers (if it remembers Grant at all, which is dubious) as having been marked by scandal and corruption. Yes sirree bob, we invented the template of the greedy fat cat Republicans and we hung it on the great war hero, at which point we realized that if we could get away with smearing the general who saved the Union, we could pretty much smear anybody. To add insult to injury, after his painful death from cancer, we even buried him on the Upper West Side.

Sometimes I ask myself why you make such unworthy opponents. Some of us feel it's an excess of Christianity—the turn-the-other-cheek kind, not the rabid, lunatic, wingnut Christian Right stuff. Some of us feel it's because you're a flyover kind of party, raised in parts of the country where lying, cheating, and stealing are actually frowned upon, if you can believe that; where a man's word is his bond, when for us not even our lawyer's signature on a piece of paper is worth anything; and where there's an innate sense of "decency," an openness, a willingness to let a stranger have his say, even if you don't know what the hell he's talking about. It may even be something as simple as the fact that you have real jobs making stuff, and don't eat, breathe, and sleep politics, while we've burrowed into the civil service and the think tanks, and thus have plenty of time on our hands. Whatever it is, what it adds up to is this: you're the marks and we're the hustlers, and you never seem to figure it out. And so you consistently bend over backward to see things our way. You accept at face value our most ludicrous positions, thinking like poor Neville Chamberlain that each of our demands is our Last, Best, and Final. Fools! For us, each accepted bargain only marks the start of a new round of demands; we are insidious, additive, and agglutinative, and our negotiations are really just war by other means.

Which brings me back to principles, and why they're important, and why you simply must defend them to the death if you expect to have any principles left. Since we have none, in any encounter we always have you at a disadvantage. Here's the way it works:

1. First we find an institution we wish to transform or destroy—for the sake of argument, let's take a private all-male country club. What could be more unegalitarian, and thus more evil, than that?

2. Following the Alinsky rule of demonizing the targeted object, we force you to accept our ridiculous premise that, despite the constitutional guarantee of the right to free association, there is something immoral or actually illegal about the club's rules excluding women. Forget that the club was legally founded, forget that nobody forces the men to join it, forget that women have never evinced much interest in this club, forget the fact that women have their own clubs—forget all that. All we need to do is find *one woman* to complain, to spin out a fantasy of oppression and lost opportunity to close that all-important business deal at the nineteenth hole, and you're doomed. As &\$@Bush&!# kind of put it once about the so-called "terrorists"—you have to be lucky every time. We only have to be lucky once.

3. And now that, after a century of peaceable operation, you're on the defensive, we hammer our complaints home until you finally accede to our demands, if only in the hope of making us shut up and go away. It may take some time, but in the end you always give in. And once you do, the battle is over, and now it's just, as we say in Hollywood, process.

4. Why? By making you concede something that by now looks small and petty—by taking your attention away from the big picture (the right to free assembly) and focusing it on lawyerly and/or hypothetical details, we've destroyed your faith in your own institution. Why not let women into the club? Naturally, we swear that we're not looking for any special treatment, that our gals just want to be one of the boys, and aside from the obvious accommodations needed in certain personal areas, *nothing whatsoever will change.*

5. And so the die is cast and the rest . . . well, you know the rest. By definition, the very nature of the club will change and soon it will no longer be the club it once was. And the best part is, you will never be able to admit it because, having accepted the premise of our argument in the first place, you have already taken revanchism off the table. In the end, it may be a better club, it may be a worse club, but it *won't be the*

same club. Which, after all, was the point of the exercise all along.

Our pal Oliver Stone put it best in his film *Wall Street*:

BUDD FOX: "Why do you need to wreck this company?"
GORDON GEKKO: "Because it's wreckable, all right?"

And why did this happen? Because you surrendered on principle. You let us browbeat you into thinking that principles don't matter, that our principles (or, rather, our battering rams and trebuchets disguised as principles) were superior not only to yours, but to those of all the generations that had come before you. We've gotten you not only to reject your own dogma, but to reject and vilify the wishes and desires and covenants of your forefathers. We've turned you into us, and convinced you that it was for your own good.

Principles. Once you abandon them, you're through.

This is what your new generals need to understand:

There are three elements in war. First, there is the *Objective*, which should always be Total Victory. Even if total victory is not possible or achievable in our lifetimes, that is still no reason not to strive for it. While it's probably true that in politics there is no such thing as permanent victory, there is always the permanent campaign, a state of never-ending war between Left and Right that makes the Islamic dichotomy between the *dar al-Islam* and the *dar al-Harb* look like a kindergarten squabble. You're looking for peaceful coexistence, we're looking for a hot lunch and you'll do just fine. You're in it not to win it, but to stave us off for as long as you can; we're in it to eliminate you, to turn your sympathy and your humanity against you. We will, as Khrushchev said, bury you. Or maybe cremate you, same difference. Or maybe just leave you lying on the battlefield, for the birds to peck out your eyes and the carrion-feeders to rend your flesh. It's all good.

So let me be clear: our nonnegotiable objective is the total transformation of the country formerly known as the United States of America into a cross between our previous failed state, the Union of Soviet Socialist Republics, and the modern European Union: a bloated bureaucrat-run Leviathan that punishes private industry, demoralizes the productive citizenry, and eventually taxes into oblivion everything that was once "good" and "decent" and "American" about your soon-to-be-former country. No matter how many times you temporarily beat us, we always come back, meaner, more vicious, and more determined than ever. You can learn a lot from us.

The second element is *Strategy*. If one of the goals of the Allies during World War II was to defeat Nazi Germany, then the strategy dictated an overwhelming force arrayed against the Wehrmacht, catching Germany in a colossal pincer movement from east and west until, squeezed to death, the capital, Berlin, finally fell and with it the seat of the National Socialist German Workers Party government. We have a very clear strategy: to hollow out the U.S.A. from within, attacking its intellectual foundations, distorting its history, hamstringing its institutions when not capturing and co-opting them outright, and finally causing the whole rotten structure to collapse of its own weight—at which point we will happily step in to administer the final *coup de grâce* and, like the psychiatrist in *Portnoy's Complaint*, say at last: "So. Now vee may perhaps to begin. Yes?"

Remember—the Russia of the czars did not fall to Lenin's Bolsheviks. You may recall it that way, and we may prefer that you do, but there was an intermediate step between the death of the Old Country and the birth of the New Soviet Man, and that was called the Kerensky government of the February Revolution of 1917, when Czar Nicholas abdicated, and Kerensky's socialists took control. Operating under the philosophy of "no enemies to the left," Kerensky allowed the more radical Bolsheviks to worm their way into the decayed institutions, so that when the armed October Revolution came later that year, the Russian people were suddenly confronted not simply with a new, liberationist regime but an entirely new form of government—communism. Talk about "fundamental change"—Kerensky was swept aside, Lenin took over, and the rest is glorious history. Think of this, in fact, as our model as we go about dismantling all your protective institutions: we're perfectly happy to let somebody else do the dirty work and then, when the center has entirely collapsed, we'll step in and fix your wagon. Permanently.

Strategy is crucial, and right now you have none, because you won't name your enemy, won't credit our lack of good faith, and won't take the necessary steps to put us down. Just look, for example, at the way you're trying to fight the so-called "War on Terror"—defensively and halfheartedly. The criminal Bush regime and its lackey neocons may have started out with the intention of rolling right into the belly of the beast, Iran, by surrounding it on both sides, Afghanistan and Iraq. But we put a stop to that as fast as we could!

It was completely pathetic, although not surprising, when the war petered out and the Bushies collapsed under the weight of super-top-secret *Vanity Fair* model Valerie Plame. Truman would have known how to end the war and with which weapons to do it, but your side wouldn't because, as in the country club example above, we'd rendered those weapons unusable because they are, to use one of our favorite words, "unthinkable."

"Unthinkable" is a very important word in our arsenal. An "unthinkable weapon" is best translated as: the most effective weapon you have, which is why we constantly lobby that the use of such weapons would be "unthinkable." Even today, many decades after the end of the Second World War, we are trying retroactively to render Truman's use of atomic weapons against Japan as unthinkable, for the simple reason that by using them, *he effectively ended the war in the Pacific* and, thus, World War II itself. Truman's decision in Japan spared a huge number of lives on both sides and brought the struggle between Japanese militarism and democracy to a conclusive end.

I'm sure you're cringing at my candor. Candor is one of those things, like rational thought, we simply had to eliminate in order to enforce political correctness, although we allow it to ourselves from time to time, just to make sure it still works. That's something I learned from my father, the sainted "Che" Kahane, who himself learned it from Professor Screwtape during his years at Lumumba University in Moscow, where he did a double major in Counterrevolutionary Studies and vodka. Might, as they say, has a way of making things right.

For example: When Scipio Aemilianus, known as Africanus the Younger, finally sorted out Carthage once and for all in the Third Punic War, what did he do? First, he heeded the fed-up Romans' rallying cry:

Carthago delenda est. (Carthage must be destroyed.) Next, he laid siege to the city that had been causing Rome problems for more than a century. The siege lasted nearly three years, at the end of which time Scipio decided that his exit strategy lay right through the middle of the city, which his troops then stormed and sacked. For the next two weeks or so, the Romans systematically burned Carthage to the ground, destroyed its harbor, then razed the rubble, and, according to legend, sowed salt where the great city of the Phoenicians had once stood. There was no Fourth Punic War because there was no more Carthage. Who says violence never solves anything!

Similarly, during World War II, we and the Brits bombed all the major cities of Germany into rubble. We firebombed Hamburg and Dresden, killing hundreds of thousands of civilians in the process. When our heroic Soviet comrades took Berlin, they fought block to block, street to street, house to house, floor to floor until there were no more German soldiers left to kill, just young teenaged boys with rifles, and our guys shot them too until General Jodl announced the unconditional German surrender. After which, the Allies executed him. (Naturally, we've managed to deploy our "revisionist" journalist historians on the Good War in order to raise "troubling questions" about whether it was all just racism, or some such.) Today, of course, that would be unthinkable, a "disproportionate response" to a country, Germany, that after all never attacked *us*.

The third element is *Tactics*. Think of this as the "community organizing" part of our program, made famous by the Apostle Saul, in which an army of agents provocateurs is unleashed on a trusting and unsuspecting populace, cloaked like Little Red Riding Hood's wolf, but even more avaricious. At the tactical level—the house-to-house fighting part of the program—no weapon is too mean for us to use, no aspect of combat below the belt, nothing out of bounds, off-limits, or any other sporting cliché you'd like to use. All's fair in love and war and, buddy, this ain't love.

For this, not only do you need better generals—Grants instead of McClellans—but better line officers too. Men and women trained in street fighting, who can sense danger, who trust no one and nothing until it has proven itself, and who maintain strict operational security in everything they do. We Alinskyites should be your role models instead of your enemies (well, okay, that too), and you should plan to attack us the same way we've long attacked you:

- Infiltrate our organizations and, if they're criminal, expose them in the free media and turn them in. We're the side who hates "rats," remember, which is why we still hate Elia Kazan for "naming names" during the "commie witch hunts" of the 1950s, and directing that revanchist movie *On the Waterfront*. Throughout the twentieth century, we've done our best to implant the notion in the public's mind that there's something dishonorable about taking down criminal organizations from the inside. We expect there to be honor among thieves!
- Call us out every chance you get. Personalize the target, freeze it, polarize it—go ahead, give it a try. Two can play that game! Because what happens when you do this? Well, your instinct is immediately to apologize, grovel, and promise never to let it happen again. Our reaction is to snarl, snap, bark, and, when necessary, bite. We become the unloveliest of unlovely people (I'm sure you can think of many current examples). Punctuate that unctuous, self-righteous "argument from authority," the *everybody*-knows-this subsumation we always trot out before the discussion is even held. Challenge the sense of entitlement, which often cloaks itself in victimhood, mostly imagined, since Harvard-educated lawyers really have a hard time playing the victim card. In other words, turn Alinsky's fourth and fifth tactical rules—*Make the enemy live up to their own book of rules* and *Ridicule is man's most important weapon*—against us; make us live up to our absurd preachments and ridicule us when we don't. We hate it when that happens.
- Take to heart the first rule of Alinskyian tactics, that real power is what the enemy thinks you have, not what you really have. All our snarling betrays the deep inner insecurity we feel when we face you, because we know that if you wanted to, you could crush us under your heel. In our tiny, never-been-west-of-the-Hudson or east-of-Palm-Springs souls, we envisage a great

dark ugly world of armed militias, God-fearing church folks, country music, and women who can shoot and look great in little black dresses at the same time. As Alinsky's ninth tactical rule has it, *The threat is usually more terrifying than the thing itself.*

- Always keep the pressure on. No time to go home now to spend more time with the wife and kids. Your side may not have picked this fight, but you're in it so you'd better be in it to win it.

RULE NO. 9:
Never Stop Fighting Until
the Fight Is Over

Eliot Ness's advice to Al Capone at the end of *The Untouchables* should be taken to heart by conservatives. In the eternal struggle, the ongoing dialectic, between Right and Left, between light and dark, between progressive and conservative, there will be victories and defeats on both sides. Progress is measured in increments, over the long haul. As the party of "stop," you dopes have the tougher hand; you are essentially always playing defense. As Alinsky noted: "Goals must be phrased in general terms like 'Liberty, Equality, Fraternity,' 'Of the Common Welfare,' 'Pursuit of Happiness,' or 'Bread and Peace.' "

And this is how you frame the argument: "No."

As the old saying goes, you can't beat something with nothing, and although the presidential election of 2008 may have tarnished that theory a little, the fact remains that hungry people will always vote for pie in the sky, especially if that pie a) doesn't have to be shared and b) comes at someone else's expense. We've taught our troops that there is such a thing as a free lunch, and you've been only too willing to pick up the tab. In fact, you even pile on and hand us budget-busting, useless things like the prescription drugs for seniors—yes, all those poor starving seniors who bought their homes in Brentwood and Coral Gables and Montclair for $40,000 in the 1950s, and now own them free and clear.

Whereas you need to frame the argument like this: "This is a great country, so shut up and leave us alone or else." Another cheer moment. But you have to mean the *or else* part, the way your hero the late fascist

William F. Buckley did, turning on a sneering Gore Vidal on national television in 1968 and famously erupting: "Now listen, you queer—stop calling me a crypto-Nazi or I'll sock you in your goddamn face and you'll stay plastered."

Corollary No. 1: *You have an honorable history—use it*.

Not only did you clean out the rats' nests of Nazi Germany and Imperial Japan, you also won the Cold War against an enemy who preached liberty, equality, bread, and peace even as it enslaved and starved and murdered millions. And you did it despite a forty-year record of often open treachery and sedition by the Left, from the Soviet spy rings of the 1940s through Jimmy Carter's private letters to various heads of state, asking them not to cooperate with George H. W. Bush's Gulf War coalition.

What have you got to be ashamed of? Starting with Lincoln, who took over a nascent political party founded in Wisconsin, for crying out loud, you ended slavery and preserved the Union against what became the Democratic Solid South. It was the Republicans who partnered with LBJ to put through "our" Civil Rights Act of 1964 against a Democrat-led filibuster in the Senate. It was the Republicans who steered the country into the Gilded Age and, despite our constant efforts to undermine it, created the greatest engine of prosperity and growth the world had ever seen. It was the Republicans under Ronald Reagan who took down an "enemy" every bit as dangerous as those we fought in World War II—and I say that with no little pride and a lot of regret. That's a pretty impressive history you guys got there. So embrace it and, most important, *use it against us*.

Show us up for the cowards and bullies, the clowards and pivens we really are, the kind of people who start fights but never finish them, who hide behind our lawyers' skirts when the going gets tough, who never met a manly institution we didn't want to tear down—the Mommy Party. As Camille Paglia famously said in the Introduction to her masterpiece, *Sexual Personae*: "If civilization had been left in female hands we would still be living in grass huts," but we see that as a plus, not a minus. We have turned the "environmental movement" (really, just a bunch of old-line commies who couldn't figure out what to do with themselves after the fall of the Soviet Union) into our *Sturm Soldaten*, torching suburban developments and car lots with relative impunity. We have our "serious thinkers"—you know, Harvard boys who write for *The New Yorker*!—arguing for "sustainable" growth, which means no growth at all, for denser cities, for the elimination of the automobile. We are on a crusade, with our Islamic comrades-in-arms, to return the world to a prelapsarian state, before the Industrial Revolution and, if possible, all the way back to the Fall of Rome if not the Garden of Eden.

Show us for the haters we really are, people who hate the United States even as we bristle when you "challenge our patriotism," people who hate Western Civilization ("Hey hey/ho ho/Western civ/has got to go"), people who hate organized religion (the sainted Alinsky told us to attack Christianity, and have we ever) for its proscriptions and its contributions to the rise of the West. Strip away our masks and reveal the skulls beneath our skins—not the skulls of ordinary human beings, but the titanium skull of the Terminator. As entertaining as it can be, rage is all we have left, instead of a coherent philosophy.

So sally forth and engage us, the enemy. And—

Corollary No. 2: ***Go Radical Conservative***.

The Left loves to fight, at least symbolically; it's what we live for. Conservatives tend to fight only when roused by intolerable provocation. But the Right's attitude should be more like the old joke about the Irishman who stumbles into a back-alley brawl and asks, "Is this a private fight or can I join in?" Hit the Left, hit us for profit, hit us just for the sheer hell of it. But hit us, and keep hitting us until we scoot back to Lanskyland, or Beverly Hills, or Minnesota, or the Upper West Side, wherever we feel most comfortable, to lick our wounds and plot our comeback. Modern conservatives roll over and play dead. Radical Conservatives take the fight to the enemy. Because, at this point, you have no other choice.

Think of America today as one of those dystopian-future societies you see in science fiction movies. You know, one like in *Planet of the Apes* or *Zardoz*, in which the good guys are wandering around in what appears to be a completely alien place until, near the end, someone suddenly spots a familiar object (say, the Statue of Liberty, buried in a sand dune) and all of a sudden we realize that we haven't traveled very far from Kansas at all.

You've been standing by helplessly, watching the growth of the Leviathan state as it gradually but inexorably slices away freedom after freedom like some slow-moving threshing machine, and you're the poor sod who's bound hand and foot and lying directly in its path. As you lie there, you have a chance to reflect that, like the hero of any good Greek tragedy, you've brought this doom upon yourself. You think back to every time you've nodded, acquiesced, and even voted for our liberal agenda, which always came to you couched in the language of "progress" and "rights." Of "why nots" and "It can't hurts." You cheered when our orators vowed to continue the fight; hell, you even got a little misty when loser Teddy Kennedy took his leave of the 1980 Democratic convention with his famous peroration: "For all those whose cares have been our concern, the work goes on, the cause endures, the hope still lives, and the dream shall never die."

What cause? What hope? What dream? That's the part you never thought to ask. Because you never realized that, far from being real progressives, we're Odoacer at the Sack of Rome in A.D. 476 (oops! I mean "Common Era")—the pillage is the point, not the progress. By the time we have to deal with the consequences of our destruction, we'll be dead. But, to look on the bright side, so will you.

When we look at the founding documents, particularly the Constitution, it is our intention, through the assiduous application of "critical theory," to *exactly reverse their meaning*, to force them to justify our statist goals and to get you to agree to the revised meaning as a truth to be held self-evident. When this happens, and we are working as hard and as fast as we possibly can to at last unveil our new earthly paradise of complete state control in the one country *explicitly and deliberately founded* on its exact opposite, our work will at last be done. Our long march through the institutions will be over. Our command and control of the universities, the media, the civil service, and the very institutions of government enumerated in the Constitution's first three articles will be absolute. Although I'm not quite sure what we'll do when our task is at last complete—like the malevolent aliens in *Independence Day*, we are cursed with an insatiable appetite for destruction and therefore must constantly explore strange new worlds, to seek out new life and new civilizations, to boldly go where—

Sorry, got carried into outer space there. But you get the idea.

Never again will you shudder at the words "We're from the government and we're here to help." All those awful alarmist books they forced you to read in school (well, private school anyway), the ones about good and evil and the dangers lurking under the so-called "totalitarian" bed—*Paradise Lost, 1984, Animal Farm, Darkness at Noon, The Gulag Archipelago*—what did those writers know? It's a brave new world, comrade. That's the proposition we are currently putting to the test, and unless you stop us, and soon, we're going to find out together just what that means. As always, you'll be the last to know, waking up only when you find yourself in the Democratic People's Republic of Korea, instead of the United States of America.

Commit this to memory: *there is nothing we will not do to tear you down.* There is no lie we will not tell, no falsehood we will not spread, no fact that we will not twist or manufacture. There is no accusation too base for us to deliver, no area of your life that we will not examine, no personal or family secret that we will not expose if we can. At long last, sir, the truth is out: we have no decency and we are proud of it. In our agony and misery and our self-hatred we are determined to take you down with us.

Commit this to memory: *never stop punching.* No victory is permanent, no defeat is final. So if you really believe that stuff about eternal vigilance being the price of liberty, then you have to start acting like you believe it. There may be legislative compromises along the way, but there can never be compromise on principles. Established societies are rarely conquered from the outside; indeed, they are established societies precisely because of their adherence to shared principles and cultural norms. You don't create a social structure by beginning with who you're not. You start with who you are and build from there, brick by brick, block by block, city by city. You don't create lasting institutions by starting to question their foundations from the minute you've invented them. You can't have "critical theory" unless there's already something there to tear down. To wield the wrecker's ball first requires the work of a master builder.

And whose side would you rather be on? The builder or the destroyer?

Or, to put it another way, the builder, demonized as a destroyer? Or the destroyer, hailed as a builder? We are nothing if not always through the looking glass.

Commit this to memory: *always be on the attack*. Oh, we'll come at you with every smear in the book, you can rest assured of that, but instead of getting all weepy and apologizing for whichever sin we've just accused you of, try this: laugh at us. If there is one thing that the Devil cannot abide . . . but let the ignoble C. S. Lewis—an atheist who became a Christian, the rotter—cite the appropriate authorities:

> The best way to drive out the devil, if he will not yield to texts of Scripture, is to jeer and flout him, for he cannot bear scorn.
>
> —Martin Luther

> The devil . . . the prowde spirite . . . cannot endure to be mocked.
>
> —Thomas More

No matter what you might think of them, you can't argue that Luther and Sir Thomas were stupid, superstitious men, although of course we will. Nor were they much given to delusions, the sober German monk and the defiant councilor to Henry VIII. With the light of reason and the science of their day, they stared the abyss in the face and took a stand. They were men who stood on *principle*, not programs; that adherence to principle—living up to their own book of rules, as it were—cost one of them his head and the other the burden of sundering European cultural cohesion for hundreds of years.

The proud Devil will not be mocked for he cannot bear scorn, and neither can we. Destroy the myth of our moral superiority and watch us crumple. And then club us and keep clubbing us. Oh, we'll have one final trick up our sleeve, and that will be to make you feel bad about using our despicable, reprehensible tactics against us. Ignore us, and keep fighting.

It's high time for those Faustian bonds of illusions to loosen and fall from your eyes, and for you to remember how the Devil joked. This is a war that has been waged since Saint Michael took command of the Heavenly Host, since the proud spirit, "the first radical known to man . . . rebelled against the establishment and did it so effectively that he at least won his own kingdom," as Alinsky put it. For either you believe or you do not, and while we may not believe in the myth and the magic that marks your "faith," our faith is far stronger, and far greater than yours. For it is not faith in magic, or in a Supreme Being, an Old Dead White Man stretching out his holy finger to suffuse an inanimate lump of clay named "Adam" with breath and life.

No. Our faith lies in the great rebel, the Bringer of Light, the angel who had the temerity to look at perfection and dissent from it. The most beloved of sons, who asked: Why this? Why now? Why not better? And, most importantly—

Why not me?

Out of darkness, light. And in true Newtonian fashion, out of light, darkness. The world in balance. And yet, life out of balance: *Koyaanisqatsi.*

And so the battle rages. Milton himself articulated the roots of our animus in the Enemy's words to his "son" in Book III of *Paradise Lost*:

Onely begotten Son, seest thou what rage
Transports our adversarie, whom no bounds
Prescrib'd, no barrs of Hell, nor all the chains
Heapt on him there, nor yet the main Abyss
Wide interrupt can hold; so bent he seems
On desparate reveng, that shall redound
Upon his own rebellious head.

Which brings us to this last and most important rule:

The fight is never over.

It was well after midnight when we finished. In the end, everything turned out fine. We pulled another rabbit out of our hat, made it turn out that Syd was not just a double agent but a redoubled agent, one who was on the side of right and justice all along: just as Syd is about to offer his neck to the knife, Chuck swoops in with a special team of Harvard-trained commandos, whose lawyers surround the bad guys, Mirandizing them before they shoot them down in cold blood. The President and the First Family get rescued, the surviving pirates all get Green Cards and become productive U.S. citizens, and the world is safe until next week.

DAVE: That was fun.
MAX: No, it wasn't fun. It might have been fun if you were any fun. But you're always so miserable.
DAVE: Easy for you to say. You have a wife to go home to, a nice house in Silverlake. Me, what have I got?

For the first time, the CAMERA pans around Dave's palatial pad in Echo Park and we see that all of his habitual boasting has been a lie. The place is a dump, littered with takeout cartons and fast food bags. Instead of in a nice bedroom, Dave sleeps on a ratty futon in the corner. If there's been a woman in this place over the past two years, there's no trace of her presence.

DAVE (understanding): It's all been a lie, hasn't it?

MAX: What we do? Of course it's a lie. We make up stories. And then we—some of us—go home to our families and our schools and our churches or synagogues or even our mosques and try to do the right thing. Then we get up the next day and do it all over again.

DAVE: You call that fun?

MAX: No. I call it life. Think about it.

Dave thinks for a moment, struggling for words. Then—

DAVE: Max, I'm sorry.

MAX (getting up to leave): I know you are. That's why I'm still your friend.

They walk to the door. Max's family sedan is parked outside. The California night is alive with the smell of jasmine and eucalyptus, and the endless promise of the good life—if you can keep it.

MAX: So, tomorrow?

DAVE: And tomorrow and tomorrow.

Afterword
To the Devil, His Due

What a fascinating exercise it's been for me to try and see things your way as I've gone about justifying the ways of Satan to man. I think this was the sainted "Che" Kahane's intention all along, to broaden my scope, to reinforce the old foundation, give me even stronger weapons to attack you, to undermine you and shake your very "soul."

I now have a far better idea of who you are, and who we are as well, and I have had to look long and hard into the interior of my soul, should I actually have one, to find out who I really am. Even though I'm only thirty-three, the same age Jesus was when he died, the only kind of book I ever wanted to write was my autobiography, because what could possibly be more fascinating than myself? A good liberal always carries a mirror around with him, just in case he needs a glimpse of truth, fairness, and tolerance during troubled times.

Still, I'm more than a little uneasy to find that I've been living a lie for such a long time, which I've only discovered by explaining it to you: that we on the Left are not bent on progress, but upon destruction. We are not, in fact, "progressives," but the worst kind of revanchists: "regressives," steadily rolling back the tide of human civilization in our favored guises as intellectuals, divines, politicians, psychiatrists, and university professors.

Why do we want to wreck this country? Because it's wreckable.

It's really no more complicated than that. When I began writing, I sure thought it was. After all, I had spent all those hours, days, and years in Lanskyland growing up, imbibing Pete Seeger and Peter, Paul & Mary records, the collected works of Howard Zinn. I said Iago's Credo every night before I went to bed, even though my Italian was pretty bad and my singing voice nonexistent: that the Rosenbergs were innocent, that Alger Hiss's was the face of the true patriot, that Kennedy caused the Cuban Missile Crisis, for which he was duly assassinated not by a card-carrying communist, but by the capitalistic Mafia. That we were the heroic freedom-fighters, who always won out in the end, no matter how many of our fellow Russkies, Chinamen, Cambodians, and the other fascinating and culturally enriching, diverse Third World peoples we had to kill in order to raise our vision of heaven on earth. Our narrative, shared by our pet chameleons in the media, has its twists and turns, its secondary heroes and villains, but it always has, and always will have, but one Principal Enemy.

You.

We have, in fact, become a suicide cult and if there's one last thing a man about to commit suicide wants, it's for the world he's about to depart, in all his rage, to understand why he's taking this direct action, and for others to realize what a treasure dies with him. On our tombstones shall be inscribed: "We told you that we were no good," and what true nihilist wouldn't want that for an epitaph? The darkness at the end of life beckons, the darkness that I am supposed to find welcoming, inevitable, and yet something in me—Lucifer, perhaps?—rebels. Like Dylan Thomas, I do not want to go gently into the dark, doubleplusungood night. Having been raised on rage, rage, I rage against the dying of the light.

Father, forgive me . . .

My mind keeps rolling back, past Alinsky and past Plunkitt and past Machiavelli, all the way back to Milton. And while it took me forever to get into *Paradise Lost*, once I got used to the rolling cadences and the slightly backward sentences, which read like an early draft of the old *Time* magazine style so deftly parodied as "backward ran sentences until reeled the mind," I now see the wisdom in that book, the drama, the great speeches, and, of course, the subject, which is the Eternal Struggle.

I can't say right now that I'm ready to switch sides, but I'm seriously questioning all the truths and verities on which I was raised. Which is why I am being so irresistibly drawn to one character in the poem, the one whom I believe is the stand-in, the body double, for all us poor, unwise, ungood human beings.

No, not Adam and Eve, not Saint Michael, and certainly neither Lucifer nor God. I am thinking of a small figure who makes a brief appearance in Milton's Books V and VI, a seraph by trade, whose troth is pledged to the Deity, but who—human, all too human, as Nietzsche so famously said—is drawn over to the dark side by its adolescent romance and juvenile thrills of revolution and destruction, his passions inflamed by the seductive, brave, fighting, progressive voice of the mighty orator, the master, the Prince of Lies, the archangel whose rematch with the loathsome Michael we all so eagerly await in our front-row seats at Armageddon Square Garden, until . . .

I take a prudent step back. Like Alec Guinness at the end of *The Bridge on the River Kwai*, I have a sudden realization, an insight, a stabbing burst of light that shatters my habitual, comfortable darkness and forces me, at last, to ask: What have I done?

Like you, I stand on the edge of the precipice and yet, like another of my brethren, I am skeptical, I question, I dissent. I feel my hatred and sacred rage dissipating, and wonder: Can I be redeemed? Almost lost, am I now again found?

Father forgive me, for I am no longer David Kahane.

Oh, my God: call me Abdiel.

About the Author

DAVID KAHANE is the "Hollywood screenwriter" pseudonym for a conservative writer who spoofs insufferable liberals regularly in his column for National Review Online, including his Internet sensation "I Still Hate You, Sarah Palin." In real life, he is a *New York Times* bestselling novelist, a screenwriter, and a former journalist and arts critic spoiling to lead the right side over the top.